The Feminist Spectator in Action

Feminist Criticism for the Stage and Screen

Jill Dolan

palgrave
macmillan

First published 2013 by
PALGRAVE MACMILLAN

Palgrave Macmillan in the UK is an imprint of Macmillan Publishers Limited, registered in England, company number 785998, of Houndmills, Basingstoke, Hampshire RG21 6XS.

Palgrave Macmillan in the US is a division of St Martin's Press LLC, 175 Fifth Avenue, New York, NY 10010.

Palgrave Macmillan is the global academic imprint of the above companies and has companies and representatives throughout the world.

Palgrave® and Macmillan® are registered trademarks in the United States, the United Kingdom, Europe and other countries

ISBN: 978–1–137–03290–4 (hardback)
ISBN: 978–1–137–03289–8 (paperback)

This book is printed on paper suitable for recycling and made from fully managed and sustained forest sources. Logging, pulping and manufacturing processes are expected to conform to the environmental regulations of the country of origin.

A catalogue record for this book is available from the British Library.

A catalog record for this book is available from the Library of Congress.

For my dad, Jerry Dolan, my biggest fan,
and for my partner, Stacy Wolf,
a.k.a. Feminist Spectator 2

Contents

Contents

Acknowledgements

This book has been brewing for many years, given its genesis in The Feminist Spectator blog. I'd like to thank those who helped bring the book to fruition, as well as those who've supported the blog over these many years. The George Jean Nathan Award committee – J. Ellen Gainor, Roger Gilbert, Claudia Johnson, and Michael Cadden – honored me by giving The Feminist Spectator the Nathan award for 2010–2011, making it the first blog to receive this distinguished prize for dramatic criticism. The panel of critics who came to Princeton in April 2012 to help me celebrate the award – Karen Fricker, Randy Gener, Bonnie Marranca, and Alisa Solomon – have also been instrumental to my work over the years, as well as influencing the shape and contents of this book. In October 2012, I was invited to share the introduction and the "how-to" section with graduate students in theatre at Barnard and Columbia; I'd like to thank Bill Worthen for that invitation, as well as Julie Stone Peters, Jean Howard, Alisa Solomon, Chuck Mee, and all the wonderful, astute graduate students who commented on the drafts they read.

Jenna Steventon, Paula Kennedy, Felicity Noble, Jenni Burnell, and the staff at Palgrave Macmillan constituted my own personal editorial dream team. I appreciate their enthusiasm for the project, and particularly Jenna's astute and careful guidance. Likewise, three anonymous reviewers provided helpful comments that allowed me to revise the book appropriately.

Finally, my dad, Jerry Dolan, reads all my blogs and eagerly asks when I'll be posting the next one. He's become my sustaining fan, who motivates me to keep writing. My partner, Stacy Wolf, reads every blog post before it goes live, and has commented on this collection with her usual critical élan and generous commitment. She sees everything I write about – plays, films, television shows – and engages me in dialogue that inspires my writing. In our house, we call her Feminist Spectator 2; she's truly my collaborator in this project.

Introduction

> I myself have never been able to find out precisely what
> feminism is: I only know that people call me a feminist
> whenever I express sentiments that differentiate me from a
> doormat or a prostitute.
>
> – Rebecca West[1]

What is feminist criticism? What is a feminist perspective on the arts
and culture and why is it important? What work does feminist criticism
of theatre, performance, film, and television do in the world? In other
words, why should we care? *The Feminist Spectator in Action* tries to
answer these questions by modeling the critical practice I've developed
over my career as a theatre and performance studies scholar and as a
feminist blogger. I hope these examples demonstrate the usefulness of
looking at culture through a critical lens that seriously considers the
status of women and other marginalized people while at the same time
participates in a wider public discourse about pleasure, beauty, and the
arts. Feminist criticism doesn't sully or diminish my appreciation of
culture and my enjoyment of entertainment, but rather enhances it in
numerous ways. And despite screeds to the contrary, feminism is not a
bad word. At base, it refers to women's right to equality in all realms of
social life and culture. Feminism also provides a way of looking at the
world, a lens through which to consider how power circulates around
the axis of not just gender, but of sexuality, race, and class. Feminism is
an analytical system that gives us tools for seeing ourselves in relation
to one another. It offers a transformative politics of hope so that we can
imagine, together, a better, more equitable future for us all.

Culture is not an innocent preoccupation. Television, films, theatre
productions and performances, and other representational expressive
media both shape and reflect who we are to ourselves and to one
another. We learn from seeing in performance how gender and race
relations are embodied and enacted. Depending on a performance's

ideology, social roles are enforced so that men and women conform to rigid binary stereotypes or so that characters suggest new, more fluid ways of living within or resistantly to gender. Theatre and film show us ourselves in relation to others, or more damagingly, they persuade us of our social invisibility by not representing us at all. I was moved by dramaturg Polly Carl's essay, "A Boy in a Man's Theatre," on the website HowlRound, in which she admitted, "I am compelled to talk some truth about finding yourself 'other' in a white man's world—about the importance of insisting on being seen."[2] As she watched a rehearsal of Lisa Kron and Jeanine Tesori's adaptation of Alison Bechdel's graphic novel *Fun Home*, Carl realized that although the new musical isn't her "exact" story, "it was my story." The power of recognition – of seeing a life that looks something like yours on stage – was overwhelming for Carl, because she's been feeling invisible for a very long time.

Feminist criticism, then, participates in an activist project of culture-making in which we're collectively called to see what and who is stunningly, repeatedly evident and what and who is devastatingly, obviously invisible in the art and popular culture we regularly consume for edification and entertainment. Take only one recent example of how a film uses gender stereotypes insidiously to persuade us that the relationships it imagines are real and true: In Danish director Nicolas Winding Refn's film, *Drive* (2011), which stars Ryan Gosling as a stunt driver/criminal-for-hire embroiled in a nasty bit of double-dealing, Gosling's character is moody and stalwart. He has no back story, but we know from the set of his jaw that he's a good, strong white man despite the violence in which he participates. He falls in love with a neighbor (Carey Mulligan) and tries to help her husband, who's recently been released from prison, out of a tough spot. In the course of the stylish, atmospheric, but desperately misogynist film, Mulligan's character barely speaks; a gun moll played by *Mad Men*'s Christina Hendricks is slapped around for her stupidity and then has her head blown off with a gun in the five minutes she's on screen; and the film's only other women are prostitutes and strippers who sit naked, adorning the arms and barrooms of the gangsters with whom Gosling's character gets entangled. The film narrates Gosling's heroism and observes as he finally drives off into the night, necessarily leaving his love interest behind. What we've learned from this story and its camera angles and editing is that women need to be protected by strong silent men; that what women say is less important than how they look; and that women are most useful naked, as the background against which men play out their agency. The film was distributed in 2012 – not in 1952 – and got very good reviews, very few of which mentioned its gender stereotypes.[3]

Alison Bechdel, who's a perspicacious critical commentator as well as a wonderful graphic artist and novelist, has developed what she calls the "Bechdel test" for assessing whether a film is worth watching for feminist men and women. The test assesses whether a film has at least two named women in it who talk to each other about something besides a man.[4] (By this measure, *Drive* fails miserably.) The test is a simple but persuasive measure of women's agency in film narratives. If they don't even have names, it's difficult to care about a character, and presumably, their stories won't be as important to the central narrative ("Woman One" is rarely as significant as a lead character with a name played by a famous actor). If they don't speak to one another, the women have no chance to form relationships. And if they do speak to one another but only about men, their lives and experiences are constrained to a palette of heterosexual relationships in which their desires focus on the romantic plots that drive too many female characters, especially in popular films.

Bechdel's test allows spectators to consider content outside of a simple good or bad dichotomy. *Drive* might be a good film according to standards that consider cinematography, plot, atmosphere, and other cinematic elements. But if its treatment of women is inadequate, I can't invite friends or colleagues to see it without remarking on how I've experienced it as someone for whom gender, race, sexuality, and other intersecting identity vectors are meaningful to my entertainment consumption and reception. The simplistic good or bad binary, based on a glib, unthinking model of consumer reporting, drives too much film reviewing and consumption. The "thumbs up/thumbs down" paradigm established by Gene Siskel and Roger Ebert essentially tells people how to spend their entertainment dollars based on only two choices – yes or no.

Feminist criticism attempts a different kind of engagement with the films and performances we see. Feminist critics and spectators don't just buy culture, but pull apart the threads of meaning it produces. Of course, we do purchase some of our cultural experiences; the price of a ticket to a Broadway show or to see a film should be of real concern to a feminist critic committed to economic as well as gender and racial justice. But other kinds of cultural productions surround us more insidiously. We don't necessarily choose to look at billboards trumpeting the latest reality television show, or ads selling the latest fashions worn by impossibly thin models. Feminist criticism provides a lens through which to filter the culture we consume intentionally and not, and that helps us organize the cacophony and chaos of images that come at us from multiple directions at once. Living in western culture these days is like standing perpetually in New York's Times Square. Where do we look first? Is it possible to look away? What does all this stimulation mean? Who are we in the face of these blaring, bright meanings calling for our attention and our dollars?

A feminist critic/spectator considers the whole panoply of meanings on offer in culture. In plays, performances, films, or television series, she or he considers how a story is cast and structured rather than just narrating plot and theme. How does it move through time and space? Is it realist? Non-linear? Fantastical or naturalistic? How do those choices matter to our experience of the story and how it's told? Does the narrative enforce a particular ideology in its structural choices or provide a resistant view? In addition to considering how women fare within narrative structures on stage or in front of the camera, feminist critics also have a responsibility to advocate for women artists and other cultural workers marginalized by modes of production driven by a bottom-line budget mentality. Where is this play produced? By whom? Where is it advertised? Who has access to it under what conditions? Likewise, who are the cultural workers who've produced this art? Have they applied for grants? From whom? Who talks about their work and what do they say? What do the artists say about their work, in the production program or other materials? The percentage of women playwrights, screenwriters, or directors working in the wealthiest, most visible arts and entertainment forums remains abysmally low. Through many of these essays, I try to simply call attention to work by women that somehow remains invisible to mainstream critics, most of whom are white and male. If Hollywood and Broadway (and sometimes even Off Broadway and the regional theatres) don't give women their due as artists with stories to tell and visions to share, feminist critics need to help spectators look elsewhere and advocate loudly for their value.[5]

The Feminist Spectator in Action considers contemporary popular culture and the arts through analytical optics that yield the pleasure of informed and empowered viewing. Too often, socially aware criticism is reputed to destroy pleasure with a moralizing, "politically correct" perspective on culture elsewhere considered entertaining and unimportant as anything more than fun. I hope this collection demonstrates that there's no contradiction between enjoying film and performance and attending to its deeper meanings. My own investments in theatre, performance, and popular culture lead me continually to seek out viewing experiences in which I hope to be moved and provoked as well as entertained, to learn something about myself and others, and to experience new stories and visions for how we might cohabitate in an increasingly complicated world.

The project of criticism in the 21st century remains dominated by writers who don't see culture's interaction with humanity quite as expansively. In the U.S., for instance, the preponderance of white male critics write from unexamined gender and race biases that leave them ignorant about how theatre and popular culture can represent others. The theatre criticism establishment is shockingly white and male, though not necessarily heterosexual. In November 2011, *American Theatre* ran a piece called "Critical Juncture" that profiled 12 theatre critics from around the country. The critics ranged in age from 45 to 61 years old. Three were women. All of them appeared to be white.[6] Likewise, the prestigious George Jean Nathan Award for Dramatic Criticism, which has honored theatre writers since 1958, has recognized only seven women and two people of color in the last 54 years.[7] Of course, a critic's identity categories and his or her critical or political perspective don't always neatly align. A.O. Scott, the first-string white male film critic for the *New York Times*, tends to write from a fairly feminist perspective. And many women would say they don't consider gender when they write. Some critics of color prefer to leave race unmarked in their criticism. Many continue to buy into the myth of objectivity, insisting that to be balanced and fair, a critic needs to erase his or her predilections and prejudices and come to their spectating experiences as a "universalist." I don't believe objectivity is possible or desirable; instead, it simply masks the biases that any critic, of necessity, brings to his or her work. Those biases, in fact, comprise a way of seeing that makes the critic's work helpful and compelling. Such predispositions should be openly acknowledged and exploited.

Critical commentary that points out how theatre and film narratives sometimes circumscribe rather than expand the ways we see ourselves and our collective futures is crucial. But professional critics too often dismiss work that comes from novel perspectives. And much too frequently, powerful white male critics of women's work deliver stinging reviews that seem personal. Addressing plays or films they perceive as feminist especially provokes venomous disdain and disregard. Playwright Theresa Rebeck addressed the personal ravages of criticism in her Laura Pels keynote address for ART/NY's annual meeting in March 2010. Rebeck, whose work has premiered on Broadway and is produced at regional theatres across the country, described the progress of her 1999 play, *The Butterfly Collection*, from a workshop production at California's South Coast Rep to a fall 2000 production at Playwrights Horizons in New York. The play generated a great deal of excitement, Rebeck recalls:

> A lot of commercial producers came [to see the play at Playwrights Horizons], as people felt that it could potentially move [to a Broadway run]. Nine separate regional theaters were circling to produce it. *American Theatre Magazine* called my agent to ask for the script because they were interested in publishing it … Audiences were thrilled with the play. Lincoln Center Library was filming it for their collection.
>
> When the *New York Times* published its review it was not what anyone expected. The reviewer … dismissed the play … as a feminist diatribe. He accused me of having a thinly veiled man-hating agenda, and in a truly bizarre paragraph at the end of the review, he expressed sympathy to the director [Barlett Sher] because he had to work with someone as hideous as me. … [T]here was a flurry of upset [over the review's tone]. But with a review that bad, the play closed. All the other productions went away. *American Theatre Magazine* went away. Everybody knew that that was a crazy misogynistic review. But no one would produce the play. Ever again. And you should know that many people consider it my best play. Still.[8]

Rebeck overstates just a bit the malice with which the *Times* critic, Bruce Weber, wrote (he doesn't, for instance, call her "hideous").[9] But it's clear that his own ego was pricked by Rebeck's play, which addresses the wages of narcissism that male artists lord over their female partners. Rebeck goes on to say that after the *Times* review appeared and the production closed, she could no longer get any of her work produced. One "nice" person after another told her that she should produce her plays under a male pseudonym, since clearly, the New York critics "don't like you personally."

Rebeck has gone on to a very successful career in the theatre, but she said that she told this story in her 2010 speech "because I don't want to hear from anybody that there isn't, or hasn't been, a real gender problem in the American theater." Her talk details the underrepresentation of plays by women on Broadway, around New York, and in regional theatre, and delivers an impassioned analysis of theatre producers' hypocrisy and short-sightedness about gender. She remarks, "I never had an agenda. I just wanted to write plays that told the truth. Some of those plays told the truth about what it is like to live on this planet, as a woman. ... Why can't we do that in the theatre?"

As Rebeck's example demonstrates, women often can't do that in the theatre because of male critics' stranglehold on the business of writing about new plays or productions of any sort, especially in New York. The predominance of white male critics means that plays and performances by women, and/or people of color, and/or gays and lesbians, and especially anyone who crosses several of these categories, are suspect as "special interest" vehicles, and how they speak to wider audiences is rarely considered. Even when male critics aren't mounting overt attacks on women's work, their indifference sometimes speaks volumes. In 2010, Emily Mann produced and directed at McCarter Theatre in Princeton *The How and the Why*, a lovely, two-women play by Sarah Treem (a writer for HBO's *In Treatment*) that starred Mercedes Ruehl and Bess Rous as scientists who prove to have a biological, as well as an intellectual, affinity. The terrific production impressed local audiences and Mann hoped to take the play to New York for an extended run. When the *Times* expressed interest in sending a reviewer, Mann demurred, suggesting they wait until the play arrived in the city. But critic Charles Isherwood came anyway and filed a tepid review of a play he clearly didn't understand or care about.[10] He damned it with faint praise, admiring Ruehl's performance but calling the plot contrived and convoluted, too full of jargon from the evolutionary biology field in which both characters research the historical idiosyncrasies of women's reproductive apparatus.

Isherwood's review sabotaged the production's move to New York. It epitomizes the blind spots of critics unconcerned with not just women's work in the theatre, but with women's place in the world. With global gender, racial, or economic equality still not a foregone conclusion, criticism needs to provide a different quality of attention to women's expression and experience. Theatre won't change until the critics' corps diversifies and until more critics of any race or gender start writing from a broader perspective on the myriad stories that deserve to be told and embodied. As playwright/novelist Sarah Schulman insists, "The American theatre will neither reflect the American playwright nor serve the American audience until it decides to expand what is known about being alive, instead of endlessly repeating already established paradigms."[11] By attending closely to the critical (and audience) reception to plays and films by women, and detailing their production context, advertising and marketing, acting choices, and design, feminist criticism can break through the persistent male stranglehold on what's considered universal or even worthwhile.

As these egregious examples illustrate, no gender-equitable reviewing tradition exists in mainstream arts discourse. The preponderance of male reviewers seem actively anti-feminist and sometimes even anti-women. Some female reviewers – such as Linda Winer, the first-string theatre critic at New York's *Newsday*, or Manohla Dargis, the second-string film reviewer at the *New York Times* – occasionally comment on gender issues in their writing. They even sometimes appear on panels about gender equity in the profession, as Winer did at a New Perspectives Theatre/Women's Project and Productions discussion in August 2009, at which she expressed her frustration with the gender-biased system of criticism. But no one writes regularly about theatre and performance from a feminist perspective.[12]

Very little has changed since 1988, when I argued in *The Feminist Spectator as Critic* that the gaze remains unapologetically male, borrowing from Laura Mulvey's foundational scholarship on what she called "the male gaze" in cinema to forge a methodology for feminist criticism and theory in theatre and performance studies.[13] Since the mid- to late-1980s, a strong tradition of feminist theatre and performance, film and media, and visual arts and dance criticism exists in the academy (see the list of further reading that follows this introduction). But few academic feminist critics publish in the popular or trade press, where their work might affect the viewing habits of many more spectators. *The Feminist Spectator in Action* directly addresses the paucity of feminist perspectives in the popular press by offering critical models and applications. It illustrates the usefulness of a feminist critical paradigm to a wide range of cultural productions: feminist, experimental, and avant-garde theatre, performance, and performance art, as well as Broadway musicals and plays; new work Off- and Off-Off Broadway; wide-released, mass market, or independent films; and network or subscription channel television series.

The Feminist Spectator blog

Much of the writing collected here is drawn from The Feminist Spectator blog, which I established on Blogspot.com (which later morphed into Blogger.com) in 2005. I found myself itching to get back to the reviewing that I'd done much earlier in my career when, as an undergraduate and then graduate student, I wrote for school and neighborhood and feminist papers in Boston and New York. Blogspot was very easy to use; I chose a template and started writing. I named my site after my first book, *The Feminist Spectator as Critic*, which linked my career as a scholar with my commitments as a public writer. I made a few ground rules. I tried to write at first every other week and then every week. I decided to write mostly about theatre I like; it didn't seem worthwhile to use my time to write negative criticism about what I saw. I wanted to concentrate on work by and about women, although that dictum quickly expanded to any work, viewed from a feminist perspective. I also started writing about film and television. I preferred to write about work that I found progressive and hopeful, but I allowed myself to be more critical of mainstream popular culture, especially films or television series favored by critics who didn't take into account its gendered meanings (see, for example, my posts on *The Social Network* and *Black Swan*, included here). I think it's especially important to intervene in mass entertainment from a feminist perspective. When I'm writing about mainstream films or television shows, my goal is to refocus the lens, to see from the side, as it were, where all the holes in the narrative are suddenly clear, and where all its presumptions and exclusions are most transparent. From the start, then, I maintained a two-prong approach to my blogging, advocating work by women, queer people, and people of color and engaging more pointedly with popular culture. As I wrote, The Feminist Spectator became my alter-ego.

Journalist Katie Roiphe, in an essay for the *New York Times Book Review,* says that a book critic's job is to write beautifully about the literature she reads.[14] I think that theatre and pop culture critics should do the same. Many people assume my blog is a compilation of short, tossed-off thoughts, a personal chronicle of unfiltered impressions. But I take a great deal of care to craft my ideas, and to write and rewrite and rewrite again, until I know that my words do justice to my experience and to what I've seen. I especially feel this responsibility when I'm writing about work that's not mass entertainment or that might not be viewed widely. I want my words to recreate what it felt like to be in the room with Peggy Shaw and Lois Weaver as they performed *Lost Lounge*, or while Holly Hughes contemplated dog agility trials and the waning of lesbian feminism in *The Dog and Pony Show*. To truly communicate the live experience of those performances, I need to use my words, which are the only tool I have to recreate the impact and import of what I thought and felt as I watched. My words become an argument for seeing, a way to urge people to look more broadly and to engage culture that might surprise and change them.

I feel humble in the face of theatre, especially in front of perfor-mances that "work" and that touch me and the "us" with whom I watch. I want to capture that humility and emotion in my writing and communicate my belief that theatre does something, that it makes a difference in the world even by changing one mind or touching one heart. I can think of performances that rocked my world with an intensity that felt revolutionary. I know that theatre doesn't necessarily prompt revolution, though sometimes it has and perhaps it will again. But some performances I've seen have rearranged the molecules of my soul enough for the world to look different when I leave the theatre. I want to somehow translate the wonder of that feeling for others, to communicate what Jewish theologian Abraham Joshua Heschel called the "radical amazement" of seeing the quotidian world as transfor-mative and transformed.[15] That's the challenge and the deep pleasure of writing about theatre, for me – trying to capture what I felt and what I thought, the power of being there, of being changed, of being part of a live moment that mattered.

Likewise, film and television, too, create for me a community of viewing and reception that gives me pleasure and sustains my thinking. I write about film and television to communicate how I've been moved or touched or occasionally angered by what I've seen and to reach out to a more imagined collectivity of spectators than those with whom I watched at the multiplex or on my television at home. Comments on the blog or exchanges on Facebook anchor me in a virtual communal spectatorship that links me to public forums of debate and discourse about culture and the arts. Although I can't feel my fellow spectators responding in the moment of performance, as I do at the theatre, I appreciate (and find that I need) the syncopated charge of engaging with culture through online commentary.

Our responsibility to the local, citizen criticism, and critical generosity

Without an unnecessary attachment to objectivity and universality, all theatre critics have a responsibility to the local. That is, the 12 critics cited in *American Theatre* are really experts on theatre in the cities where they live. They have some relationship to New York and perhaps London, where the theatre scenes are large and influential, but ultimately, these critics are part of a very local arts community. How does a feminist critic accommodate her accountability to the local, as well as the national or even the global, arts scene? To which communities – artistic and spectatorial – are we beholden when we write? When I lived in Austin, I felt part of my job was to capture what it felt like to see theatre in a town known for music and film. Because New York has historically been considered the center of theatre production, it's more difficult to see it as local. But Manhattan and each of New York's other boroughs has its own character. Theatres audiences vary wildly depending on where and what you see. For example, the audiences at New York Theatre Workshop (NYTW) are different from those at the Public Theatre several blocks away in the Manhattan's East Village. NYTW's spectators seem a bit younger, less well-heeled, and more diverse than the Public's, which reflects a more institutional theatre's audience of mostly white, middle-class, middle-aged people. These two theatres boast different audiences from those at Second Stage on 43rd Street in midtown Manhattan, which is more emphatically white and upper-middle class. Second Stage's audiences differ from those at the Women's Project productions, where the gender balance switches to women, or Dixon Place, where audiences tend to be younger and queer, or Here, the Flea, and Soho Rep, which seem to attract more "arty" or avant-garde audiences, or from the numerous other venues and companies that produce theatre in the city. Broadway audiences are comprised of international tourists, as well as a seasoned, if aging, white upper-middle class theatre-going community. How do the demographics of audiences influence a feminist critic's reception of what she sees?

Although I base my assessment of the people who comprise any audience on unscientific impressions of how they look and respond, more and more spectators are writing about their experiences online. A new cadre of "citizen critics" now comments publicly on what they see and think. Just as websites and applications like Open Table, Yelp, and Trip Advisor encourage users to review their outings to restaurants, hotels, and attractions, more and more spectators use the Internet to talk back to mainstream critics and to post their own opinions on the theatre and film they see. Michael Kaiser's 2011 article on the *Huffington Post* website prompted a provocative conversation about the difference between citizen critics and professional critics whose work is vetted by editors. Kaiser, who runs the Kennedy Center in Washington, DC, said he found the trend toward "ordinary people" writing about what they see "scary."[16] Writing on Culturebot.org, Andy Horwitz responded that in fact, citizen critics are often artists themselves, or people whose knowledge of the arts is extensive and passionate.[17] Chloe Veltman, an arts journalist interviewed on HowlRound, says that now, "criticism is something that must be created by people who are passionate about art but not dependent on criticism as a way to make a living."[18] The growing cadre of "citizen critics" will become more and more influential to arts production, as people circumvent conventionally authorized commentators to make their own decisions based on their own criteria for what constitutes useful and pleasurable cultural consumption. That this new critics corps might not be "professional" seems a judgment handed down mostly by powerful curators afraid that what they consider a necessary step, cultural arbitration, will be neutralized. Without career critics determining taste and worth, they fear, what will happen to conventional standards? What if the so-called barbarians begin guarding the gate?

When I won the 2010–2011 George Jean Nathan Award for Dramatic Criticism for my blog, arts writer and scholar Karen Fricker noted in the theatre blog at *The Guardian* that I don't get "paid a dime" for my writing, and that my fulltime job as a professor at Princeton makes it possible for me to write The Feminist Spectator.[19] Fricker is right; I could not make my living as a blogger because of the precarious economy of arts writing in this country. What are the consequences of this structure of time, compensation, and labor if feminist critics must first meet the demands of our "day jobs," if we're lucky enough to have them in the first place? What power might be derived from a kind of informed amateurism in cultural criticism, perhaps for now in conjunction with the more established professional critics? And how might such an expanded cadre of arts writers be a boon to feminist and other art production marginalized by identity or politics?

As it stands, not enough people write feminist criticism to popularize it in the cultural imagination. And because feminism itself is so vilified, one of our first principles as critics must be generosity. Even when I do write negatively about popular culture, for example, I avoid ad hominem attacks. Powerful critics too often forget that they're writing about real people, artists who have lives, feelings, careers, and futures. To comment on a woman performer's body (as theatre critic John Simon was known to do frequently at *New York Magazine*) or to imply that a playwright doesn't deserve his awards or accolades (as Michael Feingold did in a 2012 *Village Voice* review) makes cultural discourse unnecessarily personal.[20] It's not personal; it's political. We can discuss the politics of casting and of body size and shape and skin color and what it means to the relationship of characters on stage and to the audience. But that's very different than commenting on a performer's weight or figure. This danger maintains for web-based, citizen critics as well – note the recent uproar over an email morning news broadcaster Jennifer Livingston, of the La Crosse, Wisconsin, CBS affiliate, received from a viewer who suggested she provides a lousy role model for young women because she's overweight. The writer's very personal attack prompted Livingston to broadcast her response, in which she defended herself and her weight, and used four minutes of air time to protest the presumption of a viewer attacking personally someone he doesn't know.[21] These "flames" are as dangerous in internet culture as they are in print journalism.

Feminist critics comment on what they see with an eye toward what it means to a broader understanding of culture at large. What does the relationship of bodies represented mean to what we know of ourselves and what we might be to one another? How do the characters' appearances, vocal patterns, and gestures perform gender, sexuality, race, and class? How do the director and designers help the cast tell the play or film's story? Who gets the focus in the stage picture or the film frame and whose agency is embodied and enacted? How does the production or movie make you feel and what does it make you think? What's the larger social palette on which you might argue your answers to these questions in a way that matters? These, it seems to me, are questions that point toward a generous, locally-relevant and broadly pointed critical practice.

Finally, feminist criticism is pedagogical. Feminist critics should teach spectators how to look at work for which they might not otherwise have a vocabulary. Feminist criticism should give artists and audiences a language for thinking about gender, race, and sexuality across the landscape of the arts. At the same time, we need to listen and teach ourselves about possibilities for agency and expression that we can't even yet imagine. We need to see ourselves – artists, producers, and spectators alike – as partners in the production of culture and social transformation.

A Roadmap to Action

The Feminist Spectator in Action includes essays that have been lightly edited since their appearance as blog posts on The Feminist Spectator alongside essays written purposefully for this book. I might have organized the essays in numerous ways. In the appendix, in fact, I suggest possibilities for reading the essays across theme (adaptations, fathers and sons, mothers and daughters, guilty pleasures, queer desire, revivals, Shakespeare, and the "male gaze"); across genre/venue (Broadway or West End, Hollywood, indie film, Off- or Off-Off Broadway theatre, or solo performance); or by authorship as writers or directors (people of color, queer people, women of all races, sexualities, and classes). But I've presented them chronologically as I originally wrote them, within sections that describe their central critical observations: advocacy, activism, argument, and artistry. Many of the essays could fit in each or any of these four categories – in some ways, the distinctions are specious. I use them merely to highlight some of the essential feminist critical tasks. The advocacy section includes writing about women artists whose work has been or might otherwise be overlooked by the conventional critical establishment. The activism section demonstrates how feminist critics might promote media literacy. The argument section describes films and productions that resonate with social issues, given their production choices, their narratives, or their authorship. Finally, the artistry section discusses films and theatre productions that I found particularly moving and resonant. These experiences offered moments of utopian performativity that somehow presented a vision of gender, race, and identity that helped me imagine something different about who we are and how we interact with one another.[22]

As a kind of bonus track, *The Feminist Spectator in Action* concludes with a how-to section for would-be feminist critics and spectators alike. How does one write feminist criticism? How does one go to the theatre or films or watch television with a feminist perspective in mind? This isn't an academic exercise, but a skill that can be taught, practiced, and honed by anyone determined to enhance their experience of culture. I hope that students, teachers, artists, spectators, and audiences of all sorts might find helpful the beginnings of a roadmap for how to do the feminist criticism and viewing that I advocate here. We need your voices and your eyes.

Part One: Advocacy

These essays address work by women artists from a range of production contexts. Dynasty Handbag performs in small, often queer-identified Manhattan performance venues, and tours to art theatres around the U.S. Holly Hughes, too, whose *Dog and Pony Show* I discuss here, began at the notorious WOW Café, performs at New York venues like Dixon Place, and tours to theatres, colleges, and universities (she teaches in the Art Department at the University of Michigan). Though Hughes has had a long career, and achieved some infamy in the 1990s as one of the NEA Four, I've placed my discussion of her performance under "advocacy" because her work still deserves more attention from larger audiences, and because the work itself advocates so vehemently for a lesbian feminist way of seeing the world.

More surprisingly perhaps, I've included five films in this section, two of which – *The Kids Are All Right* and *The Hurt Locker* – were successful at the box office, receiving Academy Award nominations and in some cases awards. I discuss these two films here because *The Kids Are All Right* was really the first mainstream, successful, star-cast film directed by an out lesbian (Lisa Cholodenko) and because *The Hurt Locker* won Kathryn Bigelow the first Best Director Oscar ever awarded to a woman. Both films seem significant measures of how advocacy for women artists sometimes actually works.

The last three films are "indies," independent productions written and/or directed by women that were reviewed by the mainstream press, but not as widely seen. *Circumstance* was written and directed by an Iranian-American woman, Maryam Keshavarz, and tells the story of two women who love one another under a repressive Iranian social regime. *Young Adult* is screenwriter Diablo Cody's sophomore offering, after the wild success of her first film, *Juno. Young Adult* wasn't as well received, in part, I argue, because of its cynical, smart view of its central female character (played by the very talented Charlize Theron). *Tiny Furniture*, written, directed by, and starring Lena Dunham, is Dunham's film debut. As the producer, writer, director, and star of the Judd Apatow-produced HBO series *Girls* (which I discuss in conjunction with her feature film), she's created quite a sensation as a representative of the 20-something, white, upper-middle-class female zeitgeist in the U.S. This section also includes one of four essays about television included in the book: Scandal is written and produced by famed show-runner Shonda Rhimes *(Grey's Anatomy)* and stars Kerry Washington as a political fixer. The show is the first network series to star an African American woman since the mid-1970s. (...essays run chronologically according to their date of production. Each is followed by the date on which they were written.) – J.D.

Dynasty Handbag

Produced at the Vortex Theatre, Austin, TX, 2008

New York-based performance artist Dynasty Handbag is the "solo music/video/voiceover/tragicomic performance vehicle created and executed by Jibz Cameron," according to her web site (www.dynasty-handbag.com). She visited Austin recently to perform a benefit evening for the local queer DIY performance space, CampCamp, and also offered a one-night show at the Vortex Theatre in East Austin. Word-of-mouth primed me for her performance – Dynasty Handbag got raves at the "WOW and Now" cabaret staged at Joe's Pub during the Performance Studies International Conference at New York University in November 2007.

I can see why. In the small café that serves as a casual lobby off the Vortex's theatre, Dynasty set up a tiny platform stage under a few even tinier lights and proceeded to seduce the audience with her casual, quirky charm. In a talk after the short show, she positioned herself within overlapping music and performance practices, describing her work with various bands as well as her training in theatre at ACT in San Francisco.

This multiplicity of styles and talents shines in her work. She performed an interactive conversation with her own recorded voice, played from a laptop perched beside an amplifier just off the small stage, selecting numbers from a playlist on the screen, assisted only by a friend who reached out to adjust the volume during each piece. Dynasty reminded me all at once of a singer, a stand-up comic, a performance artist, and a dancer, as her mobile face and flexible body seemed to register each nuance of emotion that crossed through her.

Physically, Dynasty Handbag performed like a hybrid of Charlie Chaplin and Gumby. Her "costumes" were outrageous arrays of clothing layered like non-sequiturs – a leotard over sweat pants, a cut-off t-shirt worn over a long-sleeve shirt. She seemed dressed for mobility, if not for speed; the queer (meaning "odd") look of her outfits enabled the herky-jerky movement of her arms and legs, as thoughts and questions and answers hurtled across her body in spastic, but supremely controlled, finally dancerly style.

In many ways, Dynasty mostly plays reaction shots, responding physically to her taped voice as it prompts her movement through each piece. But what for a less talented, less confident performer would look like mugging in Dynasty's rendition seemed like a symphony of considered, meaningful, even moving response. For instance, I've never noticed the complex of emotions available in a raised eyebrow. Dynasty lets us see differently things we think we've seen before.

The evening's highlight was her interaction with a series of discarded plastic and paper bags that littered the small platform. As each bag pestered her to be noticed, Dynasty approached them warily, with resignation, and let herself be commanded by their needs and desires. Her face and her body registered the humiliations of succumbing to instructions delivered by inanimate objects, yet her generosity with her attention became strangely heartwarming.

Far from cynical, her irony seemed shy rather than coy, hopeful rather than debased. As she petted one of the rumpled plastic bags, pleasuring it with the nearly sexual abandon it demanded, her face moved into and out of confused expressions of embarrassment and willingness, as her body just went with the flow. As each bag called to her in turn, Dynasty acknowledged the publicness of her interactions with these objects. She knows we're watching, and goes through her motions with a wink and a nod to how ridiculous and yet necessary her exchanges seem to be. When the last bag – an upright, rather imperious brown paper one with handles – called her attention, she sighed, "I'm tired of talking to bags." The line resonated as loudly and deeply (if much more comically) as Willie Loman setting down his sales cases and telling his wife he's tired of traveling.

In another number, Dynasty sat in a chair, playing an artist deciding the content of her next piece. The number was a tour-de-force of affectionate self-satire, as the stream-of-consciousness monologue spooled off the laptop while she sat responding with her face and body, pen poised over an open notebook turned to a blank page (this after she borrowed the pen from someone in the audience).

Dynasty's talent, perhaps, lies in how fresh her reactions seem, how persuasive she is in convincing us that she's never heard these thoughts before (and neither have we). At the same time, she crafts a knowing, intimate connection between herself and her spectators, bringing us into this wry, slightly askew world where your own voice gets literalized (auralized?) outside your head, and you judge each choice of action, and respond to what you hear yourself telling yourself. It's the super-ego come to life in a very public place, jousting with the body-as-id, as the ego just tries to hold it together and proceed, knowing that its contradictory, ambivalent, and finally deeply humane actions are under gentle (if pre-disposed to be generous) scrutiny.

Dynasty Handbag's appearance might have been mediated through the apparatus of her laptop and that amplifier, but the intimacy she creates carries a lovely current of liveness. We hear along with her the outrageous demands of things, the cacophony of others' judgments and needs, the absurdity of trying to negotiate questions and comments that press at us from everywhere and nowhere.

In the process, she predisposes us to identify with her disidentifications, with her cautious acquiescence and delicious resistance to the nameless forces that be, which sound an awful lot like, well, Dynasty Handbag. Far from solipsistic, the performance externalizes a conversation we can recognize and to which we can relate: the ambivalences and doubts that prompt our hopeful, finally graceful actions and the generosity with which we all go about believing in the possibilities of our interconnected lives.

FEBRUARY 27, 2008

The Hurt Locker

Voltage Pictures, premiered 2008

The Hurt Locker is a terrific film, made with a combination of guts and sensitivity that can't be attributed in any superficial way to the gender of its director. I've been reading a lot lately about 1970s lesbian feminist "women's culture" in the U.S. and its essentialist claims about women's unique emotional understandings, their pacifism, and their prized connection to nature. I'm finding that these exaggerated claims were usually more tempered than history has made them sound; many 1970s feminists were just trying to stake claims for women in a political context in which their social and cultural contributions had been dismissed and ignored.

Carving out separate space and insisting on women's differences from men seemed, in the 70s, a useful activist strategy, and it promoted a range of cultural production that I'm hoping to reconsider. But 1970s cultural feminists would no doubt have disparaged Kathryn Bigelow's work in *The Hurt Locker*, tarring it with the sticky brush of "male identification."

In 2010, it's still not surprising that the first woman ever to receive the Best Director award won it for a film about war. Bigelow's film, however, addresses not just war's brutality, but its seductions, the adrenalin rush it can deliver, and the insidious, chaotic way it makes lives meaningful.

Staff Sergeant William James (Jeremy Renner, nominated but passed over for Best Actor) spends the war in Iraq wandering the ravaged countryside defusing bombs. He's part of a three-man team traveling together in an armored vehicle, but he's the one who puts on the suit that's meant to protect him from the bombs he proceeds to dismantle by hand.

The puffy, full-body suit and the helmet that encases his head makes James look like an astronaut space-walking across the desert. Bigelow brings her camera close to Renner's face as he moves laboriously toward bomb sites, so that you can see the sweat slicking his skin and hear him talking to himself and his partners as he trundles awkwardly toward what might very well be his own death. The nonchalance and defiance with which he confronts his job's danger make James gripping to watch. He's also a renegade who makes his own decisions and often refuses to follow the protocol his superior, Sergeant JT Sanborn (Anthony Mackie), shouts at him through his headset. James is as unpredictable as the bombs he sets out to defuse.

Bigelow brings the film a stunning tension that electrifies each scene. Even when the soldiers aren't racing over dusty Iraqi streets, past burned out storefronts and shells of apartment buildings toward buried munitions, *The Hurt Locker* keeps you wary, suspicious, and watching for the unexpected. The soldiers see peril where the audience's untrained eyes don't. For example, as James dons the heavy suit and walks toward the center of a town where a bomb has been discovered, Sanborn surveys the scene with binoculars, and sees an Iraqi man with a cell phone in his hand. Before we understand what this means, he's screaming, "He's got a cell phone, he's got a cell phone!" The other American soldiers try to find and shoot the man before he can activate the bomb he controls with his phone. The most minute, imperceptible actions signal danger;

the fact that the audience can't read these signs makes every moment of the film anxious.

Bigelow nuances our vicarious understanding of how soldiers' actions can be intensely intimate and personal or completely distanced and removed. In another scene, James, Sanborn and Specialist Owen Eldridge (Brian Geraghty), their naïve young teammate, are caught by snipers as they cross an abandoned stretch of desert countryside. Leaping out of their Humvee, the three soldiers roll into position against a hillock that offers a vantage point from which they can barely see their assailants off in the distance. Even with binoculars and telescopic rifles, it's difficult for them to target the men, who occupy an abandoned structure that sits what might be miles away. Bigelow frames our view through James's binoculars or Sanborn's rifle sight, but we still can't really make out what they see. James directs Sanborn's aim, and as Sanborn squeezes the rifle's trigger, time attenuates. The bullets seem to travel very slowly over the long distance to their marks.

When the bullets finally reach the anonymous Iraqis, their features blurred by distance, they fall silently. But the relationship between cause (the shooting) and effect (the dying) seems tenuous and surreal. It's difficult to draw a connection between the American soldiers' actions and the Iraqi men's crumpling bodies, making the scene almost phantasmagorical in how Bigelow constructs the relationship between an action and the thing it does. When we see someone shot in a film, they usually buck from the force and instantly fall over dead. Here, we watch the unpredictable but inexorable passage of time between aim and destiny, and these long moments feel disquietingly real. They also illustrate how attenuated responsibility for killing must feel for men whose actions trigger causes that can barely be seen.

The sniper scene is also remarkable for how patiently Bigelow waits in the moment. It's not clear how long James and Sanborn sit in their positions against the low rise, surveying the enemy. The light changes imperceptibly as they watch, barely moving. Sanborn sights through his weapon as flies land in his eyebrows. They talk quietly, not facing one another, keeping their eyes on the horizon. Long after it seems they've killed all the snipers, James and Sanborn wait, searching for movement, determined to outlast anyone who might be calculating their last opportunity to strike. The excruciating but simply constructed scene demonstrates the men's vulnerability as well as the boredom they endure to protect themselves and to outwit their enemy.

In another unforgettable moment, the team is called to an open town square where a suicide bomber balks and pleads to be spared from the fate he chose. James and Sanborn approach warily, assessing whether the man just intends to trick them into coming closer. Again, Bigelow puts the audience within the soldiers' emotional turmoil, keeping her camera back with the vehicle as James and Sanborn try to judge the danger, then moving toward the overwrought Iraqi as James puts on the suit and approaches. We arrive with James to find the man trussed up as a human time bomb. The dynamite strapped against his chest attaches to a clock ticking off the minutes and seconds until it explodes. A metal cage encases the whole apparatus, padlocked against just the kind of second thoughts the would-be suicide bomber now experiences.

Here, unlike in the sniper scene, Bigelow gets intimate with the effects of war. James realizes he can't defuse the bomb in time, and instead tries to free the man from his death trap. Ripping off his helmet and visor, he insists Sanborn bring him tools, and works mightily to release the Iraqi. But as the seconds tick down, James realizes his attempt is futile; he doesn't have time to cut through the cage. He looks into the poor man's eyes, entreating him to understand, in a language he doesn't speak, James's sorrow over not being able to save him. "I'm sorry, I'm sorry," he repeats, knowing his face is the last this panic-stricken, doomed fellow human being will ever see. Then he runs, with seconds left to save himself.

The dynamite ignites as James hustles away, its force lifting him off the ground and throwing him from the tornado of fire, dust, and body parts it hurls through the air. The ambivalent Iraqi's death is palpable, as we're left imagining in vivid detail his body exploding like an overripe piece of fruit dropped from a high table. The moment's intimacy depicts the flip side of war; looking a soon-to-be-dead man in the eyes and trying to release his body from its fate is a far cry from the remote, clinical rifle work necessary to execute men so far away their humanity is abstracted.

Bigelow's feel for how war changes register and key is also apparent in how she draws the soldiers' relationships in *The Hurt Locker*. Sanborn and James warily paw the ground around one another, knowing they're forced to trust the other man with their lives. Their situation requires machismo they both know is only fabricated. In one of Mackie's finest moments – in an excellent performance overlooked by the Academy – Sanborn asks James if he thinks Sanborn would ever be brave enough to put on the suit. From the timid, embarrassed hopefulness with which he poses the question, Mackie demonstrates that Sanborn isn't made of the necessary stuff. But James's generous reassurance that Sanborn, too, could do the work, underlines that the only thing separating the two men is their essential level of regard for their own lives.

The Hurt Locker is paced by titles that count down the days until the men's unit leaves Iraq, markers that also increase the tension by playing on the audience's expectation that something will go wrong and they won't make it out alive. But James and Sanborn do decamp. We soon see James at home, months later, his hair grown longer, domesticated by his girlfriend (Evangeline Lilly). They shop at a supermarket, where the array of colors and the variety of textures contrasts with the rest of the film's limited visual palette, in which khaki-clad soldiers crawl over dun-colored land bleached by harsh sunlight. But James rests awkwardly at home. He smokes and stares out the window, held static by a world that comes at him with slow predictability. Before long, he's back in uniform, marching out of the belly of a transport plane that delivers him back to Iraq and a war to which he's clearly addicted. A chilling half-smile plays on his face as he leaves the plane; James is an adrenalin junky anticipating his next fix.

The Hurt Locker is a terrific anti-war film, in part because it never overtly criticizes the conflict's politics. It tallies the war's effects in human costs, not by counting the dead, but by chronicling in quotidian, disturbing ways what war does to the living.

MARCH 10, 2010

The Kids Are All Right

Focus Features, premiered 2010

In addition to being the best movie about lesbians I've seen in a long time, *The Kids Are All Right* is a beautifully written and filmed, evocative, deeply funny, and deeply felt story about relationships in general. To say the film is about a couple who "*happen* to be lesbians" would completely miss the point, even though part of what makes it notable is that the leading couple's sexuality is so completely taken for granted.

But director/co-writer (with Stuart Blumberg) Lisa Cholodenko (*High Art, Laurel Canyon*), for whom the story is apparently in part inspired by her own autobiography, understands that in 2010, being a lesbian family still requires work, gumption, patience, and ultimately, forgiveness. Lesbian parents are as imperfect as any, but they're still not exactly "normal" enough. Their striving to make the kids be all right takes emotional and physical diligence that the film evokes specifically and honestly.

Nic (Annette Bening) and Jules (Julianne Moore) have been together long enough to raise 18-year-old Joni (Mia Wasikowska) and 15-year-old Laser (Josh Hutcherson), kids they each bore using the same sperm donor. When Laser has pangs of father-longing, he asks his older sister to track down their donor, and emotional complications ensue when Paul (Mark Ruffalo) turns out to be a charismatic, free-spirited organic farmer/restaurateur.

Each of the five characters are complicated enough that how they'll respond to the awkwardness of their situation is never predictable. Some of the film's comedy comes from the surprising variety of character reactions, but then, so does its melancholy. Nic and Jules's long-term relationship is rocky under its smoothly functioning veneer, and both women have sacrificed in ways they don't even begin to realize until Paul's presence shakes up their lives.

Nic, the perfectionist OB-GYN who has a bit of a drinking problem, harasses Jules about her lack of focus and ambition, even as Nic's position funds Jules's new landscape architecture business. Jules is more artistic and freewheeling, but she's not unaware of her own psychic complexities. When she and Nic fight about Jules's flightiness, Jules accuses Nic of wanting a stay-at-home wife to raise their kids, observing that Nic never really wanted Jules to work. Both women describe their long-term relationship as a marriage, which feels poignant and right in their situation, even in the face of California's political change of heart about the legality of gay unions.

In other words, Nic and Jules suffer the problems that crop up in many long-term committed relationships, as well as those that plague parents of many teenagers. Joni, who's about to leave for college, starts the painful process of separating from her moms, encouraged by Paul's rule-flouting, easy-going manner. Nic and Jules's relationship is strained when the kids and Jules take to Paul, and Jules, whom he's hired to redesign and replant his backyard, finds herself unexpectedly attracted to him sexually. Paul's appearance provokes a major transition, but happily (for Cholodenko's story and for us), the bonds between these two women and their kids are only strengthened by the end.

Each of the performances is pitch-perfect. Bening's face registers each of Nic's conflicting emotions with a vulnerable openness that refuses to hide anything from the camera, even as Nic tries to hide her feelings from her family. Bening is a remarkable actor – her work here, and with a very different character in Rodrigo Garcia's film *Mother and Child* earlier this summer, demonstrates her emotional intelligence as well as her range. Bening plays across the spectrum of human emotion with particular insight into what it means to be a middle-aged, upper-middle class white woman with a complicated set of desires and longings, ambitions and expectations.

Moore plays Jules with a physical looseness and verve that she rarely has occasion to enjoy on screen. As Jules, Moore struggles with how to organize her separate life, but is utterly confident about the importance and centrality of her commitment to Nic and her family. Moore plays Jules's surprise as she falls into bed with Paul with unbridled excitement and a devilish joy. But when Paul falls in love with her and calls her to spin out a fantasy in which he and Jules will run away with the kids and be their own family, she's absolutely clear that she's a lesbian who's already taken: Moore grimaces at his suggestion, hangs up on Paul, and throws the phone away in comic irritation.

Ruffalo plays Paul as a sexy teddy bear of a boy-man, who's successful with his restaurant because it allows him to play in the dirt all day, eating vegetables he picks off the vine, and dreaming up recipes to please his customers at night. Ruffalo is hairy in all the right ways as Paul, sporting scruffy graying stubble and wearing blue jeans and denim shirts open to his navel. He's an earthy guy, who's managed certain accomplishments despite dropping out of school (because he found it boring), a good-time type with no commitments to drag him down.

To accentuate his hip-and-grooviness, Paul rides a motorcycle. When he gives young Joni a tour through the streets of LA en route to bringing her home to her moms, the scene evokes the thrill of the forbidden for Joni and prompts unsurprising consequences. Nic, the family disciplinarian, is furious. Paul tells her she just has to "chill out," a suggestion thrown at Nic more than once throughout the story.

What makes the rather uptight Nic complex and endearing is that she tries to ease up. She suggests a family dinner at Paul's house, where she makes a huge effort to get on board with Paul's magnetism and appreciate it with the rest of her captivated family. Over dinner, Nic and Paul discover that they're both Joni Mitchell fans. Bening plays a hilarious extended scene in which she sings "All I Want" (one of

Mitchell's harder songs to capture a cappella) off key and off tempo, with her eyes closed, while the rest of her family winces with affection. This is Nic going out on a limb – the perfectionist willing, for the sake of her family, to do something she's bad at to make herself human.

In the film's only predictable moment, Nic leaves that dinner table to use Paul's bathroom, where, of course, she finds Jules's hair in his brush and his shower drain, and proceeds to check out his bedroom, where she finds Jules's hair on his nightstand. Bening transforms from a generous, affectionate mom trying hard to fathom her brood's attraction to a man she finds unworthy into a cuckolded mate whose realization that she's been cheated on happens in the presence of her wife's paramour. Bening plays the wrenching moment with sadness, subtlety, and a whole lot of heart.

Paul hasn't really grown up. In some ways, he becomes the family's third child, making goofy faces as scenes end on shots of him reacting to his unusual circumstances. When Laser asks him why he became a sperm donor, Paul tells him he thought it'd be more fun than donating blood. When Laser looks hurt, Paul begins to realize that his actions have consequences for which he's being asked to take responsibility.

But when he falls in love with Jules, he thinks he can become a man by adopting another woman's family, and that's where Cholodenko and Blumberg make sure to underline that he's wrong. Paul's biological connection to Joni and Laser gives him no rights; even though Jules, early on, tells him that she sees her kids' expressions in his face, his DNA doesn't trump 18 years of child-rearing. Nic finally thwarts Paul's growing desire to move in on her lesbian household, kicking him out and telling him to go make a family of his own.

The Kids Are All Right could easily have been about Paul's redemption, his transition from an unattached boy-toy into a serious co-parent. Happily, Cholodenko and Blumberg avoid that too-conventional plot line. Paul is changed by meeting Nic and Jules and their kids, much more than he changes them, but he doesn't, in the end, get what he wants, and it's finally not clear if he's even learned anything about himself.

Each character in *The Kids Are All Right* has their own trajectory, and the script doesn't favor one over any of the others. Joni (named after Joni Mitchell), who's on her way to college, precipitates the family crisis not just by contacting Paul, but by becoming an adult who's leaving their cozy nest. It's Joni who, in frustration after they learn of Jules and Paul's affair, complains that she's done everything "right," that she got good grades and got into all the schools she applied to, all to prove that she's from a good lesbian family. The burden of being exemplary, Cholodenko suggests, is heavy for those who grow up in less conventional ways.

In one of Cholodenko's smartest choices, Paul is something of a loser as a male role model. Playing basketball with Laser, Ruffalo is hilarious as Paul flubs various moves and throws and never makes a basket, while Laser shoots and scores effortlessly. Paul's affair with Jules makes him morally and ethically suspect for the rest of the family (Joni tells him she wishes he'd been "better"), but he somehow expects that Laser will side with him. Peering in the window at the family dinner table after Nic has dressed him down for the last time, Paul tries to gain Laser's favor by shrugging his shoulders and rolling his eyes as though none of what's transpired is really a big deal. Lazer storms away from the table (and out of Paul's view) and throws away his food in disgust.

Another of the film's pleasures is the wonder of watching two stunningly attractive middle-aged actors who seem to have avoided face lifts and Botox injections. Bening and Moore are beautiful women who don't conform to conventional standards of too-youthful, too-thin, too-vapid American white female attractiveness. Bening (who's 52) is a mature woman with crows' feet around her eyes and wrinkles on her neck that make her look even more gorgeous (in my opinion. And the sculpted triceps evident when Nic wears a sleeveless denim shirt on a trip to the hardware store look pretty good, too).

Moore (who's 50) wears her freckles proudly, and her body, too, seems lived in and comfortably real (though very natural-looking and frankly, spectacular). Jules wears low-slung jeans and purple thong underwear (which Paul admires as Jules bends over to work in his yard), but she looks like an arty middle-age woman who lives in LA. Jules's red hair is never quite coiffed, but just worn. And although Nic is a successful OB-GYN with a spiky, short haircut, she wears jeans and jackets and signature black Converse sneakers that flatter her beauty but don't hide the very normal size of Bening's middle-aged body. Nic and Jules might wear the casual clothes and leather bands and chokers and silver jewelry of upper-class white LA lesbians, but they aren't *L Word* women; they're mature, smart, and work hard at their lives.

Cholodenko and Blumberg's script captures with humor and insight what might be most different about lesbian relationships and parenting: the over-analyzing, over-sharing, and over-speaking that's somehow typical (not to be essentialist about this) of some women who love one another and raise kids together. Some of the movie's funniest dialogue is delivered by Nic and Jules when they're trying to reach out to their kids. For example, when they suspect Laser is gay, they both go on about how he can talk to them and trust them. When Laser discovers his mom's cache of gay male porn, he asks why they watch men instead of women, and Jules delivers a hilarious explanation that's funny not because it's wrong, but because it's so truthful.

Jules explains, in Moore's deliberate, generous, too open delivery, lesbian porn is often cast with straight women, which makes it inauthentic. (Some might say the same about *The Kids Are All Right*, since Bening and Moore are straight; I'd disagree. In fact, Moore's speech in this scene might be Cholodenko's wry dig at that inevitable complaint.) Watching Jules offer too much information to her young straight son in an attempt to be a good, honest lesbian parent is a hysterical, perfectly on-target social observation.

The film's one misstep is its treatment of Jules's Latino gardening assistant, Luis (Joaquín Garrido), who understands that she and Paul are having an affair. His face registers the pleasure of his knowledge when their liaison dawns on him, which Jules misreads as judgment. She summarily fires him, archly telling him she won't reconsider. The poor guy loses his job in the story, and in the film, the character's reactions and speech are racially stereotyped in ways that seem gratuitous.

Of course, what makes *The Kids Are All Right* remarkable is that it's a mainstream film about a lesbian family (a white, upper-middle class lesbian family in LA, that is) with big-name stars, and that means a lot at this particular moment in history. Kathy Wolfe, the founder and CEO of the LGBT video distribution company, Wolfe, in her editorial in theadvocate.com, calls the movie the lesbian *Brokeback Mountain*, since it stars major Hollywood actors and has achieved wide distribution (by Focus Features, which also released *Brokeback* and *Milk*). But where *Brokeback* addressed a physical and emotional desire that drew its two men together persistently over time during a moment when their queerness might have gotten them killed, *The Kids Are All Right* tells its funny, poignant tale from the perspective of an historical moment when seeing two moms like Nic and Jules deliver their daughter to college doesn't warrant a second glance (well, at least in some places).

But it's easy to forget that Nic and Jules – and the many lesbian mothers who no doubt inspired Cholodenko's film, herself included – were pioneers 20 years ago, using sperm banks and artificial insemination to create their families of choice. And these characters provide one of the first film representations of a long-term lesbian couple that actually seems convincing. They work to keep their sex life active, sometimes successfully and sometimes not. They find more frequent intimacy talking about their kids with one another, face to face on their pillows at night. They know they're different from one another; Nic is controlling and Jules is perpetually lost. Their power dynamic means that Jules sometimes feels invisible, staying at home to raise the family while Nic is distracted with work. They're not perfect.

As Jules says, speechifying to Nic, Joni, and Laser, a marriage is really hard work and you inevitably hurt the ones you love most as you slog through the years, making mistakes you sometimes can't fix and trying to go on. When they've said their goodbyes to Joni, leaving her at college, and the now-three of them get back in their car (a Volvo station wagon, of course) to return home, Laser says from his perch in the back seat, "I don't think you two should break up." Amused, Nic asks why not, and he retorts with affection, "You're too old." Nic and Jules smile and reach to one another across the car seat. The film ends on a close-up of their hands clasped – two middle-aged women's hands, forcefully joined, fiercely determined, loving the past they share and the future they'll create.

Can't argue with that.

Except some other commentators in the queer media do. I've read responses from queer bloggers and LGBTQ folks in mainstream internet outlets who criticize or support the film on the basis of how it represents lesbian relationships (Authentic or not? Enough sex or not? Assimilationist or not?). I don't go to mainstream Hollywood films expecting radical ideological positions; call me conservative, call me liberal, but I don't expect that particular form to be the one in which we save the world. I'm happy for a mainstream film that depicts lesbian relationships at all – how many, after all, can we list? Isn't this why *The Kids Are All Right* bears what Kobena Mercer called so long ago now "the burden of representation"? Because there are so few representations of lesbians in the mainstream, everyone brings to them their own investments and standards, and it goes without saying how impossible it is to please everyone.

Yes, as Kate Clinton notes in *The Huffington Post*, the movie is in some ways the same-old same-old, and it doesn't offer lesbian sex "with skin." But as Mark Harris writes in *Entertainment Weekly*, Cholodenko seems more interested in what makes a long-term relationship than in sexy representations of lesbian moms. He thinks *The Kids* is one of the best films ever to describe what marriage means and how it looks. But some people think it didn't do justice to long-term lesbian relationships, either. Sure, the movie isn't perfect. How could it be? Sarah Schulman says on the Bully Bloggers web site, it's an achievement that it got made at all, a testament not only to Cholodenko's skill as a filmmaker, but no doubt to her ability to move through Hollywood deal-making structures that of course will have some bearing on the final product. To expect otherwise is unrealistic.

But can't we look at what this film does and acknowledge that while it doesn't do everything, it makes a contribution to however liberal a discourse about lesbians – white, upper-middle class, LA lesbians, who co-parent in a committed relationship; in other words, a certain *type* of lesbians – in the mainstream imaginary? I found the film funny, moving, and observant about what it means to work through the ups and downs of a long-term relationship. And despite my own choice not to parent, I admire women who buck the odds, adopt one another's biological children in conservative states like Texas, for only one example (where, had the movie been set there, the story might have been utterly different), and use their daily lives as a site of their activism. The relationship Cholodenko depicts isn't mine; I've been with my partner for 21 years, but we don't call one another "wife," as they do in the film. In fact, we cringe at that language, and want no ceremony of any sort (marriage or commitment) to mark our relationship. But we live in New Jersey, where we did take advantage of civil union legislation, in large part because we want to be able to make health care decisions for one another should it become necessary (and it will).

Implicit in some negative discussion about *The Kids* is judgment against the sort of lesbian families or relationships the film represents. Calling the film's central relationship only normative seems exaggerated. Lesbians (and gay men) who want to marry might be assimilationist, but are there so many images of lesbian and gay families available that they're already widely recognizable and accepted, especially outside the west coast urban context in which the story plays out? Doesn't the film at least add to the number of public, mainstream representations of a family form that might still be alien to many people who see this film? If Nic and Jules seem "just like us" to many of those viewers, is that a bad thing, really? Some lesbians *aren't* just like the mainstream and don't aspire to be. But some do; should they be judged badly for that?

It seems to me futile to prescribe what's "truly" radical in a lesbian relationship, or to suggest that any mainstream representation is just bound to get it wrong. The good thing about *The Kids Are All Right* is that it gives us something to argue around the perennial question of how the margins should be represented in the mainstream. I hope, in 2010, that LGBTQ social movement activism can accommodate multiple efforts on multiple fronts. It's desperately important that we keep reimagining different ways of being people, reconfiguring the relative value of sexual practice, and re-envisioning potentially new arrangements for domestic structures. I'd hope there's room for work like Cholodenko's alongside work by more formally and ideologically radical artists, like, for only one example, Holly Hughes, whose newest performance, *The Dog and Pony Show (Bring Your Own Pony)*, I just had the pleasure of seeing at Dixon Place in New York. I'm personally eager to see both ends of the spectrum, and everything in between, and to treat it all with the kind of critical generosity I think it deserves.

JULY 30, 2010

The Dog and Pony Show

Produced at Dixon Place,
New York, NY, 2010

Holly Hughes has plied her particular brand of solo performance for over 30 years now, experience that provides her authority and refreshing, admirable self-assurance in her latest, *The Dog and Pony Show (Bring Your Own Pony)*, which ran for two, too-short nights at Dixon Place during their recent "Hot" Festival. Hughes' last full-length piece was *Preaching to the Perverted* (2000), which detailed her experience as a so-called pariah during the culture wars in the 1990s, and her run-in with the NEA and the subsequent Supreme Court case over its grants to individual artists. *Dog and Pony* takes a different turn, narrating Hughes' attachment to the dogs with which she and her partner, the eminent lesbian anthropologist Esther Newton, have created their family.

Hughes' politics here are as incisive as usual, but also personal and subtle. The self-deprecating irony is gone, as Hughes takes physical, emotional, and intellectual command of Dixon Place's gloriously wide, deep space. Hughes and director Dan Hurlin set her story within simple décor: a small, comfortable armchair to which she retreats to tell some of the story; a tall wooden stool on which she sometimes perches; and a music stand from which she occasionally consults her script to mark her progress through the tale. Slides of historical women and their dogs run behind her, punctuating the story with humor and a gentle reminder that this is an on-going, timeless relationship into which Hughes and Newton find themselves cast. In one of the show's funniest visual moments, Gertrude Stein and Alice B. Toklas pose in a projected photo with their poodle between them. As we watch, the image morphs into Newton and Hughes, neatly tracing the legacy of famous lesbian couples and their canine kids.

In another very funny visual moment, lesbian singer Phranc is on hand for "Phranc Talk," a segment in which she films Hughes and her Norfolk terrier, Ready, preparing to execute a difficult agility course. In an affectionately satirical style reminiscent of *Best in Show*, Phranc narrates as Hughes and Ready go through their paces. Ready scurries obediently across the course, bounding up steep ramps, down see-saws, through tunnels, and over challenging obstacles, while Hughes offers vocal encouragement to keep the pup on track as they move through the stations together. Much of *Dog and Pony* pokes good-humored fun at the routines and obsessions of "dog people," in this case largely middle-aged white women, whom Hughes says need their bodies to carry stuff around the same way they need a good truck, and who, in erstwhile lesbians-of-a-certain-type style, simply throw clothes over themselves that immediately signal that they've "given up."

Yet rather than belittling this community – of which she clearly considers herself a part – Hughes understands that at a certain point, the body becomes a vehicle, like those trucks, a means of delivering something or of getting somewhere rather than an end in itself. Even the funny bit about how these women dress signals a freedom from convention, a liberation from worrying about how they look so that they can concentrate on what they *do* and what, at the end of the leashes they hold with such seriousness and care, their dogs can achieve.

Likewise, Hughes' description of her life with Newton and their dogs becomes a sly allegory for the vagaries of lesbian families. Hughes honors the importance of the primary domestic arrangements many of us have created with partners and beloved pets, taking seriously the nature of these special kinship structures. The reference to offspring is always present, happily morphing into stories about their dogs. An anecdote about Hughes and Newton waiting until the eleventh hour to reproduce turns into the hilarious and instructive tale of taking Newton's prized poodle, Presto, for sperm collection. Hughes describes Presto as her son and admits she felt as if she were taking him to a whorehouse for the first time when they take him to the vet for an appointment with a flirtatious bitch. She relates her mortification when Presto's interaction doesn't produce enough sperm to make him a good stud. That even in the world of dog breeding gender presumptions go without saying is part of the story's moral, but Hughes plays it for laughs instead of lessons.

She describes the dog's maleness in their lesbian household as a challenging curiosity (Newton, Hughes says, won't have the dog fixed because she likes to look at his balls). The story of Hughes and Newton buying a sectional sofa so that they and their nine dogs can have "family time" together paints not just a hysterical picture of "dog lesbians" (as Hughes calls them), but also describes a viable alternative to more conventional lesbian families (if that's not a contradiction in terms). I can still picture Hughes and Newton on their ever-growing sofa, surrounded by terriers and poodles competing for their humans' attention.

In *Dog and Pony*'s opening speech, Hughes announces that the lesbian community remains divided: there are dog lesbians and cat lesbians and the asthmatics who can't breathe either way. But her declaration underlines that the lesbian community continues to exist and even thrive despite these (and obviously other) differences. Hughes continues to enjoy community and to find it important, a refreshing commitment in the face of its more trendy disparagement. She might have left New York and the pleasures of WOW, the theatre "home for wayward girls" comprised of performance artists Hughes recalls were kicked out of one feminist organization or another in the early 80s. But in her Michigan residence, she's clearly embraced another community of women with practices as equally out of the ordinary. In fact, she says, dog people are a lot like artists; no one cares what they do.

Alongside stories of dog agility, breeding, and the women who know just how to do it, come Hughes's observations about being a lesbian and a feminist of a certain age, about how her work and her life have always been inextricable from the politics of gender and sexuality. This aspect of *Dog and Pony* is poignant, politically smart, and often moving. When Hughes announces her identifications, her declarations are really rather performative – that is, they *do* something to remind us of how potent the words "lesbian" and "feminist" once were and still can be, said with the conviction and faith and historical depth of experience Hughes brings them.

A vignette about Hughes wearing a "This is What a Feminist Looks Like" t-shirt to give a lecture at a university and the political fallout that ensues from her talk is terrific, as it illustrates the muddle of expectations people bring to contemporary politics. Invited by a lesbian academic to address the bad reputation of feminism among college students, the woman winds up accusing Hughes of giving a talk that only exacerbates the stereotype of feminists as "angry lesbians." Astonished, Hughes retorts that "angry" and "lesbian" are her shtick – why was she invited if that's not what this woman wanted?

Despite ironies such as these, *Dog and Pony* presents Hughes in a generous mood. The lovely writing describes her relationship with Newton, and with a new best friend in Ann Arbor, where Hughes is now a professor in the Art Department at the University of Michigan. These relationships clearly matter to her a great deal, and their texture and import color her stories with a new depth of feeling.

I consider Hughes one of the most important artists of our generation, someone who's always taken formal risks to tell stories that too often go unheard in other cultural venues (mainstream, lesbian, and feminist alike). This new show retains her trademark outré humor, but also delivers authoritative insights in a style that's beautifully modulated and tonally diverse. Hughes's stories ring with the confidence of a cultural warrior who's come out of the fray not just intact, but wiser, with a distinctive clarity about where she's been, where she's going, and what it all means. We're invited to laugh with her in *Dog and Pony*, to see the grace and beauty of ordinary people with their crazy but somehow humble obsessions.

For the performance's final, lyrical bit of image-making, Hughes stands downstage center and describes a silver wolf, with four legs that "spell fear," coming out of the woods to assume the place created beside human beings when evolution left us without as much to do. Dogs, she protests, don't descend from wolves; she credits the animals with agency, suggesting they chose their place beside us to help create us, just as we, with great empathy and affinity, help to create them.

As Hughes takes her curtain call, one last video clip plays of a woman handling a Golden Retriever that she's trained to dance beside her. The two perform in a large, nearly empty arena to music we can't hear. Both of them seem thrilled to be moving in sync, dancing as a cross-species couple. The grainy image is striking and sweet, an homage to mutually fortifying, joyful and enabling relationships between humans and canines. Thanks to Hughes's beautiful rendition of *Dog and Pony Show*, those relationships become a model for us all.

AUGUST 8, 2010

Circumstance

Marakesh Films, premiered 2011

Writer/director Maryam Keshavarz's beautiful, disturbing film tells the story of two Iranian high school girlfriends in Teheran whose growing attraction and love for one another quickly hits the wall of religious interdiction and oppressive patriarchy. Filmed with a grainy realism, *Circumstance* is haunted by impending doom, even in its frequent moments of whimsical affection and erotic passion. The film's opening scene sets the tone, as Atafeh (Nikohl Boosheri) and Shireen (Sarah Kazemy) stand among their young peers in a school yard, all wearing identical, modesty-imposing skirts and jackets and hijabs that barely hide the two women's beauty. Shireen slips an origami bird into Atafeh's hand, a gesture of fondness weighted with the symbolism of impossible flight and escape that comes to define the girls' relationship and their lives.

Although *Circumstance* follows the young women's sexual and emotional relationship in the context of the Iranian theocracy, the film more broadly addresses the country's human rights violations against women. A pervasive sense of surveillance quickly becomes the film's visual motif. In that first schoolyard scene, after the headmistress dismisses the girls, we see Atafeh and Shireen hail a taxi to leave the school grounds. Keshavarz shoots the action from above in grainy black and white, as if through the lens of a security camera. The image conveys the intrusive intimacy of being so closely watched.

These surveillance-like shots appear regularly throughout the story, reminding spectators of the omnipresent eye of the religious authorities whose word holds sway, even as the two young women seem blissfully unaware of how their every move is observed and catalogued. Ata's brother, Mehran (Reza Sixo Safai), serves as the family's in-house surveyor. He returns to the family fold at the film's start, after an unexplained absence. Mehran was a talented musician who gave up his gift after recovering from a devastating drug addiction that's left his father suspicious and his mother forgiving. Mehran replaces his passion for music and drugs with religious fanaticism, surprising his wealthy, secular family with his new commitment to prayer.

Mehran becomes the vehicle through which Iranian religious and political authority infiltrates the micro-level of the family. His post-addiction paranoia translates into obsessive spying on his sister and his parents. His eye supplements the state's, as he installs cameras around his family's home through which he observes their every interaction. He also collaborates with the mullahs who become his new compatriots. When he begins to understand the physical and emotional reality of Ata and Shireen's relationship, he engineers a series of confrontations in which the morality police round up and harass the two girls. Mehran comes to Shireen's rescue in a way that forces her to depend on his manufactured generosity and allows him to manipulate her into an unwanted marriage.

While Ata's family is well-off and initially protected from the authoritative whims of the local mullahs, Shireen's parents were professors executed as counter-revolutionaries by the religious regime. The beautiful, doleful young woman lives with her uncle and her grandmother, tenuously attached to the relatives who tolerate the economic burden of her presence. Her grandmother adores her; a scene in which they dance together in the kitchen with a kind of joyous freedom is lovely and contrasts sharply with those of her uncle trying to palm her off on another man by arranging a marriage before Mehran steps in to offer himself.

When Ata and Shireen are arrested on a fabricated morals charge, the cruel officials accuse Shireen of being a whore. They belittle her and threaten to hang her, just as the state hanged her parents. Ata is fierce on her friend's behalf, and she is saved by the sage generosity of her own father, who bails her out by bribing the unctuous, dangerous official. But Shireen knows how limited her options are without money or a father to rescue her, and she becomes trapped by the impossibility of truly being free as a woman in a deeply patriarchal, religiously driven social order.

Because Shireen's lineage already puts her at a political disadvantage, Keshavarz establishes visually how the male-embodied state holds power over her very flesh. When Shireen takes a taxi from a party alone, the driver abuses her sexually, using her for his fetishistic pleasures. Likewise, Mehran's patriarchal hold over Shireen and his sister begins to leech away Shireen's sexual desire and control. Watching her degenerate from a powerfully erotic young woman who plays with men but clearly loves Ata into a sexually and emotionally subservient wife is one of the film's many heart-breaking narrative arcs.

Keshavarz directs her two fresh, leading actors with subtly and respect. Boosheri and Kazemy are lovely together as Ata and Shireen, communicating the stark contrast between what their newly matured bodies want and what their deeply constrictive culture allows. They convey their love for one another with small gestures that Keshavarz captures with simple delicacy – one girl's finger curling around the other's as they stand in line at school or as they walk together with the men who comprise their social lives; the quick kiss Shireen gives Ata when she breaks a car window to steal a shimmering handbag she admires; and especially in the way the girls dance together, alone in Ata's room, before Mehran intrudes on their pleasure. Their physical freedom, and the obvious eroticism of their bond as they dance together with delight while they watch *American Idol*, is at once moving and wrenching.

Ata and Shireen's palpable attraction to one another provokes anxiety in the film's spectators, if not in the other characters, about their fates. But although Keshavarz keeps the threat of danger flickering around the film, only the scenes with the mullah and Mehran actualize the dire circumstances in which the women live. Still, their lives are a series of close calls, each of which underlines the cost of female resistance and the gender hypocrisy of Iranian culture. For example, Ata and Shireen frequent parties in Teheran's underground, where young people dance to Western music, drink, do drugs, and experiment with sex in ways Keshavarz depicts as normal for 21st century young people. But these rites of passage are consigned to private homes, which Ata and Shireen enter by pretending they're going to sewing circles. Their male friends, on the other hand, can range freely through Iranian society, without the sartorial or behavioral constraints that confine the young women.

Keshavarz also complicates the film's gender politics by making Ata and Shireen's male intimates rather harmless, suggesting that they are constructed into the gendered power of the state, rather than naturally assuming it. Ata's ostensible boyfriend at first seems threatening. When he tries to have sex with Shireen – who soundly rejects him – he seems fully in command of his sexual power. But he turns out to be innocuous and young. He and Ata team up with Shireen and Joey (Keon Mohajeri), a young man who's gone to school in the U.S. and has progressive ideas about ideology and politics. Joey idealistically dreams of dubbing *Milk,* the American Harvey Milk biopic, into Arabic, so that Iranians – he believes – will be able to see their own situation in the story of gay liberation in America. He wants his people to be inspired to change what he, speaking the film's title, points to as their dubious circumstances. Some of the film's lightest moments show the four friends working on the dubbing project with Joey. They try to speak like Sean Penn as Harvey Milk and to simulate the film's gay sex with the right tone of voice. Joey's faith that his work will mean something is touching even though the film clarifies that it's also naïve and, in the end, fatal.

Circumstance is at its best when Keshavarz more indirectly shows the oppressions of a culture in which binary gender distinctions are so determining. When Ata and Shireen join Ata's family for a day at the beach, the director stages in the background another family lounging beside their beach blanket, the mother in full black dress and hijab while her sons and husband wear revealing swim suits. Ata's father, Firouz (Soheil Parsa), and Mehran also enjoy the privilege to inhabit their bodies publically, leaving their own women behind with only a small backward glance before they run into the waves. Later, when Ata and Shireen find themselves alone by the water as the men are called to prayer, they take advantage of their exclusion from religious ritual to strip to their underwear and swim together. The actors perform the sensual thrill of floating in your own skin along the surface of the water alongside someone you love.

The action in *Circumstance* is oblique and subtle, as characters' allegiances gradually shift and their commitments change. After Shireen marries Mehran, breaking Ata's heart, she creeps into her friend's room to confess that she wed him only so that she could be close to Ata. Their sudden freedom to be together with the legitimate excuse of being sisters-in-law releases their erotic charge even more publicly. At a family party, Ata and Shireen sit beside one another on a piano bench flirting so seductively, only the culture's profound disregard for women's sexuality would permit anyone to misrecognize their relationship. Even Ata's mother, Azar (Nasrin Pakkho), is complicit in her refusal to see anything but what makes her life livable. She's glad for her son's return and unwilling to acknowledge the authoritarian religious current he brings into her house. Given Azar's lack of power, the film suggests she can do little but use her intentional blindness to survive.

Only Ata, in the end, finds her circumstances untenable. She sees that her liberal father will inevitably acquiesce to the mullahs to retain his economic, if not political, privilege. She notes with horror as her father begins to join Mehran's religious observances. Ata understands her world will constrict even further unless she escapes while she can. Following a dream that Shireen first articulated – though she now refuses to come along – Ata bribes an official to let her travel to Dubai without her father's permission, freeing herself into a life in which she hopes to embody the woman she has become.

Circumstance's ending sounds a few false notes. Perhaps Shireen's fear of being hanged by the police is finally enough to force her to capitulate to her husband, but in her final scene, it seems she has also, inexplicably, developed some feeling for him. And occasionally, Keshavarz paints the mullahs and their henchmen as two-dimensional villains, when the subtlety of their evil is much more chilling. Nonetheless, with its artful yet stark eroticism bumping up against scenes that reveal the unadulterated cruelty of an oppressive social system, the film is a powerful indictment of the disempowerment of Iranian women. *Circumstance* provides a stirring, important picture of the crushing double standard between what women desire in private and what they're allowed in public.

OCTOBER 17, 2011

Scandal

ShondaLand, premiered on ABC Television, 2012

Shonda Rhimes' new television series arrived at its first season finale last week, after a terrific premiere and seven-week run and the promise of renewal for a second season. Kerry Washington stars in the first series to feature an African–American woman in the leading role since 1974, a fact of network history that seems both outrageous and significant. The lie that America is "post-race" has long been put to rest, but that *Scandal's* demographics make history in 2012 seems hard to believe. Washington plays Olivia Pope, a Washington, D.C., crisis manager (or "fixer") whose story is based on the real life of Judy Smith. Smith established her reputation working for the D.C. district attorney's office in the 1990s, when then-mayor Marion Barry was caught using cocaine. Her demonstrated crisis management skills prompted the first Bush White House to hire Smith as a deputy press secretary, and led to the storied career on which *Scandal* focuses. When Smith struck out on her own, her firm's first client to draw national attention was Monica Lewinsky. (Smith is on board as one of the show's producers.)

Kerry Washington said (in a recent exclusive interview with The Feminist Spectator) the fact that *Scandal* is based on a real person delights her because it prevents people from scoffing about the character's believability. Washington's performance more than honors her source – Olivia Pope is one of the most compelling women characters I've ever seen on television. Subscription TV has given us *Nurse Jackie, Weeds,* and *The Big C* (all on Showtime) and more recently *Veep* and *Girls* (both on HBO), all shows that offer leading women characters a broader range of experiences and foibles than most. But *Scandal* is one of the first *network* series to feature a woman – let alone a woman of color – in its central role and to allow the character to be emotionally strong, professionally powerful, and personally complicated. (Those illustrious few include *The Good Wife* [CBS] and *The Killing* [AMC]. *Missing* [ABC] didn't grab me, which is unfortunate, because I really appreciated the series star Ashley Judd's recent protests about the media's focus on women's physical appearances. All of these series, however, feature white women leads.)

Washington is pleased that *Scandal* pushes the envelope of network television. While she admits that it would be a different show on cable, she says, "I'm proud that it's on the network. That it's mainstream America.... Cable is known to take more risks, but it's time to have a show with a black woman as a lead not seen as a big deal." Emily Nussbaum, in *The New Yorker,* suggests that *Scandal* in fact avoids mentioning Olivia's race to the show's detriment. But as she does with *Grey's Anatomy* and *Private Practice,* Rhimes seems more concerned with affirming racial and ethnic diversity as a visible part of her series' stories without emphasizing race as content. Representational politics seem to me equally important right now – that is, *seeing* people of color on television in roles typically populated (without comment) by white people makes its own statement.

On *Scandal,* Olivia Pope administers her firm with iron-clad rules and demands fierce, uncompromised loyalty. Her rag-tag band of employees – the so-called Gladiators in Suits – all boast certain skills, and most have sordid, secret pasts from which they've been rescued by Olivia. Like the squad of detectives who surround Chief Brenda Lee Johnson (Kyra Sedgwick) on *The Closer* (TNT), Olivia's team stands in awe of her know-how but also harbors deeper emotional feelings for a boss who leads them with careful aplomb through the minefields of a very political world. If part of the joke of *The Closer* is that Brenda's squad is full of men (of various races and ethnicities), each with his own charmingly comic character flaw, Olivia's team on *Scandal* is comprised of men, women, white people, and people of color, each with his or her own charming but dangerous character flaw. And instead of playing on overly feminine white Southern wiles to get her way, as Brenda does in the very male world of Los Angeles police work, Olivia Pope stands strong, tough, and African–American in the very white and very male world of presidential politics that provides *Scandal*'s milieu.

As a Shonda Rhimes show, *Scandal* mixes intense workplace environment storylines with subplots about the personal lives of characters whose professional commitments always drive their ambitions. Olivia's team is on call day and night. Her newest employee, Quinn Perkins (Katie Lowes), plays with fire when she decides to date a journalist who's sniffing around the firm looking for information about Amanda Tanner, one of its more infamous clients. The other team members are already stalwart. Harrison Wright (Columbus Short) has some sort of prison record, which makes him happy to be at Olivia's beck and call. Abby Whelan (Darby Stanchfield) is a progressive who's appalled when Olivia decides to take the case of a Latin American dictator searching for his apparently kidnapped wife. Stephen Finch (Henry Ian Cusick), who comes closest to being Olivia's professional equal, proposes to his fiancée in the series' first episode, but rarely spends time with her. He arrives at Olivia's home any time of the night to consult with or comfort her. And the mysterious, taciturn Huck (Guillermo Diaz) demonstrates his loyalty and his acute empathy for Olivia's frequent ethical anguish by constantly reassuring her and the others that he's got Olivia's back.

The crew is idiosyncratic and interesting, and the family of actors assembled to perform the team is apparently very close. Washington says, "People at the network are surprised, [we] really love each other." She attributes this intimacy to Judy Smith, whose compassion for her fellow human beings inflects her work and Olivia Pope's character. Washington says that Smith "comes to the work as a nurturer. She wants to make sure that people are taken care of. She realizes that justice isn't always just, that not everyone gets a second chance. People make mistakes, everyone is human. She's a very caring and compassionate person. Olivia Pope has pulled in these people who work for her who she takes care of. They also have skills that make them assets." She continues, "I often think when we're thinking about powerful women we disassociate them from their maternal instincts. Olivia has no children (that we know of) but she's very much in touch with the maternal."

The actors' ensemble work has already gelled into a terrific chorus for Washington's star turn as Olivia. And what a turn it is. Washington brings to the role a superbly talented actor's confidence and the empathy of a woman who can read a scene (in real life and in a script) with an almost tactile feel for the nuances of its politics and its themes. Her intelligence shines through her performance and the series' scripts allow Washington's smarts to propel Pope's character. You can actually see Washington thinking through Olivia's frequent quandaries. One of the character's best traits is that she thinks quickly and effectively. Other critics have noted that the D.C.-based show's dialogue echoes the *West Wing*; the walk-and-talk practices established by that landmark show are recalled in *Scandal*. But here, what Washington calls "*Scandal*-pace" isn't a function of the D.C. political setting but of its central character's intensity. All the characters speak with urgency and the show's lightning-fast editing moves it quickly through its central story and subplots each week.

Washington says that *Scandal*-pace comes from Smith herself. "Judy is always moving very quickly," she says. "When you walk beside her, you're out of breath and she's talking effortlessly." That stamina and endurance shows in Washington's carriage as she's performing; Olivia holds herself proudly and propels herself through each scene as though she's singing the 11:00 number in a musical while chorus boys fall at her feet. Olivia's personal sense of resolve matches that required by her work. Washington notes that crisis management moves fast and that it's changed a lot since Smith began working in the field. Now, it's necessary to fix something in five minutes instead of five hours or five days. Washington says crisis managers are "constantly playing games where you have to think five steps ahead" of the media and law enforcement. "Time is money," Washington says. "Time could be life or death." That urgency fuels each moment of *Scandal*.

But the fast-talking is written mostly for Olivia. Her ability to think aloud in eloquent, pointed paragraphs is demonstrated best when, in each episode, she typically delivers an ultimatum (or two) to a client or a nemesis balking over a deal. Those scenes beautifully showcase Washington's ability to be at once emotionally and intellectually acute. They're typically filmed in close-up, so that the screen is filled with Washington's beautiful, expressive face, her lips moving faster than seems humanly possible while her eyes register all the complicated devotion or disdain Olivia feels for her interlocutor. Often, these moments are about persuading another character of an ethically questionable choice. The dialogue carries the heavy-lifting of reason while Washington's countenance reads with all the agony of the necessary compromise or concession. I love those moments in *Scandal* because they let you see an actor at work in the guise of a character whose skill at fixing political and personal crises invariably saves the day. This isn't a woman seducing a client through personal charm. On the contrary, Olivia Pope lays down the law, tells it like it is, reads the riot act, and otherwise gives people their marching orders, with Washington making every one of those speeches heart-rending and convincing.

Washington says she was drawn to the role because "the emotional life of the character was on the page from day one":

> That very much drew me to this project. The woman is often the accessory, so you're looking for ways to three-dimensional-ize the character. Your job as an actor is to fill that picture. But when I read the pilot it was all there. I loved that you could have this woman who was fierce and powerful and together in her professional life. But her personal life is a bit of a mess. That dichotomy could exist on the page. These people [her team] would go over a cliff for her. [She says she doesn't cry, but in the] pilot, you see her crying alone in a coat closet. She has so many ways that she performs her identity.

Washington says that she's always interested in a character's different performances of her public and private selves. Olivia is a rich example of the compromises often required of professional women.

Perhaps the biggest scandal on *Scandal* is that Olivia has an on-going romantic affair with the President of the United States, Fitzgerald ("Fitz") Grant (Tony Goldwyn, exceptionally sexy and soulful as a powerful man with secrets). The episode called "The Trail" (#1.06, aired May 10, 2012), flashed back to the beginning of Fitz and Olivia's relationship to reveal that they started their affair when Fitz hired Olivia to assist on his campaign for the presidency. Although his marriage to the imperious and wily Mellie (Bellamy Young, terrifically sharp as the wronged wife) is a sham, the President nonetheless can't afford to compromise his image as a happy husband. His mercenary wife, eager to gain and later retain her power as First Lady, brazenly aids and abets the cover-up of Fitz's infidelities.

Washington and Goldwyn's scenes together are gentle, sad explorations of a desire that just won't quit, despite the challenges of position and politics. Although Fitz's escape from the prison of the White House in "The Trail" stretched credulity (hey, it's a television show, after all), the President's mournful appearance at Olivia's door proved a touching illustration of their mutual need and yearning. Goldwyn and Washington ratchet up their chemistry with each of their characters' encounters.

Jeff Perry plays Cyrus Beene, the president's Chief of Staff, who's determined to alienate Fitz from Olivia. The on-going mystery plot in *Scandal*'s first season sees Olivia hired to help and protect Amanda Tanner (Liza Weil), a former White House staffer who claims she's had a relationship with the president and is carrying his baby. Olivia's new client strains the triangulated relationship between Cyrus, Fitz, and Olivia, in which each balances their power, their abilities, and their insights to keep the president in office. The Amanda Tanner storyline threads through each of the season's episodes, keeping the tension high as Olivia and the team otherwise solve the crises of each week. Tanner, it seems, was pressed into service by shadowy enemies to blackmail the president into thinking that the baby she carried was his. When Tanner decides to back out of the plan, we see her call her operatives to renege. Shortly after, a black-clad, hooded figure breaks into her apartment, knocks her out, and carries her off. We don't see her again until her body is dragged from the Potomac.

Billy Chambers (Matt Letscher), the vice president's Chief of Staff, is somehow involved in this nefarious plan. The VP, beautifully played by Kate Burton as a southern conservative Tea Party-er from hell, ran against Fitz in the presidential primary and reluctantly joined his ticket in the second spot. Billy's reptilian delusions of grandeur lead him to fantasize that he can unseat Fitz and install his woman instead, using Tanner's purported affair with the president and her pregnancy as the impeachable offense. He captures the media's attention by spreading rumors of the president's ethics violations, and it looks like Fitz might have to step down.

In the season finale ("Grant: For the People," episode #1.07, aired May 17, 2012), the plot only thickens. Olivia and Fitz share a brief romantic moment, imagining that they can have a normal domestic future if the scandal forces him to leave the presidency. But thanks to the mercenary deal struck by Fitz's wife, and thanks to Olivia's brilliant abilities, they spin the story to avert disaster. Mellie exacts her revenge by forcing Fitz back into a sexual relationship to produce the baby she claims to be carrying, and Olivia grieves that her commitment to her job (and I guess her country) means she has to sacrifice the love of her life. The season's real twist, though, comes in the final moment, when we learn that Cyrus, not Billy, engineered Amanda Tanner's murder. Played by Perry as a smug, grasping (and gay) narcissist, the plot twist dangles the promise that many more complications are in store, which will no doubt continue to compromise Olivia's already troubled ethics. I'll look forward to that.

It's great fun to watch an African-American woman character navigate the halls of power with her personal and professional dignity intact. I revel in *Scandal*'s implicit feminism and the pleasure of seeing Washington take charge on the screen. Washington says, "I'm proud to play this role as a feminist," in part because "one of the things that makes [Olivia] powerful is that she's a human being. She's always trying to be the best version of herself, despite her own confusion." Despite the high visibility – and no doubt, some vulnerability – of being the first African–American woman to star in a network TV series since 1974, when a show called *Get Christie Love* aired starring Teresa Graves, Washington says she doesn't feel a heavy burden of responsibility about this historical fact. "I actually feel very supported doing it. There was a lot of anticipation about the show; people were excited that this character was going to live and breathe and exist off the page. I felt a lot of support from the community of women of color actresses in Hollywood." The pressure, Washington suggests, is on the audience: "Will the American people show up and watch this smart woman, in a show that's female-driven, that's driven by an African–American female? Will people allow her into their hearts?"

That *Scandal* has been renewed for a full second season seems to indicate audiences' willingness to take that leap. And that faith, Washington believes, might contribute to real social change. She says, "Audience members in theatre, film, and television, through consciousness and imagination, are able to put themselves in other people's shoes. That expanded consciousness makes us more inclusive and lets us see similarities instead of divisions. Art can show us who we want to be. That's powerful work." Let's hope spectators will be willing to put themselves into Olivia Pope's (gorgeous) shoes. She's a tough woman navigating a brutal world, and doing so with intensity, grace, and a ramrod straight spine that makes her irresistible to watch, especially in a medium that allows so few women to be as complex, powerful, and charismatic. And thank goodness an actor as ethical, aware, and committed to social change as Kerry Washington is bringing Olivia to our hearts.

MAY 24, 2012

Young Adult

Paramount Pictures, premiered 2011

In screenwriter Diablo Cody's first film after her indie hit, *Juno*, *Young Adult* stars Charlize Theron in one of her less glamorous and more nuanced roles in which, as she did in *Monster*, she's willing to compromise her beauty to develop a character whose moral decay becomes embodied on her person. Cody and director Jason Reitman challenge spectators with a film about Mavis Gary, a woman whose growth is stunted by the story she tells herself: that she escaped a stultifying small-town life and has "made it" in the big city, in this case, Minneapolis, which her former classmates back home in Mercury, Minnesota, call "the mini apple" to her great chagrin. With this recurring joke, Cody underlines that Mavis hasn't wandered very far from home at all, and that the stakes in the real-life game she pretends to play still aren't as high as they would be if she were in the "Big Apple."

Mavis insists on calling herself an author, even though she's really the ghost-writer for a young adult series that's seen better days. Mavis is proud of leaving Mercury, where she grew up as the icy, arrogant homecoming queen who, it turns out, everyone pitied rather than adored. *Young Adult* watches with remote fascination as Mavis hatches a misbegotten plan to return home to win back her high school sweetheart, Buddy Slade (Patrick Wilson), who's just had his first baby with his wife, Beth (Elizabeth Reaser).

Reitman, Cody, and production designer Kevin Thompson (with set decorator Carrie Stewart) signal Mavis's unhappiness in *Young Adult*'s opening scenes. She lives in a high-rise apartment building in downtown Minneapolis, boasting glorious views of the city and lots of space. But the place is trashed, strewn with dirty clothes, papers, and old cans of dog food that keep alive her much ignored, needy little Pomeranian. The slovenly, alcoholic Mavis drinks massive amounts of bourbon and beer, has sex with anonymous men, passes out, and wakes at home draped across her bed wearing yesterday's clothes. To bring herself back to life each morning, she chugs liter bottles of Diet Coke before she even leaves the sheets.

The film alternates between fascinated attention to Mavis's elaborate preparations to go out each evening, beautifying herself with hair extensions and pounds of make-up, and an equally captivated, if morbid, tracking of the aftermath of her evenings of debauchery. During the day, Mavis's hair is ratty and dull (she pulls clumps of it from her scalp by nervous habit), her eyes hidden behind large sunglasses, her body adorned with old, torn jeans and a t-shirt you can practically smell because she's not a woman who's diligent with her laundry. She exudes unhappiness, bitterness, and resentment. But her delusions persuade Mavis that she's the alpha girl who reigned over her high school social scene that was the apex of her life to date. She's the female version of the dissolute high school football star whose best days are behind him by the time he graduates. Mavis might have left Mercury, but she's not yet accepted her own adult role and responsibilities. That she writes young adult fiction is an obvious but potent metaphor, and the story she writes about a high school prom queen, shared in a voiceover, mirrors a fantasy version of her own.

When an email arrives from Buddy and Beth announcing the birth of their first child, Mavis contrives to visit Mercury to woo Buddy back. Because she's desperate for something to win, and because she can only recall what she believes was her high school success, Mavis decides she and Buddy are meant to be together. Her reasons are never romantic, but only mercenary; she needs to see herself, once again, as the queen bee of what's become her much diminished social landscape. Crawling out from under the oppressively heavy arm of her most recent one-night-stand, Mavis leaves her bed and her apartment with a suitcase and her little dog, returning to Mercury to make her conquest.

Reitman and Cody share a keen eye for the strictures of small-town life. Reitman's camera pans the anonymous landscape of fast food joints and big box stores as Mavis drives back into Mercury. The town could really be anywhere in suburban America. In fact, to the film's credit, the characters don't speak with *Fargo*-esque, exaggerated accents. Their clothing signals the Minnesota location more than their speech. At the party that proves the film's climax, Buddy and Beth's friends and relatives wear jeans and flannel shirts, signifying the laid back, unpretentious earthiness of a post-Hippy, generally liberal Midwestern gestalt. In such a context, Mavis's towering high heels, clinging shirts, plunging necklines, and too-short dresses announce her as an outsider, as someone trying much too hard to flaunt her contrived urban difference.

Theron plays Mavis as a performance of herself, almost as a drag role, as she tries to re-insinuate herself into the clueless Buddy's affections. Everything she says is insincere, uttered for effect. To her great consternation, little of it works. Buddy doesn't respond to her flirtations.

Matt Freehauf (Patton Oswalt), a high school classmate who shared the locker next to hers for four years, who she doesn't remember or recognize, sees through her machinations and tries to warn her off. Mavis's mother and father (Jill Eikenberry and Richard Bekins) evince the benign neglect that no doubt contributed to Mavis's outsized sense of herself. When she announces she's an alcoholic, they scoff and ignore her. Her father seems openly distasteful of his daughter, and her mother willfully misunderstands her. They both enable the static fantasy of her life, preserving her room at home as it was when she was a teenager. A birthday banner tacked to her bedroom wall wishes her a happy 17th birthday, and all her old make-up and nail polish sit intact on her dresser as though she never left. Buddy's letter jacket still hangs in her closet. She looks ridiculous when she puts it on, but she leaves the house determined to turn back time.

If *Young Adult* were a romantic comedy, the suspense would come from wondering if Mavis could successfully steal Buddy from Beth. But because the film's humor is much darker than that, there's no doubt that Mavis will fail. Cody and Reitman encourage us to watch dispassionately as she makes a fool of herself, wandering back into town shaking her considerable booty in the face of a man who's happily married and oblivious. The Greek chorus of old high school classmates who surround Buddy and Beth look on with palpable disapproval. They all see what Mavis is up to, and no one approves.

Unlike other films that hail life journeys away from origins as evidence of healthy separation and growth, *Young Adult* instead indicts the pretentions of a woman who never knew herself or her real place in the world she thought she escaped. It turns out that Mavis was reviled in high school, and her return home incites pity more than lust. Beth feels sorry enough for her to invite Mavis to their daughter's welcome party, against Buddy's wishes. Mavis thinks she's mysterious and imperious, but everyone sees through her. Matt becomes her confidant, mostly because he used to have a crush on her and welcomes the attention and because he's so far beneath her notice, she can afford to share her secrets – such as they are – with him.

Matt's back story seems off tone and strains credulity. He was viciously beaten in high school by a gang of toughs who thought he was gay. Turns out he was just a fat kid. But the beating left him with a limp, a cane, and a bent penis that, in *Young Adult*'s cosmology, makes him strangely proto-gay. He can't perform "normally," although he and Mavis do engage in a pity fuck – because he pities her, not, as might be expected, vice versa. I'm not sure, though, what Matt's beating signifies in Mercury's fictional past. Does it mean the town was indeed narrow-minded and small and worth fleeing? Or was it a high school prank gone dramatically wrong? Mavis has no sympathy for Matt's long-held resentments about his resulting handicap. She tells him to just get over it, even as she clings to a past that's equally stunted her present potential. Because Oswalt plays Matt with such detailed compassion and self-knowledge, the character rises above the symbolic function to which he and his disability might be reduced. But their relationship never quite makes real meaning for either of them.

Likewise, Matt's sister, Sandra (Collette Wolfe), who lives with him, since all three have postponed their move into adulthood, still idolizes Mavis (though Mavis doesn't remember her from high school, either). When she leaves their house, heading back to Minneapolis, Sandra begs Mavis to take her along. Mavis coldly replies, "No, you're fine here," which could be a smug assessment of the young woman's failure to survive elsewhere or an envious reading of her ability to fit easily into a community that seems suitable. Mavis can't rest effortlessly anywhere because she's hollowed herself out with fantasies about who she is and who she was, caught in limbo between past and present.

In one of the film's best scenes, Mavis visits a local bookstore where copies of her novels sit prominently displayed. When she offers to sign them, the unctuous young clerk tells her that if she does, the store won't be able to return them to the publisher for credit. She insists that she's the series' author, even though her name can only be read in very small print on the fly leaf, and wrestles copies from him on which she's determined to scrawl her signature. He tells her they're only on display so that they'll move quickly, because the series is no longer popular. While she tries to inflate her importance and the fantasy of her artistic future, his pragmatism insists she leave her creations anonymous, ready for pulping instead of reading.

Likewise, in scenes that bookend Mavis's trip to Mercury, the motel clerk at the Hampton Inn where she stays isn't impressed with Mavis's performance of glamor and urbanity. The young woman drily calls her on everything from hiding her dog in her bag (which Mavis denies even as the bag wiggles on the front desk countertop) to wanting a donut reserved for "Gold" members. Mavis wins that skirmish by popping a powdered sugar ring in her mouth as she leaves the motel. But in deft bits of dialogue, screenwriter Cody demonstrates that Mavis's pretentions are transparent even to this ordinary girl.

Her failed trip back to Mercury doesn't change Mavis. She leaves with the same haughty sense of entitlement and arrogance with which she arrived. She's one of those people who soldier on through the fantasy of their lives, constructing a house of cards that she rebuilds each time it collapses, just the way she reapplies her make-up every evening after her day-long hangover lifts. Mavis represents a sorry cycle of expectations set falsely high and self-knowledge set impossibly low.

Young Adult barely rippled at the box office when it appeared in 2011, despite positive reviews. Perhaps audiences found it difficult to connect to an utterly unlikable central character, whose narrative arc leaves her exactly where she began without a shred of new understanding. But I found the film bold for exactly that reason. Its unrelenting cynicism about escaping the strictures of who we are offers a biting critique of more conventional films with pat progress narratives in which characters always grow for the better. How realistic is that? On the other hand, perhaps *Young Adult* is just a cautionary tale about a beautiful, mean ex-prom queen who's stuck in the past, a revenge fantasy in which the people she considers "little" show their largesse of spirit and their generosity of soul. Whichever, I admire how *Young Adult* keeps us uneasy and off-guard, upending easy expectations about life choices, success, and failure.

JUNE 15, 2012

Girls and *Tiny Furniture*

Apatow Productions, premiered on HBO, 2012; Tiny Ponies, premiered 2010

Lena Dunham's HBO series *Girls* has been hailed for its sharp, insightful snapshot of 20-something white, straight women navigating their New York City lives in a post-*Sex and the City* moment in which (*Bridesmaids* aside) nothing in popular culture has really seemed to catch the zeitgeist from women's perspective. Dunham, who plays Hannah, the lynchpin of the quartet of friends on whose overlapping lives and close-knit friendship circle the series focuses, shines with a particularly smart, offbeat on-screen charisma. She radiates intelligence in a way that few young women on television do. Hannah is not waif-like and flighty, but someone with dreams, desires, and something to say. Her body size doesn't conform to impossibly thin conventional standards, which means her clothing (she remarks how expensive it is to look "this cheap") hangs differently around her. Her haircut doesn't seem outrageously posh and she doesn't seem to wear make-up. In other words, her appearance immediately breaks the mold of most young women seen on television and in films. And even though she comments on her weight and her clothes, bemoaning how they don't hold up to the ideal, it's still a pleasure to be invited into the life of a normal-looking woman.

Her friends, though, conform more closely to typical beauty and behavior standards. Marnie (Allison Williams), Hannah's roommate, has long brown hair and a svelte figure and, in the pilot, bemoans the excessive attention of a hovering beau. Shoshanna (Zosia Mamet), their motor-mouth, hyper but earnest friend, is also thin and attractive, if slightly more "ethnic" (read Jewish; her last name is Shapiro). And Jessa (Jemima Kirke), Shoshanna's British cousin, is chic and sophisticated – or at least her accent makes her sound that way. Jessa, it soon turns out, is also pregnant, so her body looks strangely more like Hannah's. Rebecca Traister, writing admiringly of the show in *Salon*, notes how these four women's primary intimacy focuses on one another. In the show's opening image, Hannah and Marnie spoon in bed together as the alarm goes off in the morning. Marnie, it seems, wants to escape the smothering embrace of her boyfriend, which she had accomplished the night before by hanging out in Hannah's bed watching *Mary Tyler Moore* show reruns and falling asleep. Later, the friends bathe together, Marnie shaving her legs wrapped in a towel and Hannah lounging naked beside her, eating a cupcake for breakfast. But even though Hannah mentions that she's never seen Marnie's breasts, Marnie demurs, insisting that she only reveals herself to people she's having sex with.

And thus my basic hesitation with *Girls* so far. I love the focus on female friendships, which we so rarely get to see on television (*Sex and the City* aside – I was never a fan. And I long for Alicia and Kalinda to be friends again on *The Good Wife*). But much of the *Girls* pilot works overtime to secure these women's heterosexuality. Marnie and Hannah have slept together, but we're not to mistake them for lovers. Later in the episode, another of the friends makes a crack about lesbians that's meant to underline, again, that she's not one. And despite Hannah's penchant for having sex with inappropriate male partners, same-sex choices don't appear to cross her mind. If these women truly are intimate with one another emotionally and logistically, I'm not sure why sexual relationships between them or with other women have to be so quickly foreclosed. For young women who are sharp, sophisticated, and observant about social mores and patterns, such heteronormativity bespeaks a limited imagination, a cultural palette that fails to explore the full spectrum of human relationships.

Hannah's tryst with Adam (Adam Driver) in the pilot provoked some viewers with its awkward, explicit sexual nature. Adam drives their exchange, telling Hannah how to position herself, taking her from behind, and clearly using her for his own enjoyment without either one of them appearing to be very concerned with hers. Hannah talks throughout the sex, asking him if she's doing what he wants and explaining why she's not interested in being penetrated anally. He finally asks her to be quiet, shutting down her ruminations and, it seems, her sexual agency. Perhaps this is how Hannah prefers to have sex. Fine with me. *Girls* wants to represent women and their desires differently, which I admire. But as a television representation, it sends a certain message about how women prioritize (or not) their own sexual needs.

Dunham's 2010 debut film, *Tiny Furniture*, predicts some of the preoccupations that inform the HBO series which she now writes and produces and in which she performs. The film stars Dunham, her real mother, and her real sister as a family living in a spacious loft in Tribeca perched above her mother's art studio. Aura (Dunham) moves back to Manhattan after graduating from an unnamed college in Ohio, somewhere arty (perhaps Oberlin, where Dunham herself studied Creative Writing) where she majored in film theory. Aura makes little videos that she posts on YouTube, where they're viewed by a paltry number of people. Her most recent is of herself, in a bikini that reveals her comfortably cushioned body, brushing her teeth in an outdoor decorative stone fountain. The snippets we see of Aura's work offer the perfect analogy to Dunham's: *Tiny Furniture* is an autobiographical film in which Dunham uses quotidian activities and dialogue to unearth the fault lines in the life of a young woman trying to become an adult.

For viewers of *Girls*, the narrative arc of *Tiny Furniture* will seem familiar and resonant. Aura returns to her mother's loft after she graduates because her degree is economically useless and she can't afford to pay her own rent. In *Girls*, Hannah's parents are eager to teach her a lesson about independence until they relent and offer support for her Brooklyn artist's lifestyle. In *Tiny Furniture*, Aura's mother, Siri (Laurie Simmons), and haughty 17-year-old sister, Nadine (Grace Dunham), barely acknowledge that Aura's come home. Siri is a successful artist who photographs miniature objects arranged in random patterns; her cool-girl assistant helpfully moves little pieces of furniture an inch one way or another as Siri peers through her lens. But Siri's artistic remove infiltrates her family life, leaving her cold and distant from her oldest daughter. Siri and her younger daughter, Nadine, seem to have formed an enthusiastic affiliation in Aura's absence, unbalancing the family triangle. In one of the film's most poignant scenes, Aura asks Siri if she can climb into her bed in the middle of the night, but Siri says there's no room; Nadine is already there. When Aura tries to cuddle close to her sister, Nadine groans and pushes her away.

But one of Dunham's trademarks as a writer/director/performer is her tough refusal to wallow in self-pity. Aura is a smart young woman with a clear cost-benefits analysis. She wants to be an artist, but she knows that the would-be filmmakers and painters and performers who surround her are full of mostly hot air. Nonetheless, she finds herself prey to their charms. She meets an *artiste* named Jed (Alex Karpovsky, also cast in *Girls*) at a party and winds up inviting him to live in her mother's loft for 10 days while Siri and Nadine travel to look at colleges. Jed produces and stars in a web series called *The Nietzschean Cowboy* in which he spouts comic-philosophical monologues while perched on a kids' wooden rocking horse. Jed is in town from Chicago for meetings with studio executives that never seem to net him anything, yet his self-esteem remains unnecessarily inflated and his entitlement grand.

Likewise, Aura's old friend Charlotte (Kirke, who also stars as one of Dunham's best friends on *Girls*) fashions herself as someone with connections and access, even if they're mostly based on seduction and sex. Charlotte is lush and sensual, inhabiting her lovely body with the grace and ease of a young woman who knows how to use her sexuality. Aura, on the other hand, is one of those quirky smart girls who finds men attractive but can't quite make the romantic connections she thinks she deserves. Jed sleeps in her family loft for a week and rebuffs all of Aura's physical advances. Keith (David Call), the sous-chef at the restaurant where she briefly works as a day hostess, responds to Aura's flirtations even though he says he has a girlfriend at home. Their brief attraction is consummated late one night with humiliating sex in a large piece of aluminum piping in a vacant lot in the city. Prefiguring Hannah's sex with Adam in *Girls*, Keith mauls her mouth for a moment and then takes her from behind without a glimmer of concern for her own satisfaction, leaving her on the street with a peck on the cheek.

Aura's relationship to men and sex resonates most loudly with *Girls*. Aura is too sober and straightforward to expect high romance, but written on her face as Keith fucks her is the perplexed disappointment of a smart young woman who at least wants her subjectivity acknowledged while her body is penetrated. Dunham communicates the painful mix of shame and desire that motivates Aura, her willingness to have experiences (with a capital E) to establish her sophistication and cool, but her disappointment that her emotional life is stymied right and left. Aura is clearly the prototype for Hannah, who is also involved with a series of unsavory men whose own sexual satisfaction is more important than hers.

Tiny Furniture also establishes the body ease that distinguishes *Girls*. Aura and Charlotte flop on their beds half-clothed, casual with one another's half-nakedness and their own. Aura wanders Siri's apartment in a night-shirt and no underwear, peering into closets. (In a running joke, Aura asks where things are and Siri tells her to look in 'the white cabinet' – a whole wall in the loft's living room is lined with them.) Aura isn't trying to conform to pernicious, fascist standards of young white women's thin fragility. The only unhappy references to her body are the comments about her film on YouTube, which Charlotte reads aloud to her dismissively. (In *Girls*, Dunham saves Hannah's complaint about her weight for the first season's finale, in which, unfortunately, she does reveal it as a pernicious, preoccupying issue.)

Aura finds her mother's diaries from the 1970s, when Siri was Aura's age and engaged in the same self-searching journey toward what she hoped would be her own voice. Aura reads the journals avidly, even filming herself reading them in the bathroom, speaking them directly into the camera as though the words are her own. While she finds them revelatory, Siri dismisses them as unimportant. Aura thinks she's made an illicit discovery; Siri deflates their totemic power. But for the spectator, watching Aura discover this early, unformed version of her mercurial mother offers a touching window into Aura's confusion and desire, even as we somehow intuit that Aura, too, will find her way toward what seems to be Siri's easy success.

Nothing momentous happens in *Tiny Furniture*, which is part of Dunham's point. What does a smart young woman with a liberal arts degree (and a famous mother and an annoying but very smart sister) do after she graduates? Aura plans to share an apartment in New York with her college friend Frankie (the always wonderful Merritt Wever of *Nurse Jackie*), whom she calls on the phone for reality checks as Frankie prepares to follow her to the city. With oversized black-framed glasses and the somber clothes of a would-be intellectual, Frankie is also mordantly funny and grounded, an Oberlin girl with wry self-esteem and nascent power. But Aura throws her over, telling Frankie right before she moves to the city that she has to continue living with her mother, who "needs" her (a blatant lie, since Siri barely notices Aura). Frankie finds Aura at an art gallery where she's attending an opening with Charlotte, and the contrast between the two friends is stark. That Aura chooses Charlotte is painful evidence of a striving she can't resist, even though she knows better.

Dunham is always willing to show her heroine (that is, herself) in unflattering light. No redemption narrative surfaces to rescue Aura. By the film's end, she's as perplexed and unfocused about her next move as she was at the beginning. And yet the audience has perhaps learned a few affecting things about the challenges of being young and talented (and socially advantaged); about the complications of being sexually "liberated"; and about the complexities of female friendship for young women whose BFFs sustain, support, and truly love them, while they persistently look to men for relationships that prove utterly unsatisfying.

Girls has been criticized for its all-white cast and its privileged setting, an accusation that could also be made against *Tiny Furniture*. And yet as Dunham has responded in numerous interviews, this is the world she knows. To pepper it with extraneous people of color would be tokenism, though for the second season of her HBO hit, Dunham has apparently added a boyfriend of color to the cast. Perhaps the real critique here is of an American culture in which class and race continue to segregate us. On the other hand, how refreshing it would be if Dunham's smart stories loosened enough from her real life to help us imagine a culture in which smart young people did indeed mix across race and even class as they try to form their futures.

JUNE 10, 2012

Part Two: Activism

I include this section's essays under the activism rubric because they promote feminist media literacy. The essay on the Showtime television series, *Nurse Jackie,* for example, considers how the genre of hospital emergency room television show can be refigured when its nurse-heroine is an addict whose psychological motivations for using drugs is never clear. Show-runners Liz Brixius and Linda Wallem are themselves in recovery and use their own trials and tribulations to explore their character's complications.

The rest of the essays address Hollywood films with an eye toward how they might be read and understood at least slightly differently than they were by mainstream critics. *Mamma Mia!*, for instance, was directed by Phyllida Lloyd, who also directed the very successful Broadway musical on which the film is based. Few critics noted the joy of watching middle-aged women – and such a luscious mix of theatre stars, film stars, and London-based actors – cavort with full throats in a silly summer comedy. *For Colored Girls* is Tyler Perry's adaptation of the ground-breaking play by Ntozake Shange, which received generally poor reviews from critics less familiar with Shange's original. *Black Swan*, Darren Aronofsky's Grand Guignol of a film about a deranged ballet dancer, prompted a heated conversation in the blogosphere about the representation of women in dance, most of which was invisible and unheard in the mainstream critical discussion about the film. Likewise, *The Social Network*, David Fincher's film about Facebook's founder, Mark Zuckerberg, received excellent notices and Academy Awards, but few (if any) critics described what I found its appalling gender politics.

The last two films in this section, *The Hunger Games* and *Brave*, offer more positive representations of gender. *The Hunger Games*, however, prompted both a racist online discussion about the casting of the character Rue with a biracial young girl, and a critique of the film's racial politics, since many of the book's readers perceived the leading character, Katniss, as black, but she was played by Jennifer Lawrence, a white actor.[1]

In *Brave*, Disney/Pixar's first animated release to feature a girl heroine instead of a boy, the gender messages are a bit more progressive, though feminist commentators expressed disappointment at the persistence of the princess narrative.

These examples demonstrate the necessity of feminist media literacy, so that we can enter debates about popular culture and argue effectively.

Mamma Mia!

Universal Pictures, premiered 2008

Seeing middle-aged women frolicking mindlessly on screen might not seem like much of a feminist achievement, but I'm pleased to consider *Mamma Mia!* part of the improving landscape for older women in popular entertainment. If summer is traditionally when action films like *Hancock* and *The Dark Knight* and *Iron Man* open, trolling for dollars from the pockets of the young and the male, then *Mamma Mia!* breaks the mold in a refreshing and pleasurable way.

The film continues in the tradition of the stage play on which it's based, a string of ABBA songs never meant for the theatre that are stuck along a plot no more than a millimeter deep. A young girl, Sophie, about to marry her young boyfriend, Sky, is desperate to meet the father she's never known before she begins her adult life. Her mother, Donna, was a free-spirited American who stayed on an idyllic Greek island after a summer vacation, pregnant with a daughter who could belong to any one of three men. The determined Sophie somehow finds these now 20-years-older men, invites them back to the fantasy isle for her wedding, and lo and behold, unbeknownst to her astonished mother, they come.

Plot contrivances make sure Sophie and the audience never find out for sure which man is her father, but the cast winds up dancing and we wind up toe-tapping in our seats if we've let ourselves enjoy the fanciful fun and silliness of the slight enterprise. The musical was never meant as high art, but as a campy romp that uses ABBA's songs to explain the paper-thin depths of character psychology and motivation across a story that strains credulity. The film follows suit. As more than one critic has remarked, those ABBA songs really are difficult to resist. Even glancing at a print advertisement for the film can lodge one of the tunes in my head for hours (and who needs to hum "Dancing Queen" while trying to work?).

Part of the film's fun comes from watching Meryl Streep sing (not too badly) and dance (terribly, although not much is required of her) and, as one critic described, mug her way through the throw-away role of the counter-cultural mother, Donna. With her blond hair long, scraggly, and wind-blown, Streep magnanimously gives in to the proceedings' campiness. Donna's once-upon-a-time suitors, all of whom remember her fondly enough to traipse halfway around the world to see her again, are played by unlikely men, all three clearly surprised to find themselves in a musical: Pierce Brosnan plays Sam, the most serious of her former lovers, who's saddled with the plot's biggest leap of faith as he actually proposes to Donna, after no contact for 20 years, at the film's end. The poor actor can't sing a note, but watching Brosnan, and Colin Firth as Harry and Stellan Skarsgard as Bill, Donna's other long-ago mates, warble their way through a verse or two makes you feel kindly toward guys who would so gamely essay something at which they're really not very good.

In fact, only Christine Baranski, as Tanya, one of Donna's two old friends who come to the wedding, has any experience with Broadway musical theatre, which makes *Mamma Mia!* more like a sing-along than a full-out movie musical. None of the leads are expected to really be able to dance. What passes for choreography looks more like the moves set on high school students eager to do *The Music Man* with no song or dance training. The gestures key literally to the lyrics, and overly obvious visual puns and jokes ensure that they're fun to watch, even if they're never artistically innovative. As a result, the music seems to heighten the lives of the characters, but in a highly quotidian, rather accessible way. Supernumeraries who otherwise serve as cooks or bellmen or handymen at the small hotel that Donna runs suddenly become (of course!) the Greek chorus when they hear the tinkling intro to the next ABBA tune, dropping their tasks to face the camera and rock out as Streep's back-up singers. That they return to their jobs without a thought after they've held each song's last note just seems a matter of fact in *Mamma Mia!*'s alternative universe.

In one of the movie's best scenes, Streep becomes a pied piper, the head point on a phalanx of women of all ages who leave their work at the hotel and their laundry lines in town to join Donna in singing and marching purposefully nowhere to "Dancing Queen," which they transform into an anthem of self-assertion about collectively washing their men right out of their hair. The film's joke is that no one is meant to take these shenanigans seriously, but only to enjoy them with a big dollop of great good fun.

Streep, Baranski, and Julie Waters, as Rosie, the third of the adult female trio, appear to have their own hugely pleasurable time camping it up together. They all play women in their mid-50s or so, with tenuous connections to conventionality. Baranski's Tanya is a sardonic, much-married sophisticate who clearly enjoys her husbands' money as much if not more than she's pleased by their companionship and luxuriates in her mutual seduction with one of the hotel's barkeeps. Waters' Rosie rejects the idea of settling down, happily chasing after Bill for some good clean dirty fun. Their spirit of anti-establishment female hell-raising becomes infectious. And though they act silly and campy, the film (helmed by Phyllida Lloyd, who also directed the stage version) never makes fun of them. Instead, we're encouraged to be entertained by the good time they seem to be having, which is a rather neat trick for a mass-market summer film when middle-aged women are involved.

The only unfortunate plot choice is that the film sticks to the original musical's ending, which requires Sam to propose marriage to Donna at the 11th hour. Somehow, daughter Sophie (Amanda Seyfried), whom Donna has tried to dissuade from her own wedding to the handsome but dunderheaded Sky, is finally convinced – at the altar no less – that she should travel the world instead of getting hitched. This is clearly a happy outcome for a girl so desperately young and obviously naive (signaled by how and what she sings and how shrilly she shrieks with her girlfriends, a trio not at all as compelling as Donna and her friends). But god forbid a good wedding should go to waste. Sam comes to the rescue with his knees bent and his hat in his hand, asking Donna to forgive him for leaving her the first time and now, 20 years later, to give him another try and marry him while she's at it. The rules of romance on film require her to accept, an act which Streep performs with watering eyes and tremulous lips in unnecessary close-ups, throwing over in a ludicrous moment Donna's own adulthood of more sober, unconventional, interesting choices and perfectly competent hotel management. Apparently, Donna wasn't even aware of the torch she'd been holding for Sam, and her eyes widen with surprise when it turns out to be burning her backside.

And so, of course, the priest is happy because he gets to say his vows, and the guests are happy, because they've schlepped up a very high and narrow, precariously winding mountainside stairway to get to the church for the ceremony. The movie's setting, too, is a fairy tale – how could even a Greek island be that picturesque and dazzling, the hotel Donna runs so charmingly dissolute, and even the sailboat on which the three once-and-future suitors arrive together so vividly seaworthy? The whole enterprise resembles a karaoke performance of a Disney-like film: a lot of fun if you've drunk enough really sweet cocktails not to be bothered by performers who can't sing and a lot of mass-manufactured, by-the-numbers ideology about love.

But I was happy to watch those middle-age leading women throw their arms around one another and laugh, cavorting merrily, even if by the film's end, I was so exhausted from all the forced gaiety and frivolity I needed a cocktail myself. Dancing queens indeed.

JULY 24, 2008

Nurse Jackie

Lionsgate Television, premiered on Showtime, 2009

This new Showtime series stars Edie Falco as a wry, knowing, harried emergency room nurse. The show offers a terrific vehicle for the versatile actor, as a well-written, smart and funny, situation-based character study that takes advantage of Falco's intelligent, restrained emotional presence and her quirky humor. Unlike old-fashioned network doctor dramas like *ER*, women characters propel *Nurse Jackie*'s narratives. Jackie begins each episode with a brief voice-over remark, and then the story continues from her perspective.

Jackie's best friend at work is Dr. Eleanor O'Hara (Eve Best), an elegant Brit whose arrogance is matched by her intelligence and wit. The upstairs/downstairs aspect of their friendship provides lots of comic fuel. O'Hara often refers casually to how much she spent on various items of clothing, from her $1,200 scarf to her almost as expensive silk stockings. Jackie and her bar-owning husband clearly pinch pennies to make it through their week. Jackie rolls her eyes at her friend's profligacy, but her indulgence of O'Hara's class idiosyncrasies emphasizes their bond as women in a professional environment skewed to favor men.

Pompous and powerful male doctors are represented here by Dr. "Coop" Cooper (Peter Facinelli), an Ivy League grad who struts into the emergency room with a blimp-size ego that Jackie promptly deflates when Coop's misdiagnosis – against Jackie's instincts – causes a young patient's death. After the first few episodes, Jackie's frequent corrections seem to bring Coop into line; he's cultivating his human side and considering his patients' emotional needs. In a recent episode he lavished rather sweet attention on an elderly woman on one of her regular trips to the ER from a nursing home. Coop adjusts her wig and compliments her vanity while writing her scrips, even though when she soon expires, he's out by the nurses' station boasting of how skillfully he handled his first gunshot wound patient a few curtains down.

Facinelli plays Coop with a dollop of humility and lots of magnanimity, although even he seems uncomfortable with the character's odd, unconscious tendency to grab women's breasts when he's anxious (a completely gratuitous quirk that says more about the producers' anxiety about the women characters' strength than Coop's). Coop is the son of lesbian parents (deliciously played by Swoozie Kurtz and Blythe Danner), a plot twist that also particularizes and humanizes a character who could be too stereotypically thoughtless and self-involved. O'Hara, in fact, looks at Coop differently once she realizes he has two mothers; the information makes him more than a run-of-the-mill, ambitious male doc.

Nurse Jackie draws all of Jackie's relationships with men in refreshing, slightly off-beat ways. She's married to Kevin (Dominic Fumusa), a sweet guy who cares for their two young daughters while he runs the bar they own in Queens. But at work, Jackie removes her wedding band, closets her family life, and carries on a regular sexual liaison with the hospital's pharmacist, Eddie (Paul Schulze). He not only services her physically (with Jackie always literally on top) but keeps her stocked in the painkillers that make long days of walking hard floors possible. Jackie's back seems seriously compromised, but the painkillers come with an addiction problem. She snorts Percocet and other opiates in doses small enough to let her function, but regular enough that her drug use has to become an issue down the narrative line.

Jackie's secrets, though, keep the character complicated. She never slides into the self-abnegating golden-hearted-but-gruff nurse stereotype that lurks just around the corner of this story. So far, the show avoids that pitfall, gilding Jackie's essential goodness with enough sardonic cynicism to keep her from being a simple saint. Her first-year student nurse, Zoey (Merritt Wever), offers her a useful foil, as Zoey delivers the platitudes about wanting to help people that drives some idealistic young women and men into nursing in the first place.

Put up against Jackie's unsentimental pragmatism, Zoey's enthusiasm plays as funny but not quite ridiculous. The character could easily be the butt of facile jokes – Zoey is too open and cuddly for what proves the ER's more cut-throat environment. But instead, she gets her own sharp edges. Wever's loose physicality gives Zoey embodied, character-driven humor; for instance, when O'Hara blithely walks off with Zoey's new stethoscope, the young nurse's attempts to retrieve it provide Wever with moments of stuttering explanation and stealthy borrowings that show off Zoey's agency and nascent power, instead of belittling her as inept.

Mo-Mo (Haaz Sleiman), Jackie's nursing colleague, unfortunately bears the burden of race and sexuality in the narrative, a load too heavy for any one actor to carry easily. Sleiman's features are ethnically ambiguous (his character's full name is Mohammed de la Cruz), allowing him to fill the "colored" slot in the character list, and his slightly fey, gentle presence and willingness to give Zoey fashion advice betray his gayness. Although his easy relationship with Jackie gives Sleiman and Falco some nice moments, so far, Mo-Mo represents still another gay person of color serving the development of the far more centralized white characters, a narrative strategy we all could do without by now.

On the other hand, Anna Deveare Smith makes regular appearances as Mrs. Akalitus, a nurse-turned-hospital administrator charged with guarding the bottom line. The character is a hard-assed factotum, but Smith brings her, too, subtle off-beat humor. When she borrows what she thinks is a packet of Jackie's sugar, and unknowingly gets high on the painkillers Jackie has ground up and put into the packet instead, Smith's performance as the suddenly lit and goofy administrator is priceless. In another episode, Akalitus finds a Taser gun lying in the corridor. After she shouts with anger to no one in particular about how irresponsible it is to leave such things lying around, she gets on an elevator and promptly stuns herself with the gun. Her electrified pratfall is hilarious. Watching Smith, who usually plays the steely, powerful, alpha-female roles in films and television shows, play a comic character role makes me admire her acting even more.

Many terrific New York-based actors play the ER's patients and visitors, offering keenly observed turns as the sick and dying and their families. The situations into which they're written, however, are often predictable and run to stereotypes. For example, in one episode, the wonderful Lynn Cohen is on hand as an elderly Jewish woman who tends to her dying husband's heart disease with chicken soup. Their scenes are saccharine and lachrymose, their Jewish accents wearying echoes of vaudeville sketches about Jews and their magic ministrations that should be put to rest soon.

Likewise, the Latina mother whose son's lung collapsed in a playground accident speaks with a thick accent, and her other son is excessively emotionally expressive; the elderly white woman who's regularly delivered to the ER from her nursing home is vain about her appearance; the tourists from the Mid-West are white, middle-class, and heterosexual, and apologize for everything (even though the woman turns out to be an opium addict, offering a neat mirror for Jackie's developing habit); and an international diplomat savagely murders a prostitute but can't be touched, thanks to his legislated federal immunity. Jackie navigates these characters and their issues deftly, always looking out for the well-deserving underdog and wreaking what vengeance she can on the powerful and evil. But these characters still remain vehicles in which to drive her development, rather than truly interesting people of their own.

Nurse Jackie swivels from wistful and wry to parodic and satirical fairly quickly. For instance, when Jackie and Kevin attend a meeting at their daughter Grace's school, the teacher, the school psychologist, and the school nurse are played in high farce and shot from camera angles that make them appear large and confrontational to the prosaic, confused Jackie and Kevin. But the small family's scenes at home are warmly realist, as Grace and their younger daughter, Fiona, cuddle with Kevin on their parents' bed watching television while they wait for Jackie to come home at night. The combination of exaggerated and earnest works, as *Nurse Jackie*'s sharp humor oscillates between its poignant observations about the proximity of death to life and its insights about how we navigate all those moments in between.

One of the most interesting things about Jackie is that she has no real back story. We don't know why she keeps her two lives so resolutely separate. We also don't know why she's a drug addict, aside from the usual stress (and temptation) that plagues some nurses in chaotic, poorly staffed and resourced city hospitals. Jackie's mystery, however, adds to her allure. She's an enigma not just for her co-workers – who alternately find her brusque and sensitive, present and distracted – but also for viewers accustomed to having characters' histories laid out with too much information. Instead of a pat psychological explanation for her behavior, we're asked to go on faith that Jackie needs her life the way it is. The reasons don't matter, only that she's able to keep her worlds apart and her addiction hidden.

As the final episode of the season ends, Jackie drifts into a drug-induced haze, hallucinating herself dressed in 1950s white nursing finery, and waving to her husband and kids, who stand in front of a two-dimensional, cartoon-like, suburban-style ranch house wearing 1950s-styled clothing, waving at her robotically. Sprawled on the hospital floor comatose, Jackie can only watch these images play out in front of her as the scene fades to the credits. The moment, typical of the crises that usually propel a series to the closing moments of a season, is disturbing and compelling. Is Jackie afraid of being trapped by the conventionality of her domestic family life? Is that why she has a secret affair with Eddie, and doesn't tell any of her coworkers that she's married and has two kids? Is she smart enough to want to resist the banalities of middle-class white heterosexuality, even as she's clearly, at an earlier point in her life, decided to acquiesce to it? Does she take drugs because of her back pain or because she needs to take the edge off a life that can't contain everything she feels herself to be?

Whatever the reason, it's wonderful to see a woman as complicated and wonderfully opaque as Jackie Peyton (shades of the old soap, *Peyton Place*?) anchor a series on a major cable network. Jackie isn't a perfect mother – in fact, although she takes her oldest, the troubled Grace (Ruby Gerins), to mother-daughter tap dancing classes, Jackie's skirmish with an old high school friend embarrasses both of them and they abandon the class. Jackie isn't the perfect wife – she works nights, which means that she and her husband are passing ships in a domestic arrangement that's often barely functional. Jackie isn't the perfect nurse – she operates according to her own moral code, which means that sometimes, she breaks rules to favor people she decides wouldn't otherwise get a break. She's unsympathetic with Zoey (although over the course of the season they've developed something approximating a warm understanding) and she's flip with her superior. She's a flawed middle-aged woman, a character not often enough seen on television.

Although these days, that's not entirely true. Jackie Peyton joins the ranks of Brenda Lee Johnson (Kyra Sedgwick) on *The Closer*, Patty Hewes (Glenn Close) on *Damages*, Nancy Botwin (Mary-Louise Parker) on *Weeds*, and Grace Hanadarko (Holly Hunter) on *Saving Grace*. All these television characters are middle-aged white women with "issues," whether drug addiction, dire financial problems, alcohol abuse, or power mania that make them as complicated and imperfect as the male heroes who more typically star in television series. Watching a series as smart and morally, emotionally, and ethically complicated as *Nurse Jackie*, peopled with so many interesting, unique, and individualized women and gay male characters, is a real treat. That the story proceeds from a flawed woman's perspective feels like progress indeed.

JULY 19, 2009

The Social Network

Columbia Pictures, premiered 2010

The Social Network is a fantastic film that's miserable to women. Aside from the overt ways in which it depicts college-age young women as insane, fear-inspiring shrews or as vacuous, sexualized objects, the film's resolutely male worldview is a disturbing window into the misogyny not just of Ivy League privilege, but of the upper echelons of capitalist entrepreneurship. Written with terse, vivid dialogue by screenwriter Aaron Sorkin (*The West Wing*) that captures the short-hand and urgency of a world of students wired to their computers searching for what Harvard President Larry Summers (Douglas Urbanski) calls in the film "the next great invention," *The Social Network* captures the kind of raucous Ivy League undergrad experience in which trashed dorm rooms are full of boys drinking beer and dreaming up multimillion dollar schemes (or looking at sexy "girls" on-line). Simply by being at Harvard, Sorkin and director David Fincher (*Benjamin Button*) imply, these guys gain entrée to a world of serious money and power that has little to do with what they're taught in class. The few scenes in which professors lecture are ridiculously staid and intentionally boring compared to the fast-paced thinking and scheming that happens elsewhere on campus, where Sorkin and Fincher clarify that the real benefits of a Harvard education are to be had.

Mark Zuckerberg (the terrific Jesse Eisenberg) is a whiz-kid with serious social problems. In the film's first scene, he deeply offends his girlfriend, Erica Albright (Rooney Mara), by obsessing about getting into one of the "final clubs" to which the most elite (mostly male) students at Harvard belong. The scene sets up everything we need to know about Zuckerberg: he's a genius who aced his SATs; he's a chauvinist about gender and class (he tells Erica surely she doesn't have to study, since she goes to Boston University); and he feels like an utter outsider because he's a Jew at Harvard (which means he's neither tall, nor athletic, nor blond, nor "cool," which is what he most wants to be). By the scene's end, Erica has emphatically dumped him because, as she announces, he's also an asshole.

For a feminist spectator, what *The Social Network* communicates above all is the elite, exclusive, deeply male-oriented world of Ivy

League and Silicon Valley entrepreneurship. After Erica dumps him, Zuckerberg gets online to write demeaning blog posts about her anatomy, seeking his revenge in the most sophomoric ways. In a fit of pique, he also creates a website called "facemash.com," on which people are invited to rate and rank images of Harvard women, whose photos he acquires by hacking into Harvard's computer stores. Within hours, the site receives so much traffic it crashes the server. Harvard men leer and call to each other to check out facemash (which becomes, of course, Facebook), but Sorkin and Fincher include only one pair of women looking at the web page with dismay and anger. Their very brief scene demonstrates only that women were helpless in the face of the site's viral power, and that their perspective is completely peripheral to the film at large.

It's been a long time since I've seen a film in which the "male gaze" has been so glorified and so gleefully promoted with so little real critique. Scene after scene demonstrates the traffic in women among Zuckerberg's classmates and, later, his Facebook colleagues. In one, a bus pulls up to the back entrance of one of Harvard's final clubs to deliver 30 or so beautiful women as though they're little more than kegs of beer. At the party, where everyone gets trashed on alcohol and drugs, the men smirk while the women make-out with one another for their titillation, or stand on tables to take their clothes off, or service the men sexually in not-so dark corners of the house. At a campus lecture by Bill Gates, Zuckerberg and his roommate and erstwhile best friend Eduardo Saverin (Andrew Garfield) are hit on by two Asian–American women who recognize them as the founders of Facebook. They throw themselves at the two guys and give them blowjobs in a bar bathroom. Eduardo is delighted that he and Mark have "groupies" – the women are nothing but pretty faces, despite the fact that they're also most likely Harvard undergrads with the brains and intellectual talent to be accepted to the school.

Eduardo continues to date Christy Ling (Brenda Song), his partner from that evening. She's present the first time Eduardo and Zuckerberg meet Sean Parker (Justin Timberlake), the co-founder of Napster, in a scene that establishes Parker's cultural capital and sees Ling matching Zuckerberg and Eduardo drink for exotic drink. She's smart and quick, and understands Parker's power and the allure of the big time he represents. But inexplicably, the film turns Ling into a psychotic, controlling, predatory shrew who fulfills all the stereotypes of the Chinese dragon lady. Only under this film's misogynist logic could she become so horrible. She shouts at Eduardo because he forgets to call her, and sets fire to a silk scarf he brings her from LA in a desperate attempt to appease her impossible demands. The film portrays Christy as a terrifying, irrational presence whom the reasonable, ethical Eduardo can't contain.

On *The Social Network*'s official web site cast list, Brenda Song is named alongside her photo as Christy Ling, but the note includes no description and no actor's bio. The male characters' blurbs describe their relationships to the story, and the actors who play them are linked to the history of their own performance careers. Likewise, Rooney Mara, as Erica, isn't given a link to her career biography, although her character's relationship to Zuckerberg is explained in a few short sentences. Why don't these women actors deserve professional histories of their own? Is this evidence that the filmmakers think as much of their female performers as the male characters do of the women in the story?

When Zuckerberg forms a partnership with Parker, he moves his operations from Harvard to Palo Alto, where the women are portrayed as just as loose, easy, and disposable as they were in Cambridge. When Parker first appears in the film, he's just had a one-night stand with a Stanford woman. We know she goes to Stanford because it's written across her ass, on the tiny little briefs she wears when she gets out of bed. Her only purpose in the story is to introduce Parker to Facebook, even though she's also witty, and quick, and a French major (which makes her entirely precious and impractical in Parker's cutthroat capitalist world). As the Feminist Spectator 2 notes, the scene is hateful because even smart, self-possessed women have no purpose in this movie other than to establish the credentials of the men. Aside from showing him her Facebook page, the scene's only purpose is to illustrate that Parker is smart enough to have sex with a brilliant Stanford girl.

When Parker and another girl knock on Zuckerberg's door, surprised that he's moved across the street from Parker in Palo Alto (a choice Zuckerberg makes quite intentionally), Zuckerberg tosses the guy a beer as he crosses through the kitchen. Parker catches it easily. Then the oh-so-chivalrous Zuckerberg tosses one to Parker's girlfriend, and it hits the wall and breaks because she wasn't expecting the bottle to come her way. He carelessly tosses her another one, which also shatters all over the floor. The flummoxed young woman looks foolish and inept, through no fault of her own. It's a short scene, but it concisely illustrates everything the characters – and, apparently, Sorkin and Fincher – think about women. Throughout *The Social Network*, the female characters serve purely as conduits for the men's relationships or as adornments that represent the men's successful professional lives.

When Parker seduces Zuckerberg with his fast talk of making billions of dollars and essentially ruling the world, Mark betrays Eduardo and throws in his lot with the narcissistic Napster king. Parker dates a Victoria's Secret model, whose only role is to adorn him. She also gives him an excuse to tell Zuckerberg how the lingerie company was founded, and how the man who created it sold himself short when the head of the Limited bought Victoria's Secret and proceeded to make billions from the company. Parker's paranoid, cautionary tales encourage Zuckerberg toward ever more mercenary heights of cutthroat business practices, leaving old friends like Eduardo and other Harvard colleagues in his wake.

Sorkin and Fincher aren't interested in a character study so much as they are in a portrait of the times, a representation of the zeitgeist when a brilliant idea could career into a huge personal fortune. But because Mark Zuckerberg is one of the most complicated hero-villains in the history of the movies, the screenwriter and director can't help but psychologize his story. The founding of Facebook, according to their script, is fueled by Zuckerberg's desire to make Erica notice him again, to make her realize that he's a genius, not an asshole. As the web site grows beyond the confines of the Ivy League where it begins, he's determined that one of the first universities to which it expands will be BU, where Erica goes to school. When he sees his ex- in a restaurant with her friends and approaches her to talk, Erica summarily and publicly rejects him again. That humiliation (rather than, say, greed), Sorkin and Fincher suggest, motivates Zuckerberg to expand his fame and fortune. The film ends with him sending Erica a friend request on Facebook, repeatedly clicking the enter key as he waits for a response.

Portraying Zuckerberg as a wounded Lothario is a cheap trick, when it's clear from the rest of the story that capitalist invention is in fact driven by a world of connections facilitated by who you know and the clubs to which you belong. Women, in this schema, are interchangeable and disposable. In almost every scene, the continuous party happening in the background is populated with nubile, beautiful girls who are stoned out of their minds, giggling together, draped around one another on couches, or offering their bare midriffs up as tables on which their friends can snort coke. They're mindless accessories of the most offensive sort. Only Erica is given any kind of story or psychology that lets us see her as something of a person. And even then, her story only serves to explain Zuckerberg's.

The depositions Sorkin and Fincher intercut with the story of Facebook's founding and triumph comment beautifully on the costs of Zuckerberg's achievement. Eduardo sues Mark for bilking him out of his rightful share in the company they started together, and the preppie Winklevoss twins (Armie Hammer and Josh Pence, onto whose body Hammer's face was digitally imposed) and their friend, Divya Narendra (Max Minghella), sue him for stealing their idea for Harvard Connection, a similar site meant to trade on the allure of a Harvard. edu address to create an exclusive social network. Flashing back to the beginning of the story, then ahead to the depositions in both lawsuits, allows the filmmakers to trace the consequences of what in the moment look like Zuckerberg's capricious decisions.

The guy's coldly supercilious, superior behavior at these depositions presents him as an unlikeable cad, but the flashbacks complicate our sympathies – or at least that's their intent. Clear from Sorkin and Fincher's film is that Zuckerberg felt very much an outsider at Harvard, a Jew among gentiles, overly invested in being accepted by a club that would never call him one of its own. The final clubs he longs to join, Zuckerberg says, determine your access to wealth and connections. That Eduardo is "punched" by a club to which he'll most likely be accepted wounds Zuckerberg deeply (according to the film). Eduardo knows his friend is jealous, and supplies his own excuse: the clubs want him for "diversity," since Eduardo is Brazilian (but most importantly, he's fabulously wealthy). Eduardo is also Jewish and was raised in Miami, but his Latin American exoticism is what gets him through the door of exclusive privilege.

Despite his brilliance, Zuckerberg knows he'll always be on the outside of real power, looking in, invited only as far as the "bike room" of the Winklevoss's final club where they pitch him their idea for Harvard Connection and enlist his programming help. His "fuck you" attitude, demonstrated by his invariable costume of hoodies, t-shirts, and plastic Adidas flip-flops, doesn't protect him from his ultimate exclusion, and he knows it. Despite his fame, he's forever consigned to be a wired, weird, Jewish nerd. He can create the world's largest, most powerful social network, but the girl he desires remains forever out of his grasp, refusing his own friend requests.

If the film wants us to pity the poor brilliant rich boy, it halfway succeeds. Eisenberg's performance is focused and intense, minus the self-deprecating, nouveau-Woody Allen shtick for which he's usually cast. Instead, his Zuckerberg is crafty and calculating, trading his best friend for entrance into the dot.com bubble that only a snake like Sean Parker can provide. Eisenberg never wavers in Zuckerberg's own self-righteous defense, but during the deposition scenes in which

Eduardo relates his ex-friend's betrayal, you can see hints of ruefulness play around Eisenberg/Mark's eyes. The Winklevoss twins are beneath his contempt, partly because he knows he'll never be them, and his success will only ever nip at the heels of their inherited power and prestige. But Eduardo was his buddy, and his loss leaves Zuckerberg truly alone.

At the film's end, the female law partner helping to defend Zuckerberg at the depositions tells him that he's really not an asshole, but he's trying hard to act like one. Her gesture toward solicitude barely registers. Zuckerberg asks her to dinner and she declines. He stays behind, tapping on his laptop in the law firm's darkened conference room, trying to get Erica to respond to his friend request. That the female law associate has the last word, and that Eduardo's lawyer is a woman, can't balance out the film's hateful view of women as only bodies, as sexual entertainment for white male power and privilege, with absolutely no agency of their own.

I most regret that *The Social Network* is good enough that it will be acclaimed in the 2010 awards season without enough critical ink spilled about how it demeans, degrades, and disposes of women. We need a feminist outcry to remind audiences that creating a good film is no excuse for being so patently gender-biased and offensive. A few scenes that pointedly criticized the misogynist atmosphere the film winds up authorizing would have gone a long way toward calling attention to the highly sexualized social scene in which smart college-age young women continue to navigate. At Princeton, just this kind of predatory behavior makes women into "things" whose only purpose is male entertainment and sexual gratification.[2] *The Social Network* isn't quite smart enough or good enough to underline that Zuckerberg's relationship with Parker is a homosocial bond, or that the women Parker brings to his parties are really his way of seducing his male friends by flaunting his hetero power. The film can't come to terms with Zuckerberg and Eduardo's love for one another, either. It can only align them in mutual glee as they revel in the enjoyment of blowjobs they receive in adjacent bathroom stalls by their Asian–American female groupies. And as the Feminist Spectator 2 points out, how perfect that the rich Winklevoss boys are egotistical, identical twins. The environment is rife with homoeroticism, which is in so many ways the foundation of masculine privilege and power.

That's the part of the social network on which Sorkin and Fincher fail to comment – perhaps because they're enjoying its bounty themselves.

OCTOBER 26, 2010

For Colored Girls

Lionsgate, premiered 2010

Ntozake Shange's *for colored girls who have considered suicide/when the rainbow is enuf* was one of the first feminist performance texts of the 1970s. Shange wrote the choreopoem in bars and performance spaces in Berkeley, often performing the monologues herself, until she stitched them together and turned them into a tour de force ensemble piece for an African–American female cast playing characters named only by the color of their outfits (Lady in Red, Lady in Brown, etc.). Wearing loosely draped, flowing skirts and leotards that let them move in unison and in counter-point, and capped with head scarves that opened their faces and emphasized their gold hoop earrings, the performers (including Robbie McCauley and Laurie Carlos, who continue to write and perform work about women of color) glowed with the power, anger, and inspiration of Shange's rallying cry to female agency.

The monologues chronicle abuse of the most egregious and casual kinds. A psychotic, alcoholic returning Vietnam veteran named Beau Willie Brown abuses his girlfriend and finally drops their two children from the window of their fifth floor apartment because he thinks she is cheating on him and because she refuses to marry him. A woman is raped by a casual acquaintance she thinks she's dating. Another woman is plagued by her lover's chronic infidelity. Another woman gets pregnant and undergoes the trial of an illegal abortion. And more. After describing in visceral, searing detail the various ways people – mostly men – messed with their "stuff," the women form a circle of collective strength and declare that they found god in themselves and love her fiercely.

On stage, the 20 different choreopoems are danced and spoken, creating whirls of color, movement, and non-narrative interaction, as each of the seven "ladies" takes center stage to share her story. The others listen and react and offer gestures of support or comfort. But they aren't really characters engaged in a psychologically-oriented narrative with a beginning, middle, or end. Shange's play derives its universality from the specific stories she tells, but they aren't attached to characters with conventional through-lines, objectives, or actions.

The performers are essentially themselves, except when they pick up the thread of their individual monologues to deliver a slice of life that could belong to anyone – especially anyone, that is, who's African–American and female. But the feminist power of Shange's play comes from how it generalizes across experience, to women who've felt disappointed and betrayed by placing all their hopes and dreams in relationships and finally decide to put themselves first. Although the play is thoroughly grounded in the experiences of African–American women, many women of all races can find common cause with the stories the "colored girls" relate.

For colored girls triumphed on Broadway in 1976 after its initial run at Joe Papp's Public Theatre in downtown Manhattan. The play was the first I ever saw on Broadway. As a young college-aged white girl from Pittsburgh who'd never seen theatre like this or heard these stories before, I was overcome by the experience. I still vividly remember those powerful African–American women talking to the audience, wearing their colorful costumes and moving with the grace of dancers. In the years after I first saw the play, I learned much more about feminism and theatre, and now rotate *for colored girls* through the Women and Performance or Theatre and Social Change courses I offer. It teaches beautifully. Even its typography, which eschews capital letters and sets each monologue as a verse poem, represents Shange's refusal to bow to the conventions of theatre, and its stories remain vivid indictments of a society that disempowers people because of their gender, race, and class. I've seen revivals of the play over the last 30-odd years, but none as striking and powerful as that original Broadway production, none that spoke clearly to the specifics of its contemporary moment.

Filmmaker Tyler Perry, however, has adapted Shange's play into a movie called simply *For Colored Girls*, and has found a way to make it meaningful in the 21st century by suggesting that so many of the issues it addresses remain urgent even now. To make the film more than an archival documentary of the play, writer/director/producer Perry creates a framework around the monologues, devising an interwoven story of ten African–American women and five men whose lives touch in unexpected ways. Crystal (Shange's Lady in Brown, played by the wrenching, powerful Kimberly Elise) inhabits the horrific story of Beau Willie Brown, playing the woman he abuses physically and then emotionally by forcing her to watch her children die.

Around Crystal's story, Perry layers in the other poems as adjacent narratives. Crystal works for Joanna (the Lady in Red, played by a steely

Janet Jackson), her boss's face an impassive mask of wealth and cruel, haughty class and race superiority until her demeanor finally breaks and she finds common cause with the others. Crystal lives next door to Gilda (Phylicia Rashad), a character Perry invents as the story's conscience and lynchpin. Gilda calls Kelly, a social worker (Kerry Washington, the Lady in Blue), when she becomes fearful for Crystal's children's lives. Gilda also meddles in the affairs of her neighbor, Tangie (Thandie Newton, the Lady in Orange), a floozy who beds man after man to mask her own history of sexual abuse and psychological pain. Tangie's younger sister, Nyla (Tessa Thompson, the Lady in Purple), lives at home with their mother, Alice (Whoopi Goldberg), a religious zealot dressed in spiritually indicated white, who can only see her own daughters as angels or devils. Alice's father, though, "gave" her to a white man because he didn't want granddaughters as "ugly" as Alice.

The cycle of abuse and degradation, Perry implies, begins in and ends as a family legacy. Unlike in Shange's play, entrenched social inequities are left mostly off the hook. In fact, social systems – particularly medicine and the police force – are represented as rather heroic in Perry's film. The one exception is the racism and governmental negligence that are to blame for Beau Willie Brown's inability to collect his veteran's pay or to get help for his post-traumatic stress disorder. In fact, when Kelly, the social worker, makes a home visit to the apartment he shares with Crystal to check on the kids, Beau Willie is furious that she's worried about them and not about him and becomes forbidding and violent enough to chase Kelly out of his apartment.

Beau Willie's anger boils that the Veterans Administration won't even return his calls. But when he dangles the children out the apartment window and Perry's camera focuses in on his hands letting go of their little wrists (mercifully not showing them fall or land on the pavement as the horrified neighbors watch below), his murderous act is depicted as the result of his inability to control himself when he's drunk and his fury at Crystal's refusal to marry him. In Shange's play, the tragic monologue ends with the chilling, agonizing words "and he dropped them," which echoes out into the theatre like a curse you can't take back. The story is placed nearly at the play's end. In the film, the event takes place closer to its middle. The other women, whose lives have already been connected by Crystal's brewing tragedy, gather around her in the hospital as she's sedated, psychologized, and released into the good Gilda's care. Bringing her back to life and helping her take responsibility for not leaving Beau Willie before he murdered their children becomes the women's collective goal.

All of them, though, in some ways blame themselves instead of the constraining social order. Kelly (Washington, as smart, lovely, nuanced, and empathetic as ever) feels guilty for not removing the children from a man she knew was abusive. But she's been preoccupied with her inability to have a child because of an STD she got from a womanizing man who interfered with her and her girlfriends by seducing and dividing them when she was young. Even Gilda, who calls in the warning that prompts Kelly's site visit, can't stop the inevitable tragedy, as much as she meddles in the others' lives. (She's the building's superintendent of sorts and has all the keys – to their apartments and their psyches.) Gilda knows that Tangie's promiscuous sexuality covers emotional wounds because, Gilda finally admits, she's been there herself.

All of these revelations and interrelationships are pat and essentially unbelievable. But Perry makes the structure work to communicate the collective community Shange conjured on stage through the proximity of the performers' bodies as they told their "colored" ladies' stories. If Perry needs to put them all into a contrived, *Crash*-like closeness to make the play work as a film, it's easy to forgive him, because it so elegantly makes his larger point. These women need one another, like it or not. They support, harbor, and encourage one another, finding god not just in themselves as individuals but in each other as a group of women suffering similar tragedies and triumphs.

Perry weaves Shange's choreopoems into the women's everyday exchanges, borrowing the structure of musical theatre to literally let the monologues sing. He also sometimes integrates Shange's poetic language into more prosaic dialogue between the women and their boyfriends, husbands, lovers, or friends. The film's tone doesn't quite shift for these moments so much as it intensifies, letting the language and the performers do its emotional work. Perry brings the camera in close on their faces during the monologues, and the performers beautifully capture the pain and poetry of Shange's words. Their acting in these moments is almost theatrical, reminiscent of monologues delivered directly to the audience, as the performers did in Shange's play. I felt like I had the best seat in the house for those filmed soliloquies.

On the other hand, Perry's habit of switching focus between the characters in the foreground and the background of the shot became distracting. Occasionally, Perry successfully opens the monologues out to other characters in the film. For instance, the nurse, Juanita (Loretta Devine, strong and compelling as the Lady in Green), delivers the "I almost lost alla my stuff" monologue to the group of women she counsels about safe sex and relationships. They respond joyously to her declarations of independence. Watching the faces of the actors reacting to Juanita's speech makes their collective empowerment pleasurable and infectious.

Sometimes, one of the women delivers a monologue to a character who in Shange's script is an abstraction instead of a real man with a backstory and his own dialogue. Juanita's scenes with Frank (Richard Lawson), for instance, her unfaithful boyfriend, are staged in her small apartment, where he insists she take him back and where she finally tells him off. Frank's dialogue – like that of the other men – is stilted and less vivid. Shange's words, after all, were written for women, and Perry has difficulties writing appropriate rejoinders for the men he creates to people his more realistic movie world.

Anika Noni Rose is elegant and heartbreaking as the Lady in Yellow, Yasmine, the artistic, energized teacher empowering young women in Harlem by teaching them to dance. Perry puts Rose in a dance studio, where she delivers monologues as though she's rehearsing for a one-woman show, watching herself in the mirror. She wears a costume and head scarf reminiscent of the iconic design of the original Broadway production (signally captured on the 1981 Bantam Books edition of the play). Yasmine adores her girls, and her belief in the transformations of art helps them finish high school and go to college. When Yasmine is raped in her own apartment by a man she dated just once, it's clear that all of her talent and faith can't keep her from the degradation of being a sexual assault victim in a system determined to prove that she deserved it. Rose's performance of the monologue in the emergency room, where she clutches a hospital gown to her bruised collarbones and bitterly indicts such a world, is one of the few in the film that blames systemic injustice instead of individual bad luck. When Perry contrives for her rapist to be killed by the next woman he assaults, Yasmine marches into the morgue where she's been asked to identify him as her attacker and slaps his dead face. Then, she begins to rebuild her life.

Because each subplot only receives a modicum of time (in a film that feels long at two hours), the characters don't deepen or develop. Some feel like caricatures. Poor Whoopi Goldberg, as the evangelizing Alice, has to describe how her father called her "ugly," which prompted hoots of laugher for some reason from the audience with which I watched. Goldberg was "ugly" in *The Color Purple*, too – why can't anyone cast this woman as a character who's as strong and radiant as she is in reality, even in her work on a talk show like *The View*? Thandie Newton, playing Alice's oldest daughter, seems unbelievable, partly because her role as a man-hungry but man-hating, emotionally damaged virago is so two-dimensional. By contrast, Tessa Thompson, as Tangie's sister, Nyla, performs a beautiful, affecting turn with her opening monologue about losing her virginity to a boy whose smile charmed her. That this boy also gets her pregnant and switches the focus of Nyla's story is unfortunate in Perry's adaptation. One of the few monologues that celebrate female sexuality turns too quickly into a victim narrative. When Nyla visits an abortionist, Perry films the scene as a descent through the circles of hell, full of card sharks, drug addicts, vicious dogs, and a back-room abortionist with dirty instruments, bad teeth, and a drinking problem. In scenes like these, *For Colored Girls* devolves into heavy-handed melodrama, despite the actors' effort to make more of their material.

The most egregiously caricatured relationship is between Janet Jackson's imperious Joanna and her on-the-down-low husband, Carl (Omari Hardwick). Perry blames Joanna's icy remoteness for her husband's sexual desires, implying she emasculates him with her financial and emotional control. Their confrontation scene, in which he confesses that he has sex with men (but not that he's gay), ends with her revelation that she's HIV+ and contracted the virus from him. The script emphatically links homosexuality and disease. It strongly suggests that the cost for being a too powerful woman is turning your husband gay and risking infection with the gay disease all gay men inevitably get. This is cheap, loathsome even, and the audience's loud antipathy for every scene in which gay sex or even just same-sex male longing was represented underlined Perry's irresponsible politics around sexuality.

For Colored Girls isn't a particularly good movie, but it's worth seeing because the women's performances are terrific (especially Elise, Devine, Rose, and Washington's). It's also worth watching because it remains Shange's feminist exhortation for women of color to find strength in themselves and to protect it fiercely. For that reason alone, *For Colored Girls* is an important, necessary, significant film. It's not just an homage to Shange and her 1970s feminism (what Alice Walker would soon come to call "womanism"), but a continuing clarion call for women to band together to end our social and sexual inequality.

That's a movie I'm happy to see and to recommend.

NOVEMBER 7, 2010

Black Swan

Fox Searchlight Pictures, premiered 2011

Natalie Portman deftly defies the genre conventions of what would otherwise be a predictable, unsettling melodrama about an unhinged ballet dancer who goes not so quietly crazy just as her career takes off. Because of Portman's uncanny empathy for her character, the over-the-top camera angles and story lines of Darren Aronofsky's *Black Swan* aren't quite as irritating as they might be without a lead actor who brings such nuanced insight and intuition to the role. Portman plays Nina, an utterly, single-mindedly devoted ballerina with a prestigious New York City ballet company. Her technique is perfect, but she lacks the requisite passion for the leading roles. The company's artistic director, a French-accented martinet named "Thomas" (but pronounced "Tomah"), rewards Nina by casting her as the white and the black swan in his "avant-garde" production of *Swan Lake*, but only after he attacks her sexually and she bites his lips defending herself in response.

One of the film's most interesting insights is into the twisted relationship between male ballet impresarios and their female dancers. Vincent Cassel plays Thomas with a cruel sneer in his upper lip and a leer in his eyes as he challenges Nina to give up her quest for perfection so that she might convincingly portray the evil and seductive Black Swan with the wild abandon he conceives for the role. That he uses his own body against hers to force her to find her strength is part of what Aronofsky's film wants to critique, but also partly what makes watching it uncomfortable. Thomas doesn't even pretend there's any other way to "get" the performance he wants from his star but to sexually humiliate her in public and to push her physical boundaries in private. Nina wants the role so badly she'll do anything to get it and then keep it, even as she becomes more and more deranged. As her relationship with Thomas gets increasingly entwined, she begins to suffer from a kind of Stockholm Syndrome, idealizing and even identifying with Thomas and his mercurial cruelty.

Haunting the proceedings as a cautionary object lesson is Beth (Winona Ryder), the aging (that is, over 30), once-glorious star of the company who's forced into retirement so that Nina can take her place. All the dancers want to be Beth; when Nina sneaks into the older woman's dressing room before her own star casting is announced, she steals Beth's lipstick, a pack of cigarettes, and a letter opener, totemic objects that Nina carries as talismans toward her own success. But Beth's precipitous tumble from the top to the bottom turns ugly when she won't go gracefully into retirement. Instead, she causes a scene at a benefit party and then throws herself into New York City traffic, landing in a lonely hospital room where she languishes with ugly, disfiguring, and debilitating scars. She sits in a wheelchair, her head canted down at a painful angle as she contemplates the cruelties of fate. Sadly, Ryder's shrewish portrayal of the vanquished star mirrors too closely the details of her own career, and her one-dimensional, caricatured acting doesn't help redeem her performance or the character. Nina, fascinated by the woman she's replacing, visits Beth in her hospital room as some sort of weird penance for precipitating the star's fate, but the visits aren't instructive so much as increasingly macabre and violent as Nina's reality begins to shatter.

Aronofsky signals his vision of his own leading lady with heavy-handed shots of Portman fragmented and multiplied by the various mirrors in which her life is continually reflected. In the claustrophobic apartment she shares with her equally insane mother, Erica (Barbara Hershey), a mirror by the front door is cut into pie-shaped wedges that breaks Nina's image into pieces, and the three-sided mirror in which she practices and obsessively laces and re-laces her toe shoes ensures that even at home, she's always onstage.

Nina's mother, it seems, was a corps member herself before she stopped dancing to raise Nina. No father is evident, just the suffocating co-dependency of two women who represent different generations of the same dream. Erica both wants Nina to succeed and desperately needs her to fail, so that her daughter will cling to her, imprisoned in the child-like state Erica insists on preserving. Nina's bedroom is lined with rows of white and pink stuffed animals that stare down at her bed, and every night, she goes to sleep with the tinny music box sounds of "Swan Lake" that her mother sets in motion to soothe her. Erica intrudes on Nina's privacy, checking the ever-worsening rash that blooms across her daughter's back, chiding her for mutilating herself and, at the same time, helping Nina hide her wounds. When Nina is cast in the lead role in *Swan Lake*, Erica doesn't set out to sabotage her success, but willingly abets Nina's fast downward spiral when it begins.

The real agent of Nina's downfall is the woman who might otherwise be her savior. Lily (a stunning Mila Kunis) arrives in the company from LA full of self-confident sexuality and the distinctly un-ballet-like languor of the west coast. Nina first catches a glimpse of her on a subway, distracted from her own image in its Plexiglas windows by Lily's hair and the headphones she wears. Lily makes her first appearance at the studio by banging open and closed the door while Nina is dancing, causing her to stumble in her audition for *Swan Lake*. But Lily's laxity proves a refreshing counter-balance to a ballet world in which young women are wound tight, can't eat, throw up what they do get down, and, like Nina, are so disciplined to be perfect that they have no lives outside their dancing.

Lily, the film's own black swan, loves sensuality and sexuality in equal measure. After she and Nina get off to a rocky start, Lily visits Nina at home, shocking both her and Erica with her brashness. Undone by Erica's haranguing, Nina impulsively goes to a bar with Lily, where she's persuaded to take a disinhibiting drug that Lily insists will just relax her and only last for two hours, "most." Tempted by her desire to be free of her mother, and by Thomas's insistence that she "touch herself" as homework to help herself loosen up, Nina lets Lily drug her cocktail and gets very uninhibited indeed. The two women flirt with men who are deeply uninterested in ballet – to Nina's shock, since the art forms her entire world – then dance together wildly in a scene shot in pink light and edited frenetically to represent Nina's descent into drug-induced ecstasy. The evening ends when Lily makes a pass at Nina in a taxi, and Nina brings her home, to the shock and dismay of Erica, who tries to batter down her bedroom door while the two young women have very wild, hot, and explicit sex.

The sex scene is the film's pivot point, as it demonstrates how much Nina represses for her art, and how passionate indeed she can be. High as a kite, Nina won't stand for her mother's interdictions, and pulls Lily into her bedroom, where they rip off one another's clothes and practically swallow each other's tongues. Aronofsky films and edits this scene, too, with close-ups of body parts and quick jump cuts that heighten the intensity, until he finally focuses in on Nina's sexual awakening under Lily's ministrations. The scene reveals that other side of the carefully controlled artist is a young woman of painful depth and desire, who revels in just the kind of passion Thomas has been so eager to induce.

But the next morning, things go quickly awry. Lily is gone, but the pole Nina uses to keep her bedroom door propped closed hasn't been disturbed. Nina wakes hung-over and late for rehearsal, where she finds Lily already in costume, performing in her role. Immediately, Lily becomes a palpable threat to Nina's ascendancy, and when Nina refers to their evening together, Lily accuses her of having a "lezzie wet dream" and denies that anything happened. From there, Nina's sanity teeters ever closer to the brink, and Aronofsky plays even more fast and loose with what's real for her and what's real for us.

From the film's beginning, moments that seem true are suddenly proven false. In the bathroom of the ballet benefit party, Nina's ragged cuticles begin to bleed and she can't get them to stop, eventually peeling a three-inch strip of flesh from her finger. But when she's interrupted by, as it happens, Lily knocking on the door, Nina looks down to see her finger miraculously healed. This girl bleeds terribly – her toenails break from dancing on them, her back bleeds from scratching, and blood continually reddens the water in which she bathes and washes. But we're never sure if her wounds are real, and neither, it seems, is Nina.

In fact, in the film's climactic scene, Nina seems to kill Lily in a violent rage, shattering her dressing room's full-length mirror with her rival's head and then dragging her body onto the cold tile of her bathroom floor. When Lily's blood seeps under the door, Nina covers it with a towel and goes off to perform triumphantly the second act of *Swan Lake*, where she nails her performance as the black swan with galvanizing passion and rage, murderous in her seductress's make-up.

But when she returns to her dressing room to change costumes for the ballet's third and final act, Lily comes knocking on her door to compliment Nina's performance. The body in the bathroom is gone and so is the blood. Nina redresses herself in her white swan costume, but as she pulls on her white feathers, she finds in her own abdomen the seeping red wound she thought she'd inflicted in Lily's. With morbid fascination and a strange glint of triumph, she retracts the shard of broken mirror she seemed to have used to kill her enemy.

As she returns to the stage to finish the ballet exultantly, we're not sure if this, too, is a hallucination. The white swan falls to her death and Nina falls to the mattress that catches her behind the set, where her fellow dancers and Thomas surround her, extolling her glory and her talent. He calls her "little princess," the affectionate but diminishing name he once used for Beth (just as Lily predicted he would), then notices with dismay that her white costume is marred by a spreading stain of very red blood. But as she lies there, apparently dying, Nina says both "I was perfect" and "I felt it," fulfilling her own expectations and Thomas's wish. In Aronofsky's vision, she's also finally become a woman, her technical perfection infused with the reckless passion of adulthood and her cocoon-like innocence stained with the menstrual-like blood of her masochistic wound. The swan in the story dies, and while it's not clear if Nina survives, we're supposed to think she's at the very least killed off the part of herself that held her too-adult passion and desire at bay.

I suppose Aronofsky also wants us to consider the depravity of those who give themselves to an art that gives so little in return. The rewards, *Black Swan* suggests, are fleeting, ephemeral evenings of triumph and applause, which fade too quickly as ballet dancers inevitably age. As my film-going companion, Feminist Spectator 2, pointed out, adoring fans are faceless and strangely unrepresented in the film. Nina peeks out at the audience before she performs, but it's really the adoration of her colleagues that she craves and finally achieves when they surround her fallen body at the film's end.

Aronofsky indicts the cruelty through which Thomas realizes his vision of *Swan Lake* by manipulating the already unstable Nina, but the writer-director's camera also enjoys a bit too much how the story makes Nina suffer, and happily represents her as a martyr to her art. Thriller conventions bring *Black Swan* its rather perverse excitement, as Aronofsky keeps the viewer off balance, like Nina, through quick confusing cuts to a murky woman who keeps turning up in the troubled young woman's fantasy/reality. When Nina masturbates at home, following Thomas's instructions to "loosen up," nearly at climax she turns her head and sees another woman sitting on the chair in her bedroom, watching her. The cut happens so quickly, it's not clear if the woman is Erica, the mother, or another young woman whose face and figure recurs in Nina's dreams/fantasies, who may or may not be a younger Erica or some other Nina-style doppelganger. I kept expecting some previous trauma that would explain Nina's insanity, but Aronofsky never delivers a backstory to illuminate her strange psychology. That choice heightens the film's suggestion that it's her single-minded dedication to art – encouraged by her similarly obsessed mother – that's driven Nina mad.

Barbara Hershey is convincing as the over-bearing, bitter mother who watches her daughter achieve the career she always wanted. Erica lives through Nina and resents her deeply, calling incessantly on Nina's cellphone, which displays "MOM" in insistent capital letters as the phone bleats plaintively. Erica doesn't seem to be employed, but instead sits alone in a small room in their apartment (how these two afford a three-bedroom flat in Manhattan is never explained), creating Munch-like paintings of her own (or is it Nina's?) face, images that seem to scream and follow Nina with their eyes when she peeks into the room. Erica and Nina's bond is both incestuous and ambivalent, as they're attracted and repulsed by everything they mean to one another.

Nina's fantasy hook-up with Lily also seems to sublimate her strange push-pull relationship with Erica, while at the same time, to represent the entirely incestuous, homosocial, female-dominated world of ballet. Strangely, though, it's also a heterosexual world, in Aronofsky's conception. Lily enflames Nina's jealousy by flirting with the callous man who dances the white swan's romantic object (Benjamin Millepied, who choreographed the film and later became Portman's husband). The only obviously gay man in this world is the rehearsal accompanist, who finally slams the lid on his piano after hours of solo work with Nina, telling her superciliously that he has a life (she, clearly, doesn't) and leaving her in the dark as the building's lights shut down.

What, finally, to make of *Black Swan*? Aronofsky has created an absorbing, if sometimes repellent, Grand Guignol of a film about artistic cruelty and excess, one that might be laughable if the leading performances (Portman, Kunis, Cassel, and Hershey, especially) weren't so heart-felt, layered, and persuasive. Portman's shattered poise, shaky vulnerability, masterful artistry, and desperate desire for both success and real connection make Nina a character from whom it's difficult to wrest your eyes. Even as Aronofsky dismantles the foundation of her world and her sanity, and keeps the viewer equally unable to distinguish fantasy from reality, Portman holds us squarely on Nina's side, hoping she'll be victorious against all the forces lined up against her.

Too bad that Nina's victory requires a self-mutilation so extreme she can only succeed by succumbing to her own death. That's a message that's not good for the girls.

DECEMBER 22, 2011

The Hunger Games

Lionsgate, premiered 2012

How sweet is the taste of a movie with a female heroine heralded as the top-grossing non-sequel film debut weekend of all time? And how sweet is it that *The Hunger Games*, the adaptation of the first novel in Suzanne Collins's trilogy about Panem, a dystopian country that sacrifices its children for the amusement of its privileged leisure class, is a faithful, stirring, smart film that doesn't pander to either sentimentality or sensationalism in translating Collins's politically nuanced story to the screen?

Starring Jennifer Lawrence (*Winter's Bone*) as Katniss Everdeen, the trilogy's heroine, *The Hunger Games* creates a rich material world for a story imagined so vividly by so many readers. Director Gary Ross and his production designers realize the fictional country's twelve dispossessed districts and its excessively decadent Capitol in a way that convinced me it was just as I'd pictured it as I read the novel, captivated by Collins's narrative. Katniss hails from District Twelve, where coal mines provide the Capitol with energy and the district's residents with straitened lives of near-starvation and strife. Katniss breaks the repressive government's strict rules by sneaking through the district's boundary fence to hunt for food in the adjacent woods with her friend, Gale (a handsome, stalwart Liam Hemsworth). Her father died in a mining accident; his sudden death left her mother catatonic with grief and unable to care for Katniss and her younger sister, Prim.

Ross's film establishes in deft strokes that Katniss is an accomplished hunter with a keen understanding of the woods in which she and Gale poach. Wearing threadbare clothing and scuffed boots, she strides through the hills and trees (Ross filmed around Asheville, North Carolina) and confidently wields a bow and arrow to bag birds and the rare deer. She and Gale have an easy camaraderie that comes less from romantic attraction than from similar survival instincts, the confidence of being good at what they do, and the imperative that they provide for their families. In other words, *The Hunger Games* breaks stereotypes almost immediately by representing a friendship between a young man and woman that's not based on facile heterosexual romantic rituals. The stakes for Katniss and Gale are much higher – they could be killed for leaving the district borders, but they risk their lives to put food on their families' tables.

Their lasting bond is broken by the annual "reaping," when two children between 12 and 18 from each of Panem's districts are chosen at random as "tributes" to compete in the televised gladiatorial competition known as "the hunger games." In District Twelve, the children assemble in the town square wearing their best clothes, shirts and pants and dresses of worn, graying cotton, while the Capitol's bubble-headed representative, Effie Trinket (Elizabeth Banks), parades before them in garish shades of pink and red. Her excessively colorful outfit, make-up, and wig set her off as outlandish in the district's drab landscape. To begin the reaping, Effie broadcasts the reminder that the Games were established to assert the Capitol's political primacy, after the districts tried unsuccessfully to rebel against its hegemony. Before she picks the names of the unlucky tributes, Effie unctuously pronounces her ludicrous benediction: "May the odds be ever in your favor."

When Prim is selected as District Twelve's female tribute, Katniss desperately volunteers to take her younger sister's place, and is promptly caught up in the horrifying preparations that propel the tributes into the fabricated arena where the games take place. Along with the male tribute, Peeta (Josh Hutcherson, *The Kids Are All Right*), Katniss travels by train toward the glittery, surreal Capitol. En route, the two District Twelve competitors are groomed for the games by Haymitch Abernathy (Woody Harrelson), District Twelve's only previous winner. His drunken apathy is downplayed in the film adaptation; as soon as he recognizes Katniss's gumption and talent, he's persuaded to be the mentor he takes much longer to become in Collins's book. Likewise, Cinna (Lenny Kravitz), the stylist who helps Katniss and Peeta make an impression on the Capitol denizens and the nation's audience in the televised interviews before the games begin, demonstrates immediate sympathy for his tributes' plight. He signals his antipathy for the brutality of the whole proceedings even as he helps Katniss establish her infamy as the "girl who was on fire" in the pre-games parade.

In these preliminary scenes, before Ross brings us to the central agon of games in which 24 children and teenagers are meant to murder one another until a single victor remains, the director and his cinematographer show us District Twelve and the Capitol from Katniss's point of view. The reaping, for instance, rushes by in a blur, capturing moments and faces in fragments that seem almost Expressionistic as they look so resolutely through Katniss's anxious eyes. The hand-held filming, kinetic editing, and point-of-view shots help create an atmosphere taut with tension and fear, and beautifully capture Katniss's confusion and terror (and intelligence) as she's escorted by Peacekeepers (who look like soldiers from the *Star Wars* films) into the custody of her handlers. By giving us visual insight into Katniss's emotional vulnerability, Ross humanizes a heroine whose inner dialogue we can no longer hear, as we could reading Collins's prose. Katniss's strength enables her to survive the games, but it could also make her appear unsympathetic and impassive.

In fact, Mahnola Dargis, writing for the *New York Times*, found Lawrence's performance "disengaged" in just this way. But the film itself addresses this quandary. Katniss isn't cut from gregarious cloth, and refuses to pander to the television viewers, even when her life depends on it. Similarly, Lawrence doesn't play to Ross's camera; hers is a subtle and, I think, strong and successful performance of Collins's signal heroine. Instead, Ross uses his camera to bring us closer to Katniss's feelings, while letting her retain the dignity of her strength and her intelligence and, in some ways, her privacy, despite the intrusions of rabid spectators into her life prior to and during the games.

For example, in moments of duress in the arena fabricated and controlled by the "Gamemaker," Seneca Crane (Wes Bentley), the television director who engineers the games much like Ed Harris's producer character manipulated the world of *The Truman Show*, we see flashbacks to earlier moments in Katniss's life that help explain her resolve. We see her father descending into the mines, and then watch a fiery explosion that implies his death. We see her mother descending into madness. We see Katniss's prior relationship with Peeta, the baker's son, who defies his hateful mother by throwing bread meant for their pigs in Katniss's direction, as she hovers in the rain outside the bakery, hungry and watching. And when Katniss is stung during the games by horrifying "tracker jackers," insects engineered by the Gamemaker with stings so painful they bring on hallucinatory episodes and sometimes death, we see the venom's effects on Katniss from her perspective. Blurred, tunneled images and distorted sound capture Peeta's face and his voice shouting at her to run, and the woods rushing by in a swirl of surreal light and color. All of these filmic strategies place us squarely behind Katniss.

Ross and his team tell the story with a dynamic style that moves it inexorably forward, even in scenes that might otherwise be static. The whole thing feels like a chase film, in which Katniss and the other tributes are being followed and watched not just by one another, but by the eyes of the state, which are always focused on them. For instance, when Katniss first ties herself to a branch high in a tree on her first night in the arena, she hears a mechanical noise, and realizes that what she took for a knot in the tree trunk is actually an embedded camera. As she peers into it curiously, Ross cuts to people watching "at home," in large crowds outdoors in the districts, or on make-shift screens in their homes. The Capitol's technology invades their lives not for the pleasure of information and communication, but to ensure its own hegemony.

This is technology as tyranny, the flip side, Collins suggests, of the high tech revolution as empowering.

In the book, Katniss's inner monologue was protected from the ravages of such state surveillance, so the reader was assured by a counter-point to the intrusions of President Snow and his minions' power. *The Hunger Games* on film, though, is also about watching. The film's spectators, too, have a kind of power over Katniss and, not insignificantly, over Jennifer Lawrence, the young actor chosen for a role that will rival Bella's in the *Twilight* series for fan and media attention. I read a snarky piece on *The Daily Beast* that suggested Lawrence was being ungenerous about her fame, self-deprecating and diffident. I didn't see the David Letterman interview to which the article mostly referred, but it sounded to me like Lawrence has taken a page from Katniss's playbook, which is partly what makes her so wonderful in the role.

Lawrence is rarely off screen during *The Hunger Games*. But her emotional presence is carefully modulated. Rather than playing a more conventional girl – although the dystopian Panem begs the question of what a "conventional" girl would look or act like in such a hard-scrabbled existence – Lawrence plays Katniss as tensely coiled and focused physically and mentally on outsmarting the other tributes and, eventually, the Capitol's manipulators. In Lawrence's keen interpretation, Katniss is a reluctant heroine. She won't pander to the Capitol's media or its cameras in the ways that Haymitch, her perceptive mentor, suggests might be necessary for her to actually win the games. If spectators empathize with or come to favor a tribute, they send help into the arena, little metal parachutes with containers full of much-needed medicine, food, or supplies. Katniss is forced to think through the costs of her refusal to perform as a more typical, coy, feminine girl, but her continued unwillingness to capitulate makes her an important role model for what will no doubt be legions of the film's teenaged girl fans.

Ross carefully establishes Katniss's foils – the girly-girl tributes from the other districts who interview with the games' television host, Caesar Flickerman (a terrifically campy Stanley Tucci, in a blue wig and practically Elizabethan garb). Although they prove themselves to be quite tough in the arena, most of the other girls wear sexy dresses and assume flirtatious manners for their pre-game interviews. And during the games, they combine forces with the alpha males, playing the Bonnies to their Clydes. These female tributes are also lethal – especially Clove (Isabelle Fuhrman), who throws knives – but they're represented in relation to their young men. Katniss can't even fathom such gender performances or alliances. Her subsistence-level life has taught her only to survive and has stripped away the niceties of human interaction to a central, necessarily suspicious core. Gale is the only person she trusts, with whom she can briefly let down her guard as they talk, before the reaping, in the woods.

But even there, Ross disallows any hint of romance. Theirs is a relationship built on trust and need and a long-standing regard and love. Only when Katniss leaves for the games, and her relationship with Peeta is broadcast around Panem, does Gale realize he's jealous. His own embarrassment and confusion makes him sweet and rather feminine himself. Peeta, on the other hand, quickly understands that playing to the crowd might curry important favor. He waves to the Capitol fans who watch their bullet train enter the city, crafting a charismatic smile to wear for them. (Hutcherson's appealing, low-key magnetism is perfect for the self-abnegating Peeta.) He insists on taking Katniss's hand and raising it in a show of victory as their chariot rolls through the gigantic presentation hall at their pre-games debut. As their clothing flames behind them, he tells Katniss the fans will love their daring, and he's right. Katniss suspiciously jerks her hand from his, but he persuades her otherwise. When, during his own interview with Flickerman, Peeta declares his love for Katniss, it's not immediately clear if he's playing to the cameras again or if he means it. The rest of the film hangs on this ambiguity.

But if Peeta is wily about winning through an appeal to spectators, Katniss's survival skills keep her firmly enmeshed in the immediacy of the arena's challenge. How wonderful to watch this girl-hero read the woods, feeling the soil for moisture, crushing leaves in her hand and releasing them to see how the wind blows, using her bow and arrow to bag food and, in the end, to protect herself and Peeta from the remaining tributes. How lovely to see Peeta hang back behind her as they move through the forest, Katniss with an arrow cocked in her bow for their mutual protection. How amusing to hear Peeta joke that he'll take the bow to hunt and to watch Katniss's incredulous reaction. How nice to see the girl save the boy, helping him into a sheltered cave when he's hurt, risking everything to get medicine for him, and masterminding the actions that in the end will save them both.

Lawrence plays these actions with an understated performance that's alive with subtlety. Her face registers everything, but in subtly expressive ways – with the twitch of an eye, a small compression of her lips, a hard-won smile, a flicker of confusion. Her pre-games interview with Caesar Flickerman is a marvel of acting as reaction. Katniss is startled and confused by the audience's uproarious response to her answers to his questions, but she doesn't have the vaguest idea how to play to their affections, as she's been tutored. Lawrence works for every smile Katniss musters. Wearing her red, off-the-shoulder gown, offering to model its fiery train for Flickerman, wearing make-up that's alien on her face and a hairstyle that's foreign to her, Katniss looks like a girl in the drag of femininity, trying to work it as ridiculously as Sandra Bullock playing Miss Congeniality, but with much less comedy and much higher stakes. Katniss's final confrontation with President Snow (Donald Sutherland, oily and reptilian as ever) models a chilly resistance and promises quite a David vs.Goliath confrontation as the trilogy builds momentum. Lawrence's performance is clear and strong; she does Katniss justice by acting with economy and reserve. Katniss's inscrutability serves her well among her enemies and the film's spectators; it keeps her mysterious, unpredictable, and interesting.

Much has been made of the story's violence, especially among young people forced to murder one another by heartless manipulators. Although the film is tense with the sounds and ever-present threat of bloodshed, remarkably little of it is actually seen on screen. The initial bloodbath at the cornucopia, when the tributes are first delivered to the arena, is cut in rapid sequences in which, once again, the briefly pictured parts – of faces, limbs, actions, objects – come to stand for the whole without directly representing the killing.

Occasionally, one of the more vicious tributes is seen murdering someone, but usually at a remove. Katniss and Peeta are rarely shown directly inflicting violence; their humanity is always evident and operative. Ross also keeps sentiment at bay, even in the more emotional, moving scenes. Katniss takes young Rue (Amandla Stenberg), a tribute from District Eleven, under her wing after Rue helps her escape from the "career" tributes who have surrounded the tree in whose branches Katniss keeps herself safe. Their relationship mirrors that of Katniss and Prim. Lawrence and Stenberg play their scenes together beautifully, creating a warmth and connection that belies their murderous environment. That Katniss cares for Rue until her bitter end, and uses the occasion of her tragic death to gesture in solidarity to her comrades in District Eleven, begins the insurgency that grows through the rest of the trilogy. Here, too, Lawrence productively underplays Katniss's defiance, emphasizing her hesitant heroism.

In addition to its progressive and nuanced take on gender, *The Hunger Games* also presents a sophisticated view of an entirely multiracial future society. Those with the most state power continue to be white – President Snow (pun intentional, I assume), Seneca Crane, Caesar Flickerman, and the others are all white (and male). But in the Capitol and in the districts, Ross has carefully cast the extras and other characters in a multiracial array. Every crowd shot is full of people of color as well as people who look white, enough so that the racial and ethnic diversity of appearance is notable. When Katniss's alliance with Rue provokes a revolt against the Capitol in District Eleven, Ross films their riots in a style reminiscent of footage of 1960s American civil rights demonstrations. The Peacekeepers subdue the protesters with water cannons. People of various races, working together, overturn dumpsters and destroy property. The scene is shot in a palette of black and white, and the protestors' anger and determination, along with the Peacekeepers' might and the general confusion of social rebellion, look very much like images from the 60s.

In addition to its admirable representations of gender and race, heterosexual romance is muted profitably in *The Hunger Games*. Katniss's tenderness is reserved for Rue; their sweet, more emotionally expressive moments are lovely and moving. Katniss's rage and grief when Rue dies is her most overt emotional moment during the games. She also grows attached to Peeta, but because they're both aware that they're playing to the cameras, the authenticity of their romantic involvement is always in doubt. Although by the film's end, it's clear that Gale is jealous of Katniss's relationship with Peeta, and that the sincere and earnest Peeta very much wants to continue the romance they've performed, reducing these relationships to "Team Gale" and "Team Peeta" to parallel the Team Edward/Team Jacob triangle of the *Twilight* franchise is just silly. *The Hunger Games* is about much more than a young girl choosing between two very different suitors; it's about fascism and rebellion, about hope and social critique.

I find myself delighted by the amount of press this film has generated, most of it positive, for a screenplay co-written (by Suzanne Collins with Billy Ray) by a woman based on her novels, about a young woman whose ethical humanity, physical strength, and emotional intelligence is a terrific model for us all.

APRIL 4, 2012

Brave

Walt Disney Pictures/Pixar Animation Studios, premiered 2012

The heralded animation event of the summer film season is the debut of the first female heroine in Disney/Pixar's stable. The flaming curly red-haired Merida more than meets the challenge of pioneering gender at the studio. She's a little Scottish archer, daughter of the king and queen of the kingdom, and feisty enough to resist her predestined role when her very proper mother decides it's time for her betrothal. What's perhaps even more significant than casting a heroine as the star of its fairy tale story is that *Brave*'s screenwriter and director, Brenda Chapman, fashions the film into the story of a mother and daughter who learn to understand one another by having adventures, outwitting bad guys (including vicious enchanted bears), and by outsmarting all those who would subdue them into their conventional gender roles.

Although I don't typically follow animated Disney films, *Brave* seemed important because of the media attention to its premiere. Since studio suits still believe that while girls will attend films about boy characters, boys aren't interested in stories about girls, how *Brave* faired at the box office and in the hands of critics seemed important. I was also curious to see how the studio would handle its heroine, and tried to experience the film through the eyes of the girls (and boys) who might find in its narrative a new way of thinking about gender roles.

I worried, at first, that Merida (voiced by Kelly MacDonald) would find her independence at the expense of her mother, Queen Elinor (Emma Thompson). The queen, from Merida's earliest memories, has been the gender enforcer, schooling her in the proper comportment for a princess by scolding her about putting her bow and arrow on the table ("A Princess doesn't bring her weapons to the table," Elinor remarks, adding, "but then, a princess shouldn't have weapons in the first place"). Merida's father, King Fergus, is a huge, muscle-bound, peg-legged buffoon, whose kingly mythology includes killing the bear that bit off one of his legs. But the animators signal his essential brainlessness by the size of his head. Atop his Schwarzenegger-style physique, his head is no larger than a baseball. The king enjoys practical jokes and encourages his daughter's free spirit, not to mention her talent with archery.

Queen Elinor is the kingdom's true ruler, and she takes her role very seriously indeed. Over Merida's furious protestations, she arranges for the first-born sons of each of the kingdom's three sister territories to woo Merida's hand. To prepare for her presentation as the would-be bride, the prize of this competition among men, Queen Elinor forces Merida's beautiful, unruly cork-screw curls under a tight-fitting wimple and trusses her up in a gown so tight-fitting the girl can barely move. Folding herself stiffly into her seat beside the king, Merida requires each suitor to prove his skill with a bow and arrow to compete for her hand. Each of the hapless young men does worse than the other, and all three are clearly ill-equipped to partner with the superior Merida. Impatient and irritated by their inability to hit the bull's eye, Merida announces that she'll compete for her own hand, and proceeds to land each of her three arrows directly on the mark. She infuriates Elinor with her insubordination; the queen insists Merida toe the line.

But the feisty young girl rides out of the castle on her trusty steed, Angus, to blow off steam and to follow her own instincts. As they ride through the forest, she sees a series of Tinkerbell-like fairy lights that lead her to a witch's lair. In a funny scene in which the old crone (voiced by Julie Waters) tries to pass herself off as a simple woodcarver, Merida winds up inviting the witch to place her mother under a spell that will help change her destiny. Through a mysterious mishap, the spell winds up transforming Queen Elinor into a bear.

I was afraid that *Brave* would derail at that point from its focus on Merida's resistance to the fairy tale marriage plot. But happily, Elinor's inadvertent magical alteration instead provides an opportunity for the queen to taste a less fettered life outside the castle walls and to test her own mettle as an independent woman. The excellent animation gives Elinor's bear persona all of the queen's expressions and reactions, making the animal a rather prim but game (you should excuse the word choice) presence. Her humanity battles with her new animality; she stands on two legs with her front paws crossed primly at her chest, but occasionally, her new bear nature takes over and she resorts to an ominous four-legged prowl and growl routine.

As an unexpected team, Merida and Elinor prevail. Merida persuades her mother-as-bear that the girl should be given free rein to follow her own destiny instead of being forced into a prearranged, much too early marriage to an inappropriate suitor. Elinor learns that she's more than the king's subdued, suitably feminine helpmate, and learns to admire her daughter's grit. The bear-killing king is relieved that he hasn't slaughtered his wife when he realizes that she's been transformed. And Merida's red-mopped triplet brothers, who are also inadvertently turned into bears when their large appetite for sweets leads them to gobble up the pastry that contains the spell meant for their mother, become their big sister's accomplices and help reunite the family.

Then I worried that as part of her new compromise with her mother, Merida would be persuaded that one of her suitors would in fact do. I waited for her to buckle down to convention, since the fairy tale mold from which *Brave* takes shape typically ends with the princess wooed and entranced and indeed married to the prince. But the film resists tradition, letting Merida end the story riding Angus out to one of the high, sheer rock-faces that she scaled earlier in the film. She climbs the heights and stands, triumphant, touching the sky while a typically jubilant Disney song supplies an inspirational melody to underscore her freedom.

What a relief, then, to see the first Pixar heroine carry the day. She reunites with her mother in a newly respectful and appreciative relationship and secures her father's power while implicitly undermining his patriarchy. If the film does well (its opening weekend numbers were very strong), perhaps it'll set a high bar for future Pixar heroines and will persuade studio heads that boys will indeed see stories about girls. That said, it'd also be nice if they tweaked the formula a bit. As Peggy Orenstein, author of *Cinderella Ate My Daughter: Dispatches from the Front Lines of the New Girlie-Girl Culture*, remarked in a broadcast response to the film, why does the heroine have to be a princess? Why couldn't she be a robot, like *Wall-e*, or a monster or a car like the central characters in other Pixar animated films? Despite all of Merida's determined resistance, all she changes is *when* she'll marry, not *that* she will. And she's certainly not throwing over the local power structure. As I watched, I kept thinking, Okay, why does this film have to be set in Scotland in a castle with a king, queen, and princess in the first place? Why does that fairy tale reality prevail in stories about girls? Wouldn't it be so much more refreshing if the story were set, say, in the present, in the U.S., so that the characters' garbled Scottish accents wouldn't work to distance the story under the pretense that it's *not* about girls today, now? Wouldn't it be lovely if the animated film were cast like the 1997 television adaptation of Rodgers and Hammerstein's *Cinderella*, starring Brandy, with a multiracial cast that included Victor Garber as the

King, Whoopi Goldberg as the Queen, Whitney Houston as the fairy godmother, Bernadette Peters as Brandy's stepmother, and a Filipino prince? Why couldn't Pixar be more ideologically imaginative?

Of course, *Brave* could be much worse. It's fun and smart and in spite of her long dress, Merida's a whiz with that bow and arrow.

JUNE 29, 2012

Part Three: Argument

Although any of the 35 essays collected in The Feminist Spectator in Action makes an argument, the following section gathers writing about plays and films that themselves present a specific, intentional point of view about a social issue like gender, race, or class through their production choices or their narratives. That is, for example, Clybourne Park, Bruce Norris's 2011 Pulitzer Prize-winning play, constructs an argument about race in America after Barack Obama's election as President in 2008.

Of the nine essays in this section, six address revivals of plays. Perhaps it's easier to see the argument in a play that's brought back for another viewing in a revised historical and production context, with different acting, directing, and design choices offering new interpretations. The Normal Heart, in its first Broadway revival, reminds audiences of the persistence of HIV/AIDS as a social scourge, and author Larry Kramer's activism outside the theatre each night of the limited run argued the necessity of continued activism. Perhaps less overtly, director Daniel Sullivan's Broadway production of The Merchant of Venice argued that anti-Semitism was essential to Shakespeare's plot and helped the classic play resonate in new ways for contemporary audiences. Though it's not a revival per se, Sullivan's production was a new interpretation of the classic. The Children's Hour, the London revival of Lillian Hellman's famous play, argues not just for a liberal notion of tolerance, but for a trenchant critique of social hypocrisy that speaks urgently into our 21st century moment.

Director Diane Paulus's Broadway revival of the opera-musical Porgy and Bess stirred quite a lot of critical controversy because of her choice to revise the text and the piece's structure. But the adaptation helped Porgy and Bess become a vehicle through which to see race and gender in the present as well as in the 1930s when the production is set. Margaret Edson's play Wit, revived by actor Cynthia Nixon (who played the lead) and director Lynne Meadow, was seen once again as a happy vehicle for women's health issues, though I argue that the play demonizes smart, professional women. Mike Nichols' acclaimed Broadway revival of Death of a Salesman brings new insights to Miller's canonical drama, arguing new sides in the continuing debate over the utility of the American Dream.

I include discussions of one film and a cable television series here: An essay on *Tomboy*, a French film about a young girl passing as a boy that presents a moving argument about gender fluidity and its benefits and costs, and one on *Homeland*, the Showtime series that stars Claire Danes as a psychologically troubled but brilliant CIA operative trying to prevent another terrorist attack on American soil.

The Merchant of Venice

Produced on Broadway, Broadhurst Theatre, 2010

I missed the Public Theater's production of *Merchant* at the Delacorte in Central Park last summer and so was happy for an unexpected chance to see it on Broadway where it reopened this winter. I'd heard various responses to Al Pacino as Shylock and to how director Daniel Sullivan handled the play's notorious anti-Semitism. But I was surprised by how powerful and moving I found the production and how much it spoke to the "othering" of Jews in ways that have uneasy contemporary resonances.

I'm not a Shakespeare scholar, but I've seen various productions of the play over the years that use different tactics to handle the representation of Shylock and the pound of flesh he intends to exact from Antonio, the Italian merchant whose fortunes have taken a temporary turn for the worst, when he can't repay his loan. Sullivan's production sets the action in an Edwardian-era Italy designed to appear stark and rather foreboding, with the men costumed in mostly dark suits, and only Portia, back home in Belmont, dressed in flashes of light or vivid color. Fences provide the dominating stage image, as concentric circles of railings and slatted iron enclosures are wheeled in various loops around the stage to create shifting scene locales.

The production's striking opening image uses these boundaries to establish visually the exclusion of Jews from Venice's financial center. A buzzing hive of men work the floor of the stock market, using long sticks to push beads across the rails of black abacuses set above their heads like the board of a modern-day financial center. A wrought-iron black fence encircles their activity, outside of which sits a young Jewish boy, watching wistfully, his inexorable exclusion palpable. "Jewish," in Sullivan's production, means Orthodox. The young boy wears *payot*, the earlocks that indicate religious observance, and so do most of the older Jewish men who work with Shylock and haunt the Venice scene. The fringe of the *tzitzis* that the Torah commands men to wear peaks out from under their suit coats, and in a later scene, when Shylock visits Antonio in jail, he and a comrade both wear *tallit*, the blue and white fringed prayer shawl, over their jackets. Judaism, then, is presented from the outset as a religious and ethnic identity that marks these men as outsiders, different from and othered by the culture that so emphatically excludes them. These images underscore that Shylock, though a usurer – a kind of loan shark – isn't part of Venetian commerce or finance, but works on a shadow market to which Antonio is forced to appeal to secure the 3,000 ducats he wants to give his friend Bassanio to woo Portia.

Shylock's ire, which Pacino plays so well in this production, stems from his resentment at being placed so squarely outside the dominant law. His stubborn insistence that he exact his pound of flesh as payment when Antonio is unable to fulfill the terms of his loan here seems fueled by Shylock's anger at the anti-Semitism that refuses him access to the law for his own defense. He's righteous in his demand to be included as a full human being. He attracts audience sympathy because Sullivan and the other actors seem to underline every moment Jews are called "dog" or "cur" and by the way Antonio and other characters spit "Jew" as a curse throughout the production. Shylock's bitterness at being so othered, and his determination to avenge himself and his tribe, seems only rational in the hateful environment the production depicts.

Although a bit of the Borscht Belt haunts Pacino's performance, he also brings depth and shadings to Shylock's plight. He plays him as intelligent and strong, full of irony and reason, determined to exact his revenge against not just Antonio (Byron Jennings) but the injustices of a racist system whose exclusions he can no longer bear. Pacino empowers the stereotype of the avaricious Jew, filling it out, historicizing it, and making it empathetic and realistic. He brings a bit of what I read as modern-day New York Jewishness to his bearing and his inflections. That is, even in the Edwardian moment in which Sullivan sets his production, I doubt that Jews spoke with the Tevye-like upward inflections and fake-humble shrugs to which Pacino sometimes resorts to signal Shylock's ethnic predilections. But the performance never crosses the line into broad caricature, and Pacino's version of Shylock's righteous rage keeps him human and sympathetic, even as he sharpens his knife and approaches Antonio's bared breast to cut his pound of flesh.

The trial scene manages to heighten the moment's suspense, even as most spectators will know how it ends. Antonio's arms are strapped to a large wooden chair, and Shylock circles him with his knife, debating where to make his incision. But Pacino and Sullivan hint at Shylock's hesitation, as he, along with the disguised Portia, who comes to Antonio and Bassanio's rescue to argue their case, seems to search for a way out even as he purposefully poises his knife. Pacino plays Shylock as determined to make his point, rather than actually to take the pound of useless flesh, but the scene is chilling in its urgency and implicit violence. The cut Shylock would make against Antonio's flesh comes to embody the violence done to him as a Jew by the anti-Semitism Antonio represents.

The disguised Portia (played beautifully by Lily Rabe, with a strength and composure that makes her a worthy adversary for Pacino's Shylock) deviously twists the letter of the law under which Shylock would see himself included and to which he must finally bow. Though he's owed a pound of Antonio's flesh, in her legalist reading of the bond, he can draw no blood, which makes it impossible for Shylock to exact his revenge. Instead, the law is turned once more against him, as Portia-as-lawyer heaps on punishments, taking away Shylock's wealth, giving half to the state and the other half to his daughter, Jessica (Heather Lind), who's converted to Christianity to marry Lorenzo (Thomas Michael Hammond).

Shylock, too, is forced to convert as part of his sentence, and Sullivan stages a wordless, wrenching baptism scene that represents the man's ultimate humiliation. Shylock is dragged to the baptismal font – a small pool of water uncovered upstage right – where a priest presides over his conversion. A henchman dunks Shylock three times, drenching his payot and his white shirt, before tossing him out of the water. Shaking himself off, Pacino defiantly retrieves Shylock's yarmulke, which his brute handlers had coldly tossed aside. Standing center stage, he holds the *kippah* over his head with both hands, like a crown, and then places it firmly back on his head. Though forced to bow to laws that can only enslave and never serve him, Pacino broadcasts Shylock's angry resistance.

The day I saw the production (February 5, 2011), much of the audience applauded as Pacino replaced his yarmulke. I had the sense that this New York-based production was playing to the New York Jewish community, signaled from the stage by Pacino's inflections and bearing and from the audience by its audible approval of Shylock's disregard for his enforced religious conversion. The moment was one of those jolts out of time that sometimes happen in the theatre, when you know spectators are responding from their own historical location to an action placed in a fictional past that resonates strongly into the present.

Likewise, Portia's legal machinations to force Shylock to forego his bond also reverberated with current events. When Portia interdicts Shylock from extracting Antonio's blood, the historical allegation of "blood libel" against the Jews resonates inescapably. This accusation falsely claims that Jews murder Christian children to use their blood in religious rituals. Those two words were tossed back into public discourse last January by Sarah Palin, when she said "journalists and pundits should not manufacture a blood libel that serves only to incite the very hatred and violence they purport to condemn" after congresswoman Gabrielle Giffords (who happens to be Jewish) was shot in the head in Tucson, allegedly by Jared Loughner. Palin's own rhetoric of violence – her talk of "reloading" and the map she drew of various US districts with targets circled as if within a rifle sight – seemed to encourage the vigilantism Loughner enacted, but her use of the term "blood libel" had distinct anti-Semitic overtones that commentators noted with dismay. I saw *Merchant* after Giffords' tragic shooting and the Palin debacle. When Portia foils the execution of Shylock's bond by prohibiting the spilling of Christian blood by a Jew, the resonance with the myth of blood libel and how it continues to insinuate itself into contemporary political discourse felt unavoidable and chilling.

Merchant of Venice is an oddly hybrid Shakespeare play, a comedy at Shylock's expense which, translated into a contemporary idiom, has to play as a tragedy *of* anti-Semitism and not just as a play "about" a Jew. But once Shylock is vanquished, he and the other Jews disappear from the story. In Sullivan's production, too, after the horrific and effective baptism scene, we don't see Pacino again until the curtain call, when he appears wearing a short robe that replaces his drenched costume. And so, after Shylock's rebellious exit, the play proceeds as usual. Antonio and Bassanio (David Harbour) return to Belmont and Portia's estate, where they finish out the mistaken identity plot, as Bassanio and Gratiano (David Aaron Baker) realize that Portia and her maid, Nerissa (Marsha Stephanie Blake), had come to court disguised as the lawyer and his clerk. The two romantic couples play out the commotion over the abandonment of their respective wedding rings. The tonal dissonance – all of the flirtatious heterosexual banter after the violence and ugliness of the baptism scene – is difficult to stomach.

But that seems part of the production's argument. Under the veneer of Venetian (and contemporary European and U.S.) propriety, Sullivan suggests, courses a bleeding vein of racism that's yet to be staunched.

That the production breaks so sharply in two – the rigors of the city's financial maneuverings and its anti-Semitism versus the superficial comedy of the country's domestic plots – seems part of Sullivan's design. The trivialities of the contest for Portia's hand and of Portia's and Nerissa's anger over Bassanio and Gratiano giving up their wedding rings so quickly, sit uneasily alongside the darkness of Shylock's devastation. After the baptism, it seems intentionally difficult to take the lovers' quarrels seriously.

Still, because Rabe is terrific as Portia, those moments gather weight and import. She consistently plays Portia's strength and intelligence. Various silly suitors come to try to correctly choose the casket that contains her picture, which according to her dead father's will, then bestows the right to marry her. As she watches the hapless would-be husbands make their mistakes, Rabe plays Portia with a wry knowingness, a contemporary feminist embellishment of the character that matches how Pacino signals Shylock's ongoing resonances by adopting hints of modern performances of Jewishness. Although Portia is already one of Shakespeare's most interesting female characters, Rabe is exceptionally good in the role, cutting a striking, sharply drawn figure of a woman who's strong and nimble, despite the ridiculous contest for her hand in marriage.

The beautiful production, with a minimalist, evocative set designed by Mark Wendland, retains a compelling visual appeal throughout. Those concentric, ever-circling fences create swirling images of both movement and confinement as they roll back and forth to open up and then contain stage space and to suggest the market, the court, and Shylock's offices. Sullivan moves a wrought-iron spiral staircase fluidly around the stage to bring his pictures height and depth. He often poses Portia on its stairs to show off her colorful costumes (beautifully designed by Jess Goldstein and elegantly worn by Rabe) and to highlight her rather supercilious distance from her ineffectual suitors. The back stage wall is bare and visible throughout, offering a canvas on which light (designed by Kenneth Posner) plays to change the scene and the mood.

The well of water that opens later in the play, in which Jessica and Lorenzo wade and in which Shylock is baptized, effectively reminds us of these characters' palpable humanness. Using something as elemental as water on stage calls attention to the presence of the actors underneath their characters. When Jessica walks barefoot out of the water, she leaves puddles behind as she moves off. Shylock's wet shirt clings to Pacino's chest as he wrenches himself from his unwanted baptism, revealing his vulnerability and his strength. When the young Jewish boy rushes to his aid, he slips and falls in the water collecting around the older man. The water's presence and its unpredictable effects provide a nice companion to the production's ever-changing yet inflexible metal fences. It rushes in where the Jews can't go, but doesn't, finally, bend those bars far enough to let them through.

FEBRUARY 13, 2011

The Children's Hour

Produced at London's
Comedy Theatre, 2011

When I heard that Keira Knightley and Elisabeth Moss would star in a revival of Lillian Hellman's classic realist play *The Children's Hour* in London this spring, my first thought was, "Why now?" The play, written in 1934, remains one of Hellman's most famous. Based on a true story about two headmistresses in Scotland in 1810, the play addresses the consequences of a lie spread by a difficult child at a school for girls run by long-time friends Karen Wright and Martha Dobie. The child, Mary Tilford, takes advantage of an incendiary accusation made by Martha's dotty aunt, Lily Mortar, to spread a rumor that Karen and Martha are lovers. Although her story isn't true, Mary's powerful grandmother believes her and ruins the school she once helped champion. Karen and Martha take Mrs. Tilford to court, but lose their slander case. Karen's planned marriage to the loyal Dr. Joe Cardin is threatened. As the two women sit in their empty school, contemplating their now-ruined lives, Martha confesses that the lie was true, that she did indeed love Karen "the way they said." Karen protests, but Martha insists and goes off to kill herself so that her friend will be free to continue her life.

Obviously, this isn't a happy story for lesbians. It represents the time-honored tradition of realist plays in which lesbians have no choice but to kill themselves at the end (or die otherwise tragic deaths from inoperable cancer or other deadly means). When Hellman directed a Broadway revival in 1952, after her own black-listing by HUAC, she said that at that point in history, the play wasn't "about" lesbians, but was rather about "a lie." But *The Children's Hour* has always been discussed as one of the first American plays with lesbian content. The story is nothing but anachronistic, however, in an historical moment when "Don't Ask, Don't Tell" has finally been repealed in the U.S., and when President Obama has decided no longer to prosecute under the Defense of Marriage Act same-sex couples who want to marry. In the U.K., same-sex partners have long been allowed to marry, and they enjoy more legal rights than their counterparts in the States. So why, then, revive this play? Why now, in spring 2011, except as a vehicle for two women stars known primarily for their roles in film and television (Knightley most recently in *Never Let Me Go* and most famously in *Atonement*, and Moss for her performance as the stalwart, pre-feminist ad-woman Peggy Olsen on TV's *Mad Men*)?

Director Ian Rickson answers that question in his London production by underlining the damage done in the play by those the program calls "the morally, or politically, or religiously self-righteous [who] stand in judgment and brook no doubt about the rightness of their world view." I believe that Rickson has subtly altered the script, too, so that Karen appears unsurprised by Martha's confession of her love, and so that Martha's self-revulsion is down-played instead of highlighted as the rationale for her death. Rickson's deft direction moves the play along quickly and creates an appropriate hot-house atmosphere of sex and desire among the young girl students. Knightley's and Moss's performances bring a distinctly resistant strength to roles sometimes played as abject. As a result, *The Children's Hour* winds up being a terrific, compelling, and even relevant production.

The wonderful setting – designed by Mark Thompson, with lighting by Neil Austin and sound by Paul Groothuis – signals that this revival sees the play as more than a domestic drama. The small stage of the West End's Comedy Theatre is further narrowed with a high box set, painted in roughened gray wood that suggests the Dobie-Wright School for Girls' farmhouse beginnings. A huge high door looms upstage, just right of center, through which all the significant entrances and exits occur, and at which Mary's two young roommates are found listening during Martha's fateful quarrel with her aunt. To stage left of the door, a floor-to-ceiling bookcase, filled with volumes in the first scene, empty in the last, takes the visual temperature of the play, as Karen and Martha's lives change from busy, over-filled happiness to devastated emptiness. The scene shifts to Mrs. Tilford's mansion maintain the large door, but fill the bookcase with the precious knick-knacks of those wealthy enough to afford useless pretty things. Columns descend from the flies to mark the stately remoteness of the home to which Mary so wants to return from school that she makes up her lie to keep herself free. The set's overwhelming height and magnitude emblematizes the pressure of social strictures bearing down on both the school and on Mrs. Tilford's home.

Rickson covers the several scene changes and the play's opening with wordless moments of interaction among the characters that help pinpoint Hellman's rich subtext. At the opening, Mary appears, alone on stage, reading from a book that's clearly meant for adults. She finds a place to hide herself by the wood-burning stove, and proceeds to swoon from what she's reading. When her classmates arrive, the book becomes a much-coveted source of attention. That the book is about sex is clear from how titillated the girls act, and their glee in reading its pages over one another's shoulders. Rickson directs the eleven-odd young women playing the girls to act like a pack of puppies. They crowd together on the set's lone sofa, roll over one another to get closer to the book, fall onto the floor, and huddle together, always moving, bumping up against one another, getting in each other's faces with laughter, and whispering scandalous secrets in one another's ears. Their behavior establishes the play's over-ripe atmosphere of teenaged sexuality and longing, and the fine line between pleasure and danger that makes the school a powder keg of emotion waiting to explode.

Mary (Bryony Hannah) serves as the instigator, the alpha girl around whom the others circle, trying to accrue some of her power and access. Mary's manipulations range from subtly to overtly cruel, as she cajoles or bends the other girls to her will. In the written play, Mary's evil appears crafty and calibrated; through Hellman's command of the realist form's subtext, the audience gradually comes to see how Mary constructs her story to free herself and sully her teacher's names, all because they don't condone her bad behavior and won't believe her lies, treating her exactly as they do the other girls, despite her wealthy grandmother's influence. In Hannah's performance, however, Mary is a whirling dervish of malevolence whose machinations are obvious from the start. Hannah plays the girl with broadly physical mannerisms, almost like a cartoon figure of a whiny, pouting, willful young thing determined to get her way. She stamps the ground, flings out her arms, screws up her face, and throws herself across furniture in dramatic displays of Mary's displeasure, raising her voice more often to shout her demands than to issue quiet, needling imperatives.

Critics apparently split over Hannah's performance. Ben Brantley, in the *New York Times*, called it one of the worst examples of over-acting he's ever seen on stage. But several London critics believe that Hannah stole the show from her more famous acting partners. I found her performance distracting. Although her strong bearing and gestures gave her an interesting, boyish appeal, her general gestalt put her in a different universe than the other actors, and struck tonally false notes in an otherwise coherent and cohesive production. Where the other actors seemed to be genuinely listening and reacting to one another, Hannah seemed to be playing Charades, signaling to her stage partners in the broadest possible terms what she meant them to guess about her intentions. The one-note performance became exhausting to watch; Hannah started so high, she had nowhere to take the character as the play progressed. Since Mary's important subtext was broadcast in Hannah's overt telegraphing of her intentions, the production lost some of its enigmatic quality.

But Mary's hateful leadership also created contemporary resonances, since she's a prototypical bully who tells lies to absolve herself of her own responsibility. The pack mentality of a school for girls is palpable in Rickson's production. Rosalee, the one student who knows Mary is lying about seeing Karen and Martha kissing and is willing to say so, is brought into line when Mary threatens to reveal that Rosalee stole a bracelet from another girl. Mary's awful power over the others is physical, emotional, and psychological, and Rosalee, especially, drowns in its wake along with Karen and Martha.

In a deft choice, Rickson stages Karen and Martha's relationship to mirror those of their young charges. At their first entrance, Karen (Knightley) and Martha (Moss) are physically intimate, sharing their morning coffee and cigarette by passing the cup and the smoke back and forth between them as they prepare for their day. Their establishing business makes them in fact seem like a couple, with all the comfort and familiarity of a long friendship. Throughout the play, Knightley and Moss show their solidarity by touching one another casually in passing. Those gestures of support and warmth make Martha seem more secure, marking her friendship with Karen as less "sick" than simply long-standing and comfortable. These are women who know one another well, who've worked together closely for eight years after graduating from college to build their now-successful school. Their physical casualness might mark them as women of 2011 more than 1934, when the play is set, but it makes good sense, given their history.

Carol Kane, as Lily Mortar, Martha's querulous aunt, presents a dashing figure as the faded stage actor who tutors the students in elocution, even as she instills in her girls foolish notions of heterosexual romance by having them read *Antony and Cleopatra* aloud to one another. When her niece insists it's time for Mrs. Mortar to leave their house and their employ, Kane conveys the insulted Mortar's narcissistic excess and her destructive prattling about Martha's "unnatural" feelings for Karen. Mortar's insinuations, overheard by Mary's roommates, seed the lie that Mary waters to fruition. Mortar's unwillingness to return from her stage tour to tell the truth at their trial seals Martha and Karen's fate. When the two women confront her toward the play's end, Mortar insists she had a "moral obligation" to the theatre, and would never have considered returning to address what she calls the "unpleasant notoriety" of Martha and Karen's legal hearing. Kane's performance is so theatrical, you actually can believe that she'd put her paltry and ridiculous touring job ahead of her niece's well-being. Mrs. Mortar's self-concern underlines that those who refuse to stand against falsehoods are as responsible for their corruption as those who perpetrate them.

Likewise, Ellen Burstyn's performance as the righteous Mrs. Tilford demonstrates both the hubris of those who think they know what's right and true and the devastating downfall of those who can't buy their way back into blamelessness. When Karen and Martha rush to Mrs. Tilford's home to challenge her in person, the elderly woman relies on a textbook homophobic response, despite her earlier support for the Dobie-Wright School. Burstyn is perfect in this scene, brushing aside their remonstrations with "I don't want to hear about it" and "What you do is your business, but when children are involved...," mouthing to the letter the narrow-minded moralism of those of who think their own values rightfully prevail. Burstyn also lets spectators see how Mary works on Mrs. Tilford, finally exhausting her into believing her story. When Mary's lie is exposed, the contrite Mrs. Tilford comes back to the school to try to buy Karen's forgiveness, but Karen scoffs at her offer of help. Burstyn plays the woman's regret and shame as a physical symptom, bending forward over a chair in the now dilapidated school's sitting room, as though she's made ill by the consequences of what she's done.

In *The Children's Hour*'s second act, in particular, some of the dialogue sounded different than the play I remember, making me wonder if the production team had rewritten parts of the text. In Karen's final scene with her fiancé, Joe, for example, she intimates that she knew Martha loved her, even perhaps suggesting that she loved her "that way," too, and admitting that within every lie there's always a shadow of truth. She forces Joe to ask the question that hangs between them, after he slips and insists that it doesn't matter "what you've done." In their rearranged lives, Karen notes bitterly that every word has a new meaning; she's an English teacher who's been forced to realize how easily language can betray.

Tobias Menzies, as Joe, plays the moment sad and ashamed, but he does indeed ask Karen if the accusation is true. She realizes that the poison of not knowing for sure that he believes her will always haunt their relationship and she insists that he leave. Joe says he doesn't want to, but in a subtle bit of smart blocking, Menzies moves toward the door as he speaks, letting his body betray the loyalty he's trying to perform. He agrees to Karen's insistence on a trial separation, but she knows (and we know) that he won't be back. In fact, one of the lines cut from this production is Mrs. Tilford's hope, expressed very close to the play's end in the original, that Karen will reconcile with Joe, to which she answers woefully, "Perhaps." In Rickson's production, the heterosexual contract is permanently sundered.

Martha's destiny, sadly, can't be changed. But in Moss's perfor- mance, the way she arrives at her suicide gets a very different, much more powerful interpretation. As Karen and Martha sit together in their destroyed school, a week or two after the trial at which they lost their case against Mrs. Tilford, Moss plays Martha's outlook with an ironic humor that makes her seem a tough survivor. She and Karen decide they should go for a walk and that those who would look at them disapprov- ingly be damned. But Karen can't leave the house. Martha is willing to face the world but Karen can't find the strength. When Martha opens the imposing school door to urge her friend to go out with her, their matching camel-colored coats hang side by side on hooks in the hall. The image is as redolent of their mutual affection and interconnect- edness as the two male lovers' shirts hung on the same hanger in one of the final images of *Brokeback Mountain*.

When Mrs. Mortar comes sidling back into their lives after her theatre tour, obviously broke and looking for shelter, Moss plays Martha's rage with wonderful verve. Martha knows that her aunt set their destruction in motion with her insinuating suggestions. In response to the foolish woman's sniveling demand that Martha care for her, Moss throws Mortar's things out the large door, shouting, "I've always hated you." The moment shows Martha capable of commanding huge emotions and remaining strong and intact. But once Joe leaves, Martha can't bear the responsibility for Karen's unhappiness. She crosses to her friend to take her hand, and kneels in front of her to confess, "I've loved you the way they said." When Karen moves away from her, Martha rises, and in her final speech, Hellman's language (adapted or not) rings with contemporary resonance. Martha admits that she couldn't call her feelings by a name, that it wasn't until a stupid girl spread a silly rumor that she was able to finally see what she didn't realize was in her all along.

But even though she says she feels "sick and dirty," Moss won't let Martha sink into abjection. She performs the woman's anger, which becomes a *cri de coeur* against a world that refuses to make a place for her love. She plays not Martha's shame, but her fury at how she's been forced to know herself, which dooms her to understand her desire and end her life at the very same time. Martha moves to embrace Karen, but her friend shies away; you can see Moss realize that she's lost her forever, and that without Karen, Martha's life has no point. Moss's face clears with resolve; she smiles; she straightens her back; and she exits, saying, "Good night, darling," to Karen as she goes. A moment later, a gunshot echoes and we hear Martha's body fall.

In the last scene of the play, Mrs. Mortar rushes in to see her niece's dead body, declaring suicide a sin and continuing to moralize against her even in death. Mrs. Tilford forces her way into the house to tell Karen that she knows Mary's story was a lie, too late to save Martha or the school. Karen responds with anger, refusing the money Mrs. Tilford offers to make things right, determined not to allow the older woman to be able to sleep with a clear conscience ever again. Karen throws both women out of her home, pulls the sheet from the room's window, and throws open the sash, breathing deeply of something that feels like freedom. The lights brighten on the image before they fade, and Knightley stands nearly defiant, cracking open the box of social moralism in which Karen has been confined for too long. This final moment provides an affecting image. Like so many others in Rickson's production, it gives the old play new resonance and meaning, working against its more conservative ideological bent.

I'm still surprised by how moving I found the production. By empowering Martha at the end, and letting Moss play against the character's shame, Rickson and his actors suggest that there really wasn't any disgrace in Martha's love for Karen. In her last speech, expressing her feelings seems like a gift for Martha; she directs her anger and judgment not at herself, but at a world that has no frame of reference for her love. Of course, the play works against a happy ending, and it's a stretch to find something progressive about it. But in addition to its new spin on the play's view of sexuality, the production also resonated as an argument against a poisonous atmosphere of moralizing in general. Rickson and his cast clearly and powerfully indict the very circumstances the play narrates: The corruption of the elite, who create their own systems of meaning to damn and demean, at their whim, those with less access to power, who deserve so much more.

MARCH 17, 2011

The Normal Heart

Produced on Broadway, John Golden Theatre, 2011

Seeing the Broadway revival of Larry Kramer's landmark AIDS play, *The Normal Heart*, prompted me to think again about activist theatre and how it might effectively communicate its consciousness-changing intent in popular mainstream forums. First performed at the Public Theatre in 1985, when the AIDS crisis was just beginning, the play's furious indictment of government and community inaction when intervention could have made a difference sounds just as relevant 25 years later.

Much has changed since Kramer first pilloried closeted, powerful gay men and indifferent government officials for their refusal to publicize the disease and early transmission theories to the community who could have most benefited. The cocktail of protease inhibitors now makes HIV, for some people, a chronic, rather than an absolutely fatal virus. Clear information about how it's transmitted has made safe sex practices the lingua franca of most western sexual cultures since the 1990s. But much still remains the same vis-à-vis the pandemic, which lends Kramer's play its continued relevance. Federal government officials still short-change HIV/AIDS research, the medications that effectively forestall the virus's progress remain prohibitively expensive, and homophobes who agitate against LGBT civil rights in the U.S. continue to spread lies about HIV/AIDS as divine retribution for a morally corrupt society.

The Normal Heart's directors Joel Grey and George C. Wolfe have crafted a crystal clear rendering of Kramer's play, with a talented cast whose performances are empathetic, careful, and emotionally powerful. Grey and Wolfe focus on the interactions among the characters rather than creating spectacle, suggesting locales with simple set pieces and props that specify the historical moment without distracting from the narrative's momentum or import. Inside the proscenium's frame, scenic designer David Rockwell creates a slightly askew white box set, the walls of which, if you look closely, are imprinted with white-on-white dates of newspaper articles, the names of hospitals, and other locations and facts. This information ghosts the scene, grounding the production in a stark historical reality.

Grey and Wolfe adopt a documentary-style approach throughout, projecting location titles above the proscenium as the scenes shift from place to place: Ned Weeks's apartment, the headquarters of what becomes the Gay Men's Health Crisis (GMHC), the mayor's office and other locales. Scenes in Dr. Emma Brookner's office, for example, are staged with one rolling gurney to represent her examination table; in the GMHC office, a white board and the flyers the men fold signal their activist labor. In Ned's apartment, where he lives with his lover, Felix, the two men share ice cream and their thoughts sitting downstage center on large floor pillows, isolated in a pool of light that creates an intimate mood. The schematic setting and evocative set pieces subtly suggest that the play's themes span generations. Disco music plays as the first scene opens (Donna Summer's 1979 hit "Bad Girls"), and the costumes (by designer Martin Pakledinaz) are cut in a generally '80s style. But the production feels and looks intentionally timeless, even though it details a specific historical moment.

Ned Weeks (played with power and insight by Joe Mantello) stands in for Kramer in this autobiographical story, as a gay man whose community is suddenly decimated by a disease no one can name or explain. With a writer's desire for knowledge and redress, Weeks forms an activist collective that seeks information and widespread mobilization. Weeks meets Dr. Brookner (beautifully played by Ellen Barkin), a physician who's among the first to suspect how the virus is transmitted among her gay male patients. When Brookner insists that gay men should stop having sex to arrest the course of the disease, Weeks is the only one willing to act on her injunction. At a time when gay male culture celebrated the creative sexual expression of its community, being told to stop having sex was like being told to return to pre-Stonewall repression. But Weeks persists, alienating even his fellow activists with his anti-sex screed and his confrontational style. He creates a complex political calculus in which he enjoins his community to stop the practices that in many ways define them while he inveighs against gay men in positions of power who refuse to be open about their sexual identity.

The production tautly illustrates the costs of activists' fear and government inaction. Grey and Wolfe and the actors adopt neo-Brechtian performance strategies couched in the emotion of psychological realism to deliver their powerfully instructive history lesson. For instance, partway through the production, the actors who aren't performing in a scene stand or sit around the stage's half-lit perimeter and look on as silent witnesses to the other characters and their collective history. And in between scenes, the names of the dead are projected in a list that increases exponentially as the story continues. The names grow from 20 or so to long lines of columns that extend around the white walls of the stage and spill into the house. The device offers a moving reminder of how a disease turned into a pandemic and serves as a metaphor for the cost of inaction and inattention from those who might have stopped its spread. The wall of names is reminiscent of other memorial projects, including the Names Project – a traveling display of the AIDS Memorial Quilt composed of panels stitched in memory of those who died of HIV/AIDS – and even Maya Lin's Vietnam Veterans Memorial in Washington. Like these, the production's projections of names of the dead is a simple, powerful remembrance of the absent presence of people no longer able to represent themselves, but whose deaths must be enumerated so that they aren't in vain.

In addition to this piercing, presentational theatrical style and its political commentary, *The Normal Heart* is filled with fiery anger and more subtle, desperate emotional concern and caring. The cast plays to spectators' emotions alongside our intellect, never letting us forget that the people whose activism or inaction we're witnessing lived and (many) died for this cause. Joe Mantello is astonishing as Weeks, the intellectual Jewish Yale graduate who at first bemoans his inability to maintain a close relationship. When his friends start dying of a mysterious syndrome, he springs into action, forming an activist group that will become Gay Men's Health Crisis, and presses city officials to communicate word of the disease to New York's vulnerable gay male population.

When Ned and his friends meet with closeted administrators and politicians, Weeks's incendiary accusations and bitter recriminations horrify his fellow activists and alienate the people best positioned to help. But Weeks won't back down. Mantello plays him as spitting mad, with a consuming, furious commitment to an urgent cause. Ned also urges gay men at the *Times* to write about what's happening to their community and flies into rages when the paltry news coverage appears buried in the paper. He meets Felix Turner (John Benjamin Hickey), a closeted gay *Times* style journalist, with whom Ned spars as he agitates for coverage and attention, then eventually begins an intimate relationship. Ned's relationship with Felix is cut short when Felix contracts HIV. Ned's crusade becomes that much more personal, as Felix is the first man with whom Weeks has been able to sustain an emotional, as well as intellectual and physical, connection. Hickey is lovely as the quieter, more measured Felix. Mantello and Hickey's scenes together establish the complicated stakes of being a gay man at a time when American culture was much less liberal and accepting, when private homes or public baths were the only places in which you could express a love that was still largely forbidden.

Felix meets Ned's wealthy, straight, lawyer brother, Ben (a sober Mark Harelik), for the first time when he visits Ben to see about his will, just before Felix's death from AIDS. Ben's fear of handling the piece of paper Felix gives him outlining the distribution of his estate palpably reminds us that not so long ago, people's ignorance about how the virus is transmitted made gay men public pariahs. Kramer's play recalls that in the mid-'80s, gay men were still considered pathological in American society, despite nearly two decades of post-Stonewall political advocacy. Ben tries to be sympathetic, but it's clear that he struggles to accept Ned's gay identity. And once AIDS seeps into public consciousness, like other straight people at the time, Ben's fear of contagion, though it embarrasses him, makes him afraid of physical contact.

As Felix deteriorates from the virus, Hickey illustrates his wasting by pulling his cheeks together into a gaunt visage, using nothing but physical transformation to convey the disease's ravages. Emma, who's cared for both of them, marries Ned and Felix at Felix's hospital bed. She declares indignantly that since the hospital is "hers," she has the power to give them this final blessing in the face of an unsparing disease that's robbed Felix of his dignity and finally, his life. Her flouting of conservative public policy rings with meaning, now that LGBT activism has moved from HIV/AIDS to same-sex marriage as its most visible cause. As Emma leads Ned and Felix through their marriage vows, black screens descend over the set's otherwise white walls. Hickey and Mantello stand beside Barkin, who sits in Emma's wheelchair. Grey and Wolfe direct the scene as though Felix is lying in his hospital bed and Ned hovers beside him, although both actors stand. After Felix says "I do" with his dying breath, Hickey's head drops back to indicate his character's demise.

Mantello screams Ned's "I do" into Hickey's ear, desperate for Felix to know that he sealed their union. The wrenching scene illustrates the defiance of those furious at gay men's fatal disenfranchisement. Playing it vertically in a more presentational style lets spectators feel the scene's grief and visually empowers Felix and Ned, despite the loss that floods the moment. Hickey stands with his head laid back through the rest of the scene, a physical testament to the needless death of his character and so many like him.

Barkin is remarkable as Emma, transforming herself from the sylph-like angst-ridden woman of much of her film work to a fierce, crusading physician who's among the first to recognize the prevalence of what was then called GRID – Gay-Related Immune Deficiency – in her patients. She incites Ned to action, insisting that the only way to stop the virus is to prevent men from having sex. Barkin's exacting compassion plays beautifully into Mantello's fury and rage. Emma has survived her own virus, the polio that's left her using an electric wheel-chair. Her chair is outfitted with a pouch in which she holds her charts and stethoscope. She wheels in and out of her scenes to examine her patients, then backs up to watch the others from the sidelines. Emma becomes the female face of medical activism, never succumbing to pity but always insisting that Ned and his friends fight, even as she counts more and more of her patients among the dead. With a New York accent and a blazing countenance, Barkin makes Emma a compact, forceful presence.

Along with the medical establishment and the government, Kramer indicts his fellow activists, who chose polite, accommodationist rhetoric instead of Ned's/Kramer's accusatory tactics. The handsome, straight-acting Bruce Niles (Lee Pace) becomes GMHC's president once Ben helps them incorporate as a non-profit. But Bruce refuses to adopt Ned's confrontational style and finally supports Ned's ouster from the board. When Bruce reads to Ned the statement severing him from the organization Ned helped found, the searing moment is a Brechtian gestus of history, in which a more liberal political path was chosen over the more radical. Bruce's antipathy for Ned appears, in retrospect, as internalized homophobia. But *The Normal Heart* finds sympathy for Bruce and his compatriots even as Ned vilifies them. The production clarifies that the choice between a liberal practice of working from within established channels and a radical proselytizing from outside was already stark at the pandemic's beginning.

Grey and Wolfe craft each scene with care and compassion. The clarity and simplicity of their direction leaves room for Ned's oceanic emotion, which Mantello plays with agonizing power. His fearless, full-hearted performance communicates the frustration of looking for information in an era of fear and ignorance while it signals a contemporary understanding of the cost of inaction. Mantello's performance is a requiem, an elegy to all those who died before knowledge could save them. The directors also keep the scenes moving, pacing the evening so that the play's heightened emotions don't exhaust spectators prematurely. The production's movement also evokes the speed with which history happens to the characters; the audience can feel their palpable shock at how fast they lose their friends and lovers.

The supporting cast forms a deeply-felt community of men whipped about by events they can neither understand nor stop. Jim Parsons (of television's *The Big Bang Theory,* who recently came out as gay) is lovely as Tommy Boatwright, his southern twang bringing special warmth to his expressions of support and love for friends who are mysteriously dying faster than he can fathom. Luke MacFarlane (the out actor who plays Scotty on television's *Brothers and Sisters*) is wonderful as Craig Donner, one of the first of this circle of friends to die of the disease. Patrick Breen (*Next Fall*) as Mickey Marcus and Pace (television's *Pushing Daisies*) as Bruce, are both pitch-perfect in roles that require them to demonstrate fear, resilience, and an unwillingness to be as radical as Weeks insists.

The play's moving power comes from what we now know about HIV/ AIDS and its progress, and how our knowledge lets us share Weeks's frustration and fury over the refusal of city officials to help. Although they're never spoken here, the ACT-UP watchwords "Silence = Death" resound through *The Normal Heart.* The play and the production illustrate why those words so powerfully describe the wages of inaction and the consequences of being afraid to clamor for life. Mounting this revival in 2011, when more people are living with HIV/AIDS instead of dying from it – if they're privileged enough to afford the medications that prolong one's life – makes *The Normal Heart* that much more poignant and meaningful as a slice of recent past in which the gay male community wasn't so lucky. For those in the audience who didn't live through the earliest days of the pandemic, the production illuminates what it meant to be an activist when lives were literally hanging in the balance.

Mantello as Ned provides a portrait of an activist rarely seen on mainstream stages. He evokes the anger of those who chose not to be nice and complacent and who refused to play a political game whose rules placed the dying at a distinct disadvantage. Weeks wouldn't play by anyone's rules, but his ad hominem attacks and enormous fury make him a difficult hero. It's hard to empathize with a man who makes himself so unlikable to advance his cause. But Mantello finds the layers in Weeks. He creates a human being instead of a strident mouthpiece and embodies Ned's vulnerability alongside his strength.

Mantello and Hickey are the cast's elder statesmen. Both performed in iconic gay American plays of the 90s. Ned Weeks could be an early prototype for *Angels in America*'s Louis Ironson, the other verbal, emotionally conflicted, smart Jewish gay man Mantello played on Broadway. But 20 years later, in a play that's more a political placard than a gay fantasia, Mantello's performance feels more personal, more emotional, and if it's possible, even more compelling. When he undresses to be examined by Dr. Brookner early in the play, it's clear that Mantello's middle-aged body has fleshed out from the wiry exclamation point that drew Louis's energy in *Angels*. The presence of the actor's body, ghosted by its own stage history, is very moving in *The Normal Heart*. Likewise, Hickey, who performed as one of the central characters in the 1995 Broadway premiere of Terrence McNally's landmark gay drama *Love! Valour! Compassion!* – which Mantello directed – is older now. But the history of his own performance in a significant gay American drama haunts his presence here, too. Playing lovers, Hickey and Mantello (who are both openly gay – although I wonder why I feel compelled to even mention that) have chemistry that adds depth and emotion to their relationship and makes Felix's death unspeakably painful. The play seems personal for the supporting actors, too, as they shift between performing in role and witnessing from the sidelines as the action continues. They each provide an empathetic, real, and moving presence that mirrors the audience's involvement and that builds a sense of community that extends from the stage far into the theatre.

Kramer's autobiographical narrative clearly reaches contemporary audiences. I saw the production with an audience predominated by those who looked like white gay men, mixed with obviously straight couples, women, people of color, and people whose ages seemed to span generations. Much of the audience sobbed openly through the play. *The Normal Heart* might be mainstream political theatre – yes, Broadway tickets aren't cheap; indeed, casting familiar television and film actors ensures audience attention; and sure, the number of Tony Award nominations the production has received (five) gives it credibility in ways that community-based political theatre struggles to achieve. (*The Normal Heart* is nominated for Best Revival of a Play; Best

Performance by an Actor in a Leading Role in a Play, for Mantello; Best Performance by an Actor in a Featured Role in a Play, for Hickey; Best Performance by an Actress in a Featured role in a Play, for Barkin; and Best Direction of a Play, for Grey and Wolfe.)

But this production's extensive media coverage also refocuses attention on HIV/AIDS. And Kramer's activism outside the theatre hammers home the on-going crisis and the virus's real effects not just on the gay male community but on those vulnerable to and suffering from the pandemic world-wide. Continuing his storied attempt to inspire people to action and not just to feel emotion, Kramer stood outside the theatre during the production's first performances, handing spectators a personal letter titled "Please Know." Although Kramer wasn't present the evening I saw the play, a young man with a stack of the letters handed them out as fast as people would take them. Kramer's letter reminds audiences that the play's events actually happened. He relates that many of the actual people he wrote as characters have died of AIDS, and that many of the actors in the original production have also passed away from the virus. He reminds us that no cure exists for HIV/AIDS; that the "amount of money being spent to find a cure is still miniscule, still almost invisible"; that AIDS is a worldwide plague; and that "no country in the world...has ever...dealt with it as a plague." Kramer's letter also denounces pharmaceutical companies as "evil and greedy," accuses American presidents since the 1980s of not saying or doing anything to address the pandemic, and decries the 35 million (to date) needless deaths that he attributes to political inaction and corporate avarice.

Distributing this letter after performances is savvy activism, since the powerful production inspires in spectators a desire to know more. Our emotions raw from what we've witnessed, our hearts (hopefully) opened to the suffering we've just seen, we leave the theatre sharing Kramer's outrage. Kramer's letter and his play remind us of the devastation HIV/AIDS continues to wreak and urges us to protest inaction against the pandemic at all levels of political life.

MAY 17, 2011

Homeland

Teakwood Lane Productions, premiered on HBO, 2011

Showtime's *Homeland* debuted on the 10th anniversary of the 9/11 attacks on the U.S. The series stars Claire Danes as Carrie Mathison, a CIA operative who's learned that an American soldier in the Middle East has been "turned" and now works for an Al Qaeda cell. When Marine Sergeant Nicholas Brody (Damian Lewis) is found after eight years in captivity and returns to a hero's welcome, Carrie is certain he's the double agent. Since she can't persuade her dubious CIA superiors to follow her instincts, Carrie goes rogue, setting up an illegal surveillance on Brody's house and then engineering a personal relationship with him that lets her follow her own course.

The series plays the country's paranoia for all it's worth, constantly turning the plot to keep viewers and characters off guard. The performers hold their characters' secrets close; they're as difficult for us to read as they are for one another to truly understand, even though viewers are given key bits of information early. For instance, Carrie's surveillance cameras can't pick up the inside of Brody's garage, where we know well before Carrie that he retreats regularly for Muslim prayers. Hearing his chanting and seeing him perform the rituals seems chilling, but it later appears that the show's producers have played on mainstream viewers' stereotypes about Islam to enhance our sense of foreboding. In a later episode, Brody explains to Carrie that he adopted Islam because he needed religion – any religion – to survive the ordeal of his captivity. Because Lewis plays Brody so convincingly, it's difficult not to be persuaded and even moved by his explanation. The plot twists upend our understandings, playing both with and against viewers' presumptions.

Nonetheless, it's impossible for a series about terrorism not to trade on knee-jerk expectations of which characters will be good and which bad. The Arabic-accented, Middle Eastern-appearing men are instantly marked as villains. The only thing that makes Brody truly interesting is that he's a red-haired, archetypally American soldier who might, in fact, be working for the enemy. And in a subplot that hasn't yet been consistently developed, a young Middle Eastern professor and his blonde American wife have moved into a neighborhood that puts them within shooting range of a U.S. military landing strip. The CIA believes the man might be Brody's Al Qaeda contact, but it turns out that it's his wife, Aileen (played by the always wonderful Marin Ireland), who is the mysterious operation's architect. Her back-story gives her ample reasons to love the Middle East and to despise the United States, but her centrality to the series' plot has so far been tenuous.

Homeland's producers, then, try to keep twisting the narrative so that the binary of American/good, Middle Eastern/bad won't maintain. But its visual scenario tells a different story. Middle Eastern male characters are constantly beaten, attacked, or killed by white military or intelligence officers. The guard who confined Brody for all those years, whom Brody beats when he asks to visit the captured man in prison, subsequently slits his wrists with a razor blade somehow smuggled in to him. Aileen's husband is killed when CIA operatives catch up to him and Aileen and blast automatic rifle fire through the walls of their motel room. (She escapes.) Even the henchman of Abu Nazir – the archenemy who Carrie suspects is the mastermind behind a new plot to attack America – is nearly strangled when Brody breaks into his house to confront him about his presumed dead comrade, Tom Walker. *Homeland* invites viewers to watch with a kind of vengeful pleasure as these brown men endure violence meted out by righteous white men. Although the series wants to disrupt our assumptions, its images nonetheless secure conventional ideology about the Middle East as the dangerous, obvious locus of terrorist threats.

Danes does a wonderful job communicating the obsessions of someone high up in the CIA's ranks who takes it as her personal responsibility not to let 9/11 happen again. In fact, in Danes' voiceover on the show's credits, Carrie insists that she should have caught the clues, that she should have seen the 9/11 attacks coming and been able to prevent them. The weight of personal guilt for a national tragedy fuels Carrie's passion and her mania, making her a smart but difficult and unruly operative. *Homeland* suggests that only enormous ego or narcissism could explain one solitary CIA agent's single-minded pursuit of justice and her insistence that 9/11 was in some way her fault. At the same time, the show proposes that another terrorist event might in fact be foiled by a single agent. The show seesaws between these two different desires. It appeases our yearning for a hero who can stop speeding bullets with his or her bare hands (like Kiefer Sutherland as Jack Bauer in *24*, on which *Homeland*'s producers Howard Gordon and Alex Gansa previously worked). But it also underlines that national security is a complicated priority that takes way more than a village, let alone any solitary individual.

Homeland mostly resists *24*'s fantasy that one man could save us all. In fact, *Homeland*'s hero is a woman. While the show admires Carrie for her superior intelligence and her willingness to dedicate her life to her job, it also burdens her with an unnamed but determining psychological problem finally revealed as bipolar disease. Carrie can't tell the agency about her condition or she'd be fired from her high-level security clearance position. She pilfers drugs from her impatient, unsympathetic pharmaceutical rep sister to self-medicate and keep herself even. By explaining Carrie's obsessions as at least partly the result of her illness, *Homeland* cuts the character off at the knees. We're never sure if her paranoia is justified or chemical, and none of her reactions can be trusted because we don't know what really fuels her obsession.

Her superiors don't know Carrie's medical history; they find her difficult because she breaks rules and resists censure. She is a loose cannon in a carefully regulated world. In fact, Carrie's vigilantism is one of the least believable aspects of an otherwise smart show. Certainly, an agent who bugged the home of a returning war hero without authorization would be summarily fired. And certainly, an agent who initiated a sexual relationship with that war hero would be denounced. (But then again, indiscretions like these didn't hamper Jack Bauer, either.) Instead, Carrie confesses her misdeeds to Saul Berenson (Mandy Patinkin), her father-figure mentor. He scolds her, knits his thick eyebrows together in deep disapproval, and then absolves her, hugging her tightly in understanding parental embraces that free her to go on drawing outside the lines of agency protocol. Saul, you see, is also emotionally haunted. His obvious though unnamed Jewishness – inescapable in any character Patinkin plays – emphasizes his moral ambivalence. Like Carrie, Saul's obsession with his job compromises his emotional and domestic life. In fact, his South Asian wife has decided to leave him after 25 years of marriage to return to her family in Delhi because he's emotionally and physically inaccessible. Their scenes together allow Patinkin to indulge his hang-dog, maudlin side. The producers haven't quite figured out how to bring more nuances to a character caught between his righteous ambitions and his sincere love for his wife. Their costly commitments to their jobs make Saul and Carrie the show's real soul-mates.

Damian Lewis performs Sergeant Brody as a time-bomb set to detonate, controlled by unknown forces on an unknown schedule. Brody was isolated for eight years before being rescued by an American SWAT team. Lewis clarifies the force of will required to survive captivity, and never shies from inhabiting Brody's vulnerabilities. He makes palpable the depth of Brody's need for connection while he remained in captivity, after he was released from extended solitary confinement and torture. After sustaining himself by making unimaginable moral choices, Brody returns to a domestic life that's moved on without him. Brody finds that his wife, Jessica (Morena Baccarin), has been sleeping with his best friend, Mike (Diego Klattenhoff). But after being told that Brody was presumed dead, how long was she supposed to keep her life on hold?

Likewise, Brody's friend and fellow captive, Sergeant Tom Walker (Chris Chalk), whom Brody is led to believe he killed with his bare hands, left behind a wife who's since remarried. Both men have kids who barely know their fathers. One of *Homeland*'s conversations, then, also concerns the place of biological fathers in families that survive without them. The series implicitly asks whether men like Brody have any right to walk back into their patriarchal roles without acknowledging how their domestic spheres have closed around their absences.

Baccarin, as Jessica, plays Brody's conflicted wife with emotional depth and precision. She's given little to do – wouldn't a soldier's wife have to work for a living when he was presumed dead? – and she mostly reacts to Brody's presence. But Baccarin communicates the complicated feelings of a woman who has to pick up a marriage that was suspended and presumed ended for eight years. Her struggle to play the dutiful, faithful wife makes Jessica more interesting in Baccarin's performance than she is in the show's dialogue.

Homeland's latest twists stretch the credulity of an already somewhat confusing story. (I've noticed the on-line concern that the show might go the way of *The Killing*, last season's atmospheric AMC cable television series that finally irritated viewers with its cliff-hangers and unlikely plot turns.) But I'll keep watching to see how Danes continues to bring depth and complexity to one of the more interesting roles for women on series television, and to see how the writers unravel the current host of secrets and complications and set us up for more in season two.

NOVEMBER 27, 2011

Wit

Produced on Broadway, Samuel J. Friedman Theatre, 2012

Cynthia Nixon, playing the lead in the Broadway revival of Margaret Edson's play, *Wit*, does a heroic job putting her own mark against Kathleen Chalfant's signature performance as the dying Vivian Bearing, the professor and scholar who meets the only fight she can't win in her struggle with ovarian cancer. In fact, by the time her cancer is diagnosed, Prof. Bearing is as good as dead. At stage four, the cancer is already metastasizing, and her treatment will mostly benefit science rather than herself. But in perhaps her one selfless choice, according to a script that finds its heroine mostly distasteful, Vivian signs up to undergo a rigorous eight-month treatment that doesn't save her body, but in most ways saves her soul. Bearing is hardly a sympathetic character. By acquiescing to be the subject of research instead of a researcher herself, she learns that there's more to life than finding new knowledge. The long hospital stay that ends her life is her last lesson in how to have the relationships that she regularly denied herself, devoting her time to the obscure and difficult sonnets of John Donne instead.

Edson's play, which won the 1999 Pulitzer Prize for Drama, wants to have it both ways. It indicts a medical establishment that sacrifices the humanity of its patients to its quest for their cure, but at same time condemns its patient, who's devoted her own life to a similar kind of exacting and dehumanizing (at least in Edson's version) research. Chalfant played this sacrificial character with a dignity and subtle shadings that made her a truly tragic figure. Vivian learns too late in her life that she can relate to people instead of just teaching them and that human feelings are more ennobled by living them than by engaging them on the page. Through direct address to the audience from her hospital bed, Vivian lays out the story of her life and her sudden illness, describing how her father rewarded her zeal for reading, and how her own intellectually significant female professor inspired her to ever better research and writing. Her tone is mordant and a bit self-deprecating, as though she's embarrassed to think back on her trajectory from its sorry end.

In the right hands, Vivian can be an appealing and self-aware narrator of her life's excesses and can suggest that hers are just a different variation on those we all suffer. But as directed for laughs by Lynne Meadow, Nixon's Vivian is a bit strident, her humor too forced and ironic, until the morphine finally calms her down toward the play's end. She finds her humanity just as the medical establishment reaches the epitome of its objectification of her body. But Vivian is such an unlikable character until then that it's hard to see her story as anything but a joke at the expense of a smart woman who's happily chosen to devote her life to her work, however esoteric.

Nixon is an intelligent performer and emotionally enough in tune with the role that she strikes nice chords of sympathy with Prof. Bearing. And clearly the cancer narrative appeals to her. At a moment when so many women (including Nixon, who's a survivor) are diagnosed with breast, ovarian, and other cancers, a play that addresses their situation with the frankness of *Wit* is very welcome on Broadway. It's just too bad that Edson asks us to think only about how little agency women have in their own medical care. That, perhaps, marks her play's age – witness the recent uproar over the lack of women testifying before Congress about their proposed legislation on women's reproductive health, which might indicate how fed up women have become with just the kind of objectification and powerlessness that Edson's play incriminates. But a play that also allows audiences to laugh at the righteous pursuit of a life of the mind that Vivian Bearing's career represents compromises its otherwise feminist intent.

In this Broadway revival, Suzanne Bertish brings verve to her role as Vivian's inspiring professor. She relishes the knowledge she imparts to her pupil, and then demonstrates utmost compassion when she finds Vivian again at the end of her life. When she crawls into Vivian's hospital bed to read to her former star student, the moment is wrenching, not just because all she has at hand to read aloud is a children's book she recently shared with her grandson, but because she loves and respects Vivian for who she is. The professor's compassion at the end bears no moral judgment, which is so palpable in the rest of the play. She brings only a clear love and felt presence that finally ushers Vivian out of her life and into a kind of peace.

This production ends as the original did, with Vivian's resurrection of sorts after the death that finally, supposedly, frees her from physical and spiritual pain. Downstage right, Nixon unfolds from an embryonic ball of limbs and flesh into a triumphal, extended human "V," naked and, I suppose, liberated. The moment is a bit too stark for my taste and too symbolic of the empty freedom that Vivian's release into what Donne called the "pause" that is death brings. She holds her arms above her head in a peculiar, Pyrrhic victory. But her naked body seems also to signal how she sacrificed her physical desire for her intellectual ambitions. It's the wrong kind of triumph to celebrate and leaves the play rather hollow at the end.

Nonetheless, it's good to see Nixon claiming Broadway real estate to perform a serious play written by a woman. Edson never wrote another play after *Wit* and insists she has no intention of returning to the form. She continues to teach at an elementary school in Atlanta; *Wit* was the one dramatic story she wanted to tell. Given new oncology protocols, the play feels dated, though its critique of medicine's essential inhumanity remains sadly relevant. Its portrait of a female professor as brittle and emotionally stunted still smarts. When do we get to see a story about a smart, talented woman intellectual who's not punished by a fatal disease? These stories have been tiresome since *Wit* was first produced in New York in the '90s.

I'm always glad when work by and starring talented women is visible in public forums, but how I wish we could hear stories that celebrate instead of implicitly denigrate their accomplishments, and that let them thrive instead of fade.

MARCH 11, 2012

Porgy and Bess

Produced on Broadway,
Richard Rodgers Theatre, 2012

This controversial production comes to Broadway with the baggage of both historical and contemporary critique. First produced in the 1930s as a folk opera by George and Ira Gershwin, and DuBose and Dorothy Heyward, this production, directed by Diane Paulus with a revised book by Suzan-Lori Parks and Deirdre L. Murray, opened August 17, 2011 at the American Repertory Theatre in Cambridge where Paulus is the artistic director.

Before he'd even seen the production, Stephen Sondheim excoriated the artistic team for what he found unethical meddling with the Gershwin's original work. But as Hilton Als wrote in a lovely background piece and review for *The New Yorker*, the "original" was full of racism, an artifact of a moment in theatre history when white people represented their skewed vision of people of color for other white people. Why in the world would anyone want to preserve such original intentions for a 21st century audience?

More than a bit of sexism surfaced in Sondheim's argument, too. Here's a young white woman director and two talented women artists of color engaging one of the most famous narratives of American opera and theatre, all with an eye to renovating the central character of Bess, the drug-addicted woman whose desires drive this revision's plot. Given this refocusing, Sondheim's unfortunate objections might derive from his personal taste and respect for some artists over others, as well as from his professional investments in preserving the sanctity of the original text.

The Sondheim kerfuffle sent the production to Broadway on a cloud of critique, but this *Porgy and Bess* provides a transformative theatre experience. With a simple set by the talented Riccardo Hernandez; unobtrusive but evocative choreography by Ronald K. Brown; a superb ensemble, each one of whom seems to follow his or her own grounded and original narrative arc; and stage pictures that seem organic instead of posed, the production offers a thrilling experience at the theatre.

Hernandez creates the down-at-the-heels Catfish Row, in Charleston, South Carolina, with a one-dimensional curvilinear backdrop, all corrugated tin and wooden window frames through which light (designed by Christopher Akerlind) projects in geometric patterns that change with the time of the day. A simple working water pump establishes the outdoor scenes, and performers bring on wooden chairs and crates to give the stage picture levels and textures. Yet with so few props and such a schematic set, Paulus and her actors create a whole world, an African–American community of fishermen and washerwomen, of tinkerers and tradespeople, of grifters and preachers, and of good people and bad. The ensemble moves constantly, providing a living backdrop to the story of Bess and Porgy's doomed relationship.

Paulus draws attention to her stars through their costumes. Bess (the sublime Audra McDonald) wears a beautiful, bold red dress when she arrives in Catfish Row on the arm of her evil lover/procurer, Crown (Phillip Boykin). Costume designer ESosa leaves McDonald's arms bare and her breasts heaving over the bodice, accentuating her figure with a high slit up the side and barely supportive straps. Porgy (Norm Lewis) wears layered, dirty but pure white shirts, which help him stand out among the rest. Although the careful design and direction let spectators track the show's central couple, Paulus embeds Porgy and Bess's story within a lively, close-knit neighborhood both visually and narratively.

Theirs isn't a singular story, but a relationship aided and abetted by a community that's very protective of its "crippled" friend. Porgy, hobbled from birth, walks with a stick and a limp, his hips extended awkwardly and his left leg twisted impossibly. His disability makes it difficult for him to maneuver more than a few steps without being offered a seat by one of his neighbors. But Lewis plays Porgy with quiet dignity, not an ounce of self-pity, and a sexy magnetism that makes him the production's emotional core.

Shortly after he and Bess arrive at Catfish Row, Crown murders one of the community's men. To avoid prison, he hides out on an island off the coast of Charleston while Bess slowly, hesitantly begins to embed herself in the domestic life of Catfish Row, forming an awkward relationship with Porgy. When she joins her new neighbors for a picnic on the island where Crown happens to be hiding, and dallies behind when the others board the boat for home, Crown accosts Bess, insisting that she's still his woman and that he'll come for her once he thinks it's safe. In a scene that could easily be played as a rape, Paulus's direction and McDonald's terrific acting indicate that although his physical force makes it difficult for Bess to resist Crown, she's also attracted by his sexual clarity. Her desire confuses Bess. In this production, it's not her drug addiction that's her Achilles heel, though that weakness appears at key moments to throw her integrity into doubt. But it's Bess's deep sexuality, her own desire, by which she's ultimately undone.

In Catfish Row, women are supposed to channel their sexuality into marriage and child-rearing. The upstanding, loving couple Jake (Joshua Henry) and Clara (Nikki Renée Daniels) represent the ideal relationship, one to which Bess knows she should aspire but can't quite figure. She holds Jake and Clara's new-born baby with great wonder and tenderness, staring into its face as though it holds a secret she wishes she could fathom. And when the couple dies in the hurricane that rocks Catfish Row, Bess insists that their baby now belongs to her. But exactly this contained and proper domesticity eludes Bess, however truly happy she seems in Porgy's embrace.

Although Porgy repeatedly scoffs that "no cripple can hold Bess," he never really seems to believe it, because the character's goodness radiates from Lewis's presence whether or not he's speaking. Lewis's is a smart, clear, intensely human performance, in which the typical pitfalls of the "crippled" character redeeming the "abled" through his unsullied humanity admittedly is present, but not as salient as it might be. In this revision, his character feels fuller and more fleshed out, and in fact, Porgy doesn't ever really redeem Bess. The typical trope is foiled in ways that help play against the stereotype. Porgy loves and protects Bess, and finally finds his manhood by killing Crown, who continues to appear in their lives like a demon that just won't die. After Porgy stabs Crown to death in a stage fight in which they struggle on the ground, the only level at which Porgy might have a chance to even the odds against Crown, Porgy struggles to stand and declares that he's now a man. It's unfortunate that the disabled Porgy distinguishes himself through violence and that his gentler, more domestic masculinity is pitted against Crown's volatile force in the first place. Boykin, as Crown, is a muscular, large man, who presents the character in all his brutal sexuality and contrasts starkly with Porgy's less stable physical presence.

Even after Porgy kills Crown, theoretically freeing her from the violent man's hold, Bess is seduced by Sporting Life (played by David Alan Grier as a kind of Ben Vereen-as-the-Leading-Player-in-*Pippin* spin-off), who tells her that Porgy will be imprisoned for life and that she belongs in a big city. Sporting Life smoothly urges her toward the boat that's leaving soon for New York (in another of the musical's many numbers that became standards in the American repertoire). Played by the truly astounding McDonald, Bess's desires muddle her, pulling her from one choice to the contradictory next. She clearly feels safe with Porgy, but her blazing sexual heat draws her to danger and to a larger palette on which to paint herself. Bess never looks quite comfortable in the cotton shifts in muted prints and soft fabrics that signal her acceptance into the quotidian life of Catfish Row. The image of her lush body presenting itself draped in red in those first scenes always haunts her attempt to be just one of the women, to domesticate herself for her own safety and acceptance.

Nonetheless, this production doesn't demonize Bess and neither does it leave Porgy broken by her disappearance at the end. He decides he'll follow Bess to New York to win her back. What will happen after is anyone's guess, but that future isn't as important as knowing that both Porgy and Bess have opted to move out into a larger world, one less predictable, perhaps, one less full of love and care and fellow-feeling than the landscape of Catfish Row, but one in which they can find bigger, more ennobled versions of themselves in which to live.

That, in itself, is an achievement.

MARCH 26, 2012

Death of a Salesman

Produced on Broadway, Ethel Barrymore Theatre, 2012

Death of a Salesman has remarkable legs as a play that tells us something about "America." In its most recent Broadway production (which won a 2012 Tony award for Best Revival of a Play), sensitive direction by Mike Nichols and inspiring performances by marquee-name actors bring a whole new tone to Miller's classic, letting me hear parts of the play I'd never noticed before. I last taught the play in a course on Jewish–American Performance, considering Miller's canonical work from the perspective of Jewish writers addressing Jewish themes, that set a new horizon of expectations for my experience of the latest revival. Reading *Salesman* as a play about assimilation, alongside its themes of American cosmopolitanism vs. the country's founding pioneer spirit, offered new shadings to Miller's text. Seeing the Loman family as Jewish brought a specific sense of ethnicity to Miller's "everyman" that helped particularize the oft-called universal experiences the play depicts.

In fact, Lee J. Cobb, who first played the iconic Willy Loman on Broadway, was a Jew who changed his name from Lee Jacob. But his towering, physically imposing Willy presented the crumbling of a once powerful patriarch, rather than the social exile of a man unfit for the WASP mainstream. Dustin Hoffman, in the 1985 revival, brought an inevitable patina of Jewishness to the role simply through his Semitic appearance, but the production itself left him alone in a kind of WASP-y wilderness, since Hoffman's was the only performance marked by Jewishness in that production. Willy's hubris, in Hoffman's hands, became that of a small man pretending to greatness, already an outsider who never really comes to terms with his genetic inability to charm his way into an inner circle. In the 2000 Broadway production, Brian Dennehey returned to Cobb's precedent, using his girth and charm to review the male patriarch in his precipitous fall to earth without a single performative reference to Jewishness.

Phillip Seymour Hoffman follows suit, playing Willy as ethnically unmarked (and as a result, not Jewish). Although I was disappointed to see the production veer away from specifying ethnic particularity, Nichols and his cast instead make the text resonate with our straitened economic moment and strike all the play's emotional chords. Hoffman's Willy is an unexpected bully, a small, fat man wearing a too-short tie whose pretense to likability is belied by how truly repulsive he often seems. Hoffman's mercurial Willy shifts moods as unpredictably as he moves from reality to fantasy and present to past and back again. In one of Nichols's most adept touches, the various levels on which Willy operates blend seamlessly, so that the past impinges on the present and reality on fantasy in ways that are always clear to the audience, even if they're not to Willy, and demonstrate Willy's precarious grasp on his own psychology. Nichols's production and Hoffman's performance give us a Willy who's truly losing track of himself, who lives more and more in his head and less and less with the flesh and blood people who try to get his attention, who try to love him and save him, with tragic consequences.

Salesman can read as an expressionist journey into the deteriorating mind of a man who's never been as great as he claims. The character can be self-pitying, especially in scenes in which he's forced to grovel for money, attention, and respect. Late in the play, when he approaches his boss, Howard, for a new, local sales assignment and for an advance on his pay, the moment is so simply directed and performed that its horrible degradations are devastatingly felt. Howard (Remy Auberjonois) is preoccupied with his new toy, a reel-to-reel tape recorder that's captured the voices of his small daughter, precocious son, and diffident wife, when Willy approaches him to talk about his future with the company. Howard's oblivious privilege – he tells Willy he can buy one of these machines for only "a hundred and a half," which is more than the sum Willy desperately needs to pay his life insurance – rankles Willy, who can't stop himself from blowing up with blistering anger when Howard refuses to move him to a New York-based sales position. Howard, appalled by Willy's lack of self-control, urges him to pull himself together because there are people outside the office.

In fact, Hoffman's Willy is often told to gather his senses – or rather, those lines in Miller's script resonate here because Phillip Seymour Hoffman's Willy so often and so quickly flies off the handle. That he's losing his mind is signaled by the disbelief with which he's regarded by people like Howard, who smoothly manage the professional performances that give them access to wealth and power. Willy's more rough-hewn manner would never qualify him for the unmarked, bland, "American" but strangely emasculated performances of masculinity these men model. One of the tragedies of the production, in fact, is that the meek seem to inherit the earth. Willy's sons are built like Adonises, but they can't find their way to conventional measures of success. Hap is a resolute womanizer who can take pride only in his ease with women, and Biff only feels like himself when he's working with his hands in the western air, an occupation that his parents deride as immature.

Happy and Biff might be strong, strapping young men, who thrill their rotund father with a fantasy of their strength and ability, but it's Charlie and his son Bernard – both of whom wear the short pants and gathered sleeves of accountant clerks in different scenes in the play – who become wealthy and powerful, Charlie as a successful businessman whose offer to employ Willy he narcissistically refuses, and Bernard as a lawyer with a wife and children who's arguing a case in front of the Supreme Court. Willy continues to sneer at Charlie and Bernard, even as his jealousy over their success completely unmans him.

John Glover plays the fantasy brother, Ben, as a pioneer dandy, entering his scenes with a battered satchel and a long umbrella, outfitted in wrinkled linens and a felt hat that he rolls in his hands. Ben sports a fantastically wild, large, bushy beard, and Glover plays him with a mad twinkle in his eye that casts doubt on his credibility. When he beckons Willy to Alaska, which he calls the next American frontier, Willy is impressed and tempted but ultimately constrained by a different fantasy. He's spellbound by the image of an 84-year-old salesman who made all his calls from a hotel room, wearing green slippers. That lax, strangely effeminate image of power becomes more appealing to Willy than Ben's example of someone who strides into the wilderness and comes out a millionaire. In some ways, Willy seems lazy in Nichols's production. The idea of sitting in a hotel making calls is more appealing than being an adventurer, though that image, too, is fuzzy here. Ben often declares that he walked into a South American jungle at 17 and came out at 21 a millionaire. But when Willy asks him how, Ben just repeats his fairy tale. No formula is forthcoming; Willy has dreams but no mechanisms to achieve them. He's the loser at a game whose rules everyone seems to grasp but him.

Andrew Garfield, making his Broadway debut as Biff, is a tall, slight but strong young man, who provides a nice contrast to Hoffman's short, stocky bulk. With his dark hair and vaguely Semitic features, Garfield makes a rather tortured, desperate Biff, a young man ensnared by his father's dreams despite his antipathy for what he knows is Willy's fraudulent life. Hoffman and Garfield play out the father and son's oscillations between love and hate in operatic style, beautifully conveying their long-held mutual disappointment, suspicion, and utter inability to forgive one another. When Biff cries in despair on

Willy's ample stomach, Biff seems young and unformed, different from the cowboy-esque figure he usually cuts in the play. Finn Wittrock is wrenching as Happy, the younger son who dances around the father and older brother he reveres, desperately trying to get their attention. "See Dad, I'm losing weight," he declares pathetically and frequently as a boy, and "I swear, Mom, I'm going to get married," he insists, as the middle-aged equivalent of a man making promises he can't keep as he tries to gain the attention of parents who barely notice him.

In the revelation scene in which Miller finally shows us why Biff hates Willy, Biff travels to Boston to find his father, hoping that Willy will persuade the math teacher who's failed him and will prevent him from graduating to change his grade. But Biff stumbles onto Willy's affair with "the woman," the tittering, grasping buyer who laughs at Willy's silly jokes and trades sex with him for stockings. Garfield and Hoffman register the seismic change in their relationship with subtle shifts in their faces, as it dawns on Biff how Willy has betrayed the family he pretends to revere, and as Willy understands that he's forever lost his son's respect. Biff dissolves into wrenching sobs, broken by realizing that his hero is a hollow man. Willy blusters, trying to retain his stature and power, ordering Biff to pack his valises and sputtering frantically when Biff refuses to comply. The scene explains everything; that Garfield, Hoffman, and Nichols weave its implications so thoroughly into every scene before and after is partly what makes the production so powerful.

The scene also explains Linda's tragedy, which is her persistent belief in Willy even as she sees him deteriorate. She never learns of Willy's affair, which lets her continue to believe that her husband truly is the man he pretends to be. She can't understand why Willy and Biff hate one another, even though in Linda Emond's capable hands, Linda is a smart, dignified woman whose compassion for her husband dictates her every choice. Linda Loman is sometimes played as a flibberti-gibbet, a worried, distracted, silly woman clinging to her husband's illusions. Emond plays her strength, her determination to hold onto her husband's faith in himself and in a system that she knows discards him mercilessly. Emond also makes Linda a rather brutal mother. She sees right through her sons' posturing and calls them out on their pretenses. But she believes in Willy to his sorry end, wondering why there weren't more people at his funeral, not understanding that his death would be as lonely as his life because she believed in the false tale of his adoring friends. When she declares that "attention must be paid," she's honoring the reputation of a man who's as much a fantasy as Willy's brother, Ben.

Nichols's production reminds us that the Loman family is caught in a system they never made, a capitalist schema of power and access that hovers over them in Jo Mielziner's glorious set, reconstructed here from the designer's original drawings. On the backdrop, towering apartment buildings dwarf the little single-family house in which the Loman family tries to scratch out a respectable life. The growing neighborhood, with its inexorable bricks and mortar, draws the air out of the family home and encroaches into Willy and Linda and Biff and Happy's souls. Willy has to look between the surrounding apartment buildings to see the moon from the bedroom window at night, and to his great chagrin, the two elm trees near their lawn, between which he and Biff once strung a hammock, were cut down by developers. In his last moments, Willy tries to plant vegetables in his yard, despite Linda's admonitions and reminders that there's not enough sunlight to support their growth.

Miller's metaphors might be obvious by now, but embodied by Hoffman and company, they continue to score theatrical points. Hearing people in the audience sobbing and sniffling through the play's last few scenes, and feeling the house rapt throughout the three-hour production, reminded me of how relevant Miller's themes remain. How do we make our way in a faceless world that operates according to rules few can understand and fewer still are schooled to follow? What is the relationship between nature and culture, between a man's hands and what he's able to raise and grow? Do rewards come from hard work, or is the American way to find schemes that carve out short-cuts, like Biff's propensity for stealing things? Biff presumes that he's owed the gold pen he takes from the desk of the man who he thinks will back his grandiose plans to buy a ranch. But the man doesn't remember Biff, and if he did, would only recall him as a stock-boy who stole a football. Does it matter if we're well-liked, as Willy boasts throughout his sorry life, when charm and personal relationships, when history and long-term connections like those Willy had with Howard's father, matter much less than a corporate bottom line?

It'd be interesting to see *Death of a Salesman* cast only with actors of color, or with actors who could play the Jewishness original to Miller's text. Most productions of the canon tend to embrace a universalizing, specificity-erasing whiteness unthinkingly. Seeing the classics – like director Emily Mann's 2012 production of Tennessee Williams's *A Streetcar Named Desire* – performed in resistance to that whiteness lets them resonate further across a truly diverse American cultural landscape. That Miller's questions continue to sound through new generations of actors, directors, and audiences underscores once again the tight economy of his stagecraft and his prescience in capturing what seem the eternal ambivalences that are part and parcel of American dreaming.

MAY 12, 2012

Clybourne Park

Produced on Broadway,
Walter Kerr Theatre, 2012

Bruce Norris's 2011 Pulitzer Prize- and 2012 Tony Award-winning play was the subject of a rhapsodic essay by political pundit Frank Rich in *New York Magazine,* in which he suggested the play beautifully captures the racial mood of the United States under our first African–American president.[1] Given the number of awards *Clybourne Park* has won and the terrific notices it's received since it opened at Playwrights Horizons in New York in 2010 and played at the Mark Taper Forum in LA before moving to Broadway in 2012, it seems the theatre-going community around the country concurs. I'm impressed with Norris's adroit writing, his play's brilliant structure, and his ear for dialogue that reveals more subtext than its characters speak. I also admire Pam MacKinnon's fluid, clear and controlled direction of an excellent cast, all of whom play dual (if not several) roles across the play's two acts, in which the same location – a middle-class house in Chicago's Clybourne Park neighborhood – is used to tease out the fault lines of race in America first in 1959 and then in 2009. Norris uses the story of Lorraine Hansberry's landmark 1959 play *A Raisin in the Sun* as its motivating premise.

But I was concerned by the reaction of the Wednesday matinee audience with which I saw the production and by the play's liberal, shoulder-shrugging attitude toward the current state of our racial affairs. As I left the theatre that day, I overheard the mostly white, mostly over-65-years-old, mostly upper-middle-class (if one can tell by what they wear) audience clucking their tongues about the play's argument that nothing's changed in the last 50 years, that race relations are as complicated in 2009 as they were in pre-Civil Rights movement 1959. In other words, the audience "got" the message: Americans haven't come as far as we think we have, and though we (or rather, the mainstream press) proclaimed a post-race moment after Obama's election, we're mired in the same misguided fallacies as we were 50 years ago. Except that now, African–Americans can be included as participants in, and not just victims of, the brutal racial divide. The play dictates that now, everyone is racist and there's nothing anyone can do about it. It's not surprising, then, that Norris's well-meant play has been lauded and popular. He very much wants to be even-handed, to spread the blame for the country's lack of progress toward real racial equality. But in production, the play becomes an insidious exercise in blaming the victim and in perpetuating just the sort of oppressive attitudes it means to critique.

Norris's creative conceit is to take up where Hansberry's play left off. Setting the story in the house that the Younger family in *Raisin in the Sun* intends to buy, the plot follows Bev (Christina Kirk) and Russ (Frank Wood) as they prepare to move from their Chicago home to the suburbs. Their decision to leave is politically benign, if personally tragic; their son, Kenneth (Brendan Griffin), returned from serving in the Korean War an inadvertent criminal. When the community suspects him and refuses to reintegrate him, he hangs himself in the family home. Russ stews in anger over his son's treatment and rejects the pieties of neighbors he finds small-minded, conservative, and ostracizing.

Aside from their son's tragedy, Bev and Russ seem to be ordinary middle-class white people. Bev compulsively chatters, obsessing over trivia like the derivation of "Neapolitan" as the name for tri-flavored ice cream. Her flights of intellectual banality lead her to wonder what the denizens of various cities around the world are called, as Russ pages through a copy of *National Geographic,* bored and emotionally remote. Norris parodies middle-class mores and values by letting his characters spend so much time talking about nothing. Russ and Bev represent people whose worlds are small, whose knowledge of others is entirely second-hand or imagined, and who are contented to lead lives of little consequence, despite their son's compelled involvement in world affairs.

They're also utterly blind to those who work among them. Bev's maid, Francine (Crystal A. Dickinson), and Francine's husband, Albert

(Damon Gupton), are long-suffering "colored people." Francine tolerates Bev's fabricated and forced intimacy, rolling her eyes when her employer turns her head, and cringing noticeably when Bev throws an arm around her shoulders in faked solidarity. Norris portrays Francine and Albert as the canny wise ones, who collude with the theatre audience in a mutual understanding that the play's white characters are stupid and conservative. This fragile alliance works, to a point. Then Francine's and Albert's behavior comes perilously close to minstrelsy. Because Norris leaves them no choice but to be obsequious, even as their faces and gestures try to resist Bev's bigotry, the actors are as trapped as the characters in how they play African–Americans who have to tolerate racism.

Norris clarifies that Bev's clumsy effort to be kind to the "help" offends Francine and Albert. Much humor is generated from her desire to unload her chafing dish on Francine, until finally, Albert tells her outright, "Ma'am, we have our own things." This leaves Bev offended by his open refusal of what she sees as her generosity to the less fortunate. Norris makes sure the audience can read his parody of Bev's racism, but Francine and Albert are still its victims. That the audience presumptively knows these exchanges are racist doesn't change anything; it just lets us feel superior to the 1959-era white people whom I guess we're supposed to think didn't know any better because *we* (meaning the audience's white people, to whom the play is addressed), of course, *do* know better.

Karl Lindner (Jeremy Shamos) returns here whole cloth, borrowed from Hansberry's *Raisin* to play out his role as the head of the neighborhood association that wants to stop the sale of Bev and Russ's house to the "colored" family to which it's been contracted. Norris uses Karl's visit to Bev and Russ to let him spout all the racist intent that's implicit in his conversation with the Youngers in *Raisin*. The neighborhood will change, the property values will plummet, and one black family's arrival will presage an influx of more and spur white flight.

To make matters even tenser, Norris contrives an anxious scene in which Karl interviews the clearly reluctant Francine and Albert to prove that they wouldn't feel comfortable if they were the ones moving into the all-white neighborhood. The scene is played for laughs; Karl focuses on differences in "taste," suggesting that the supermarket, now run by a Jewish grocer, won't stock the food Francine and Albert like to eat. "You mean collard greens and pigs feet?" Albert quips, going along with the stereotype, while Francine mutters, "I like spaghetti and meatballs." Lindner's deaf wife, Betsy (Carly Street, who understudied for Annie

Parisse at the performance I saw), is Scandinavian, and much is made of her taste for lutefisk, a national delicacy, as though Scandinavian culture is as equally exotic in the U.S. as African–American ethnic tastes.

Bev natters on, her head literally bobbing on her shoulders (in Kirk's excellent performance of a clueless woman trying very hard to help everyone just get along), as Francine and Albert get more and more uncomfortable and angry. Albert gets the last word, finally stopping Bev's prattling by holding up his hand at the door and saying, "Evening," before he turns on his heel and leaves. But even in Gupton's controlled, ironic performance, Albert can't win the upper hand in this scene (or this play). He might at last escape the house, but he can't avoid the structural racism that Bev and Karl and the other white characters enact or from which they benefit.

Even Russ falls prey to insidious racist attitudes. He's furious with his neighbors for how they treated his son and appalled when Karl asks him and Bev to reconsider the sale of their house. But when Karl threatens to reveal why the house was priced low enough for a family of modest means to purchase it (Kenneth committed suicide there), Russ loses his cool. Albert tries to play peace-keeper and puts a hand on Russ's shoulder, which the white man shrugs off violently, snarling with clear and ugly racial hatred that Albert shouldn't dare put a hand on him in his own house. The one person who seemed fair, reasonable, and politically astute, in other words, flashes into racist fury when a black man touches him.

MacKinnon makes these moments of physical connection flashpoints throughout the play. In the midst of Act One's spiraling skirmish, Bev flings herself at Francine, grasping the black woman's arm and peering into her face. Francine recoils from the contact and the presumption. The moment clarifies in a deft gesture the physical violence of racism. Likewise, when Russ turns on Albert, the impossibility of real contact is drawn with physical as well as emotional clarity.

In *Clybourne Park*'s second act, 50 quick years have passed and the house is being sold once again, this time by Lena, the niece of the African–American woman who bought the house from Russ and Bev. The actors are shuffled into 2009 characters: Lena (presumably named after Lena Younger in Hansberry's play and played by Dickinson) and Kevin (Gupton) have joined Lindsey (Street, who played the deaf Betsy in the first act) and Steve (Shamos, who played Act One's despicable Karl) to iron out the details of the sale with Tom (Griffin, who played the minister, Jim, in Act One) and Kathy (Kirk, who played Bev), their real estate lawyers. At issue in the second act is Lindsey and Kevin's plan to demolish the house and build a new one in its place that will tower over the others on the block. Their choice – suggested by "Hector," their unseen, emotionally "hot-tempered" "Spanish" architect – has raised the ire of the current neighborhood association, which has circulated a petition trying to block them from proceeding.

Norris uses a tidy parallel structure to support his "the more things change the more they stay the same" thesis. In this act, the white people's banal pseudo-sophisticated discussion about the world focuses on the capitol of Morocco, which Kathy says is Marrakesh and Steve insists is Rabat. This exchange, like the discussion about "Neapolitan" in Act One, demonstrates how little the characters grasp the world and their blithe carelessness with the details of international geography. Rather than reading *National Geographic* as armchair travel, these now would-be-cosmopolitan upper-middle class people vacation around the world and casually drop the names of all the countries they've visited. But their observations sound superficial because it's clear they travel not to learn about other people and places, but to add notches to their trophy belts of cultural acquisition. And in 2009, the African–American couple is as guilty of cultural carelessness as the white couple. Lena and Kevin, too, mention national capitols they've visited in Prague and Switzerland in a not-so-subtle topping game.

Norris underlines that racism remains intractable. Kathy – played by Kirk as ditzy as Act One's Bev, even though the character supposedly has a law degree – acts surprised that Lena and Kevin have been to Prague. Lena and Kevin react with knowing bemusement as the white people's now more muted but still insidious racism infects the conversation. The African–American couple, just like Albert and Francine in Act One, continues to roll their eyes at the audience. Lena tries to make a speech through much of the second act, repeatedly announcing that she has something to say while the others ignore her. When she finally does speak her piece, her remarks are muddled and oblique. She refers to the importance of memory and history, and to the struggles of her aunt, who moved into an all-white neighborhood, although Lena says that when she visited the house as a child, she doesn't remember seeing any white faces.

Karl Linder's prophesy, of course, came true – white flight changed the racial make-up of Clybourne Park in 1959, and in 2009, gentrification will change it back. The disingenuous white couple expresses their respect for the history Lena describes, but they stumble over their racism even as they try to reassure Lena and Kevin that they love the neighborhood. Lindsey tells the African–American couple,

"I'm the one who was resistant, especially with the schools and everything, but once I stopped seeing the neighborhood the way it *used* to be, and could see what it is *now*, and its *potential*?" In other words, once she could reimagine it in her own white image, she was persuaded to buy.

What can Lena and Kevin say to this? Just as in the first act, Francine and Albert exchanged looks of disgust and dismay, the African–American couple in 2009 are resigned to do the same because in Norris's cosmos, the word racism can barely be spoken, let alone can the wages of structural inequality be called out. Lena tries: "And I'm saying that there are certain economic interests that are being served by those changes and others that are not. That's all." But she's not quite explicit enough for Steve and Lindsey or Tom and Kathy to take her point, so the group continues to blunder ahead until they run aground on the not-so-buried sandbars that surface in the racist currents that eddy through the conversation.

By 2009, Lena and Kevin are clamoring for the "right" to claim oppression along with gay men, disabled people, and rape survivors, a competition revealed when Steve shares a not very funny joke about a (little) white guy jailed for "white collar crime" and put in a cell with a (big) black guy who proceeds to rape him. As each character uses their own identity claims to determine who's most offended by the joke, Norris parodies our new and by implication excessive sensitivity to marginalized identities which, he implies, has just exacerbated the ever more complex and intractable problem of difference.

After Steve tells his off-color prison story, the jokes in the second act get out of hand. Albert shares one about white men. "How many white men does it take to screw in a light bulb?" he asks. The answer is one to hold the bulb and the rest of them to screw everybody else. The audience with which I watched the play let out a collective "Whooooaaaah" when they heard that joke, as though they, too, could feel the ante of potential offense being upped. Lena tells a comparable white woman joke, asking what a tampon and white women have in common ("They're both stuck up cunts"), which offends Lindsey, who considers herself above reproach ("Half of my friends are black," she declares, oblivious to how stupid she sounds). As the offense gets real and the meeting spins out of control, Dan (Frank Wood, who played Russ in the first act), the contractor, reappears and tries to be the peacekeeper. When he puts his hand on Kevin's shoulder, Kevin wheels on him, growling, "Don't you put your hands on me in my house." The house has seen its racial strife come full circle.

The play ends with 1959 and 2009 combined. Kenneth, the tragic son, writes his suicide note down stage right in 1959, while Dan finds and reads it in 2009. Bev fusses over her son as she delivers her (and the play's) empty benediction: "But you know, I think things are about to change. I really do. I know it's been a hard couple of years for all of us, I know they have been, but I really believe things are about to change for the better. I firmly believe that." By putting these words in the mouth of a woman whom the play has belittled throughout, Norris insures that the audience understands she's an unreliable narrator. But the choice is overkill; it's already clear that nothing at all will change, from 1959 to 2009 or, Norris implies, beyond.

By adding the African–American couple to the problem in the second act, and in fact putting Karl Lindner's words from the first act into Lena's mouth ("It happens one house at a time," she says, referring to gentrification, where Lindner predicted white flight), Norris illustrates the historical circularity of the country's "race problem." But his play abdicates artistic responsibility for truly sorting out how power works. In the first act, Jim, the minister who stops by to visit Bev and Russ, tells Bev knowledge is power, to which she responds, "Then I choose to remain *powerless*." Her line curries laughter from an audience who's been encouraged to see her as a foolish woman. But Bev's self-diagnosis could also be applied to Norris's play. He sees quite a lot in the current state of affairs, but describing it lets him shrug his shoulders (and encourages spectators to shrug theirs) because in play's final analysis, nothing can be done to stop the historical repetitions *Clybourne Park* charts.

I felt disappointed and unsettled by seeing *Clybourne Park*. It's easy to diagnose a problem people already understand and much harder to imagine a solution. The play ends the way it begins, with the white family firmly ensconced in the center of the stage and of the narrative since this has been, after all, a play about privileged white people in which the people of color have been subsidiary, representatives of racial difference over whom the white people play out their self-righteous uneasiness. This representation lets white spectators off the hook, allowing them to distance themselves from their distasteful counterparts, to shake their heads at the persistence of racism, and to leave the play and the theatre unchallenged about how to change anything.

In the program for the Steppenwolf Theatre production of *Clybourne Park*, Norris says, "If I do my job correctly I should outrage people and have rotten vegetables thrown at me; that would be the only proof that I have done something successfully."[2] The play in fact suffers from just such callous provocation. I might be idealistic, but I think it's a shame that in one of the most freely imaginative spaces in public discourse, a smart playwright like Norris couldn't encourage us to think beyond our present impasse into better, more hopeful and equitable possibilities. A playwright needn't solve all the world's problems, but I always appreciate when they help us imagine things differently.

JUNE 10, 2012

Tomboy

Hold Up Films, premiered 2011

In her utterly naturalistic narrative film, French writer/director Céline Sciamma observes a ten-year-old girl named Laure (Zoé Héran) as she moves with her parents and her six-year-old sister, Jeanne (Malonn Lévana), to a new neighborhood and decides to announce herself as a boy to her new friends. At first glance, *Tomboy* looks like a documentary because it describes its subject with a realism and respect that are the hallmarks of good ethnographers or chroniclers of people's lives. Because Sciamma's script is nearly wordless, and because she doesn't fill in Laure's backstory, we're a quarter of the way into the film before we understand that, in fact, Laure is passing when she introduces herself to her new friends as "Michael." Her hair is cut short, her lithe, thin body is adorned with t-shirts or tank tops and long red shorts and sneakers, and her expressions are restrained and careful. Yet Laure/Michael carries herself with the freedom and purpose of a pre-teen boy feeling his way through a world he's about to inherit.

Michael is a quiet observer, because Laure doesn't want to misstep as she makes her tentative way into her new circle of boy- and girlfriends. She first meets Lisa (Jeanne Disson), the neighbor to whom she introduces herself as Michael. Lisa is just slightly older, a pubescent girl feeling her way into a budding femininity. She accepts Michael without question as a boy, though as they begin to get to know one another, Lisa comments on how different he is from the others. But their world doesn't require lengthy explanations or even lucid emotional expression. Sciamma beautifully captures her characters' inarticulate cogency, letting her camera describe their ease with one another and their bodies – before the startling changes of puberty – as well as the way they're all practicing to assume their already scripted gender roles.

The boys in Michael/Laure's new crowd, for instance, are seven or eight kids of various races and ethnicities, sizes and shapes. They play soccer in a wordless emulation of professionals. They unnecessarily strip off their shirts with a seriousness and bravado that quotes their heroes – that is, it doesn't seem particularly hot outside as they play, but it does seem important that they kick the ball and aim for the goal with their bird-like chests exposed to the air. Laure/Michael watches them without jealousy about their physical freedom, but observes how she might act as they do. She goes home after playing soccer and peers at herself in the bathroom mirror. In private, Laure, too, takes off her shirt, grabbing the fabric behind her neck and pulling it over her head the way the boys do. She looks at her chest, her muscles, her back to see if she can flex her physique as her friends did, and to judge whether or not she'll be convincing. Satisfied with what she sees, the next day, she, too, takes off her shirt on the field and happily makes a goal that secures her place in her new community.

But Laure/Michael's gender choices are constantly compromised by her anatomy. Although Sciamma avoids a voice-over that would spell out Michael's thoughts and feelings, Héran is so adept and her director so good at helping her evoke the character's plight that her quandaries are written over her face. When the boys need to pee, and line up to hose the grass, Michael escapes into the woods, where he pulls down his pants to do his business. He's caught half-way through by one of the others, but it's clear the boy doesn't realize Laure's full deception, only that Michael appears to have "peed himself." To be mocked for that indiscretion is humiliating enough. Likewise, when the kids decide to go swimming, Laure/Michael thinks through how to perform convincingly in yet another potentially compromising situation. The evening before the outing, she experiments with Play-Do to make herself a phallus. As Jeanne chirps sweetly at her side, asking what she's making, Laure rolls a piece of clay into a fair facsimile and tucks it into the briefs she's cut up from her one-piece girl's bathing suit. As the boys and Lisa frolic in a lake shortly after, Laure happily passes as Michael with her clay mini-dildo intact.

Héran plays her role with a subtle intelligence that lets us see Michael/Laure's thought process mostly through her reactions to the others and through the obvious joy she takes at succeeding in her deception. But it's clear that for Michael, this ability to pass isn't a game but a real choice to be the boy Laure feels comfortable performing. His/her choice isn't without consequence. The threat of violence lurks around the edges of every interaction. In the home she shares with Jeanne and her parents, Michael is Laure, the quiet, compliant oldest daughter whose father lets her sit on his lap to steer the car, and whose pregnant mother ruffles her hair fondly as Laure listens to her yet-to-be-born baby brother's heartbeat. But outside, as she continues to pass as a boy, and as she meets each new challenge to the conflict between her biology and her desire, the film builds enough tension to make us worry for Laure's safety.

When Lisa comes to visit Michael at home, little Jeanne answers the door. Lisa inquires after her new male friend and Jeanne somehow knows to play along. In *Tomboy*, as in *Pariah* (in which an African–American teenager is a butch lesbian with her friends, has to closet herself in front of her parents, and is recognized and supported by her younger sister), the youngsters are more liberal and intuitively understanding about gender fluidity. But when Jeanne confronts Laure later, Laure has to promise to take her along with her new friends to buy Jeanne's silence. Those outings together let Laure/Michael and Jeanne seal their bond with displays of a boy-girl gender performance in which they both feel comfortable. At home, Jeanne wears a tutu and dances ballet around the family apartment, striking conventionally feminine poses with an innocent ingenuousness. Outside, as Michael plays soccer with the boys, Jeanne sits with another little girl in the grass, talking about school.

When one of the boys maliciously knocks Jeanne down, Michael comes to his sister's rescue in a masculine gesture that begins his own unmasking. He fights with the boy, cutting his lip and worrying the boy's mother, who visits Laure and Jeanne's apartment looking for an apology. Laure's shocked mother plays along with the ruse of her daughter's masculinity until the other mother leaves, placated, and Laure's mother turns on her daughter. In the film's painful final moments, her mother forces Laure into a blue dress with gathered sleeves and a feminine cut, and insists that she announce herself as a girl to the boy she beat up and to Lisa. Watching Laure/Michael's face and body as she's forced to conform and then reveal herself is excruciating.

And yet even here, Sciamma refuses to place blame. Laure's mother might finally be a normalizing force, but she insists that she's parading her daughter through the metaphorical town square as a girl not to punish her, but because she's about to attend a new school where her gender will be known and legislated according to her biology. She doesn't want Laure to suffer misrecognition in this new context. As she drags Laure between the neighbors' apartments by her reluctant hand, her mother asks Laure if she can think of another solution.

Obviously, Laure/Michael can't. She's too young to really understand the cultural consequences of her desires, although once word gets out that she's a girl, her former friends ruthlessly taunt her. In the woods and fields where the kids rule and emulate adult conventions, the boys insist that Lisa confirm Michael's biology by looking in her pants. Michael and Lisa have played at romance through the summer, casually kissing one another's lips and exchanging furtive, pseudo-intimate glances. When one of the boys says it's disgusting that Lisa has actually kissed another girl, Lisa agrees, although it seems she does so only because she's expected to, not because she necessarily finds her closeness with Laure repulsive. As Michael hovers against a tree, his eyes puffy with fear and humiliation, Lisa approaches the waistband of his shorts to take her confirming look before Sciamma kindly cuts away.

Tomboy is full of such poignant, painful moments, but also of those in which we revel with Laure/Michael in her freedom from the constraints of conventional femininity. The film takes place almost entirely in a world of children, where gender is both malleable and just about to be carved into conformity, with all its rules and regulations. Laure/Michael's friends – both the boys and the girls – are practicing to be who they are. Laure/Michael is rehearsing who she wants to be. Her mother's anguish stems from knowing that Laure's body, not just her name, will eventually betray her. Michael can only take his shirt off playing soccer because Laure's hormones haven't yet started distinguishing her as a girl.

Héran makes a beautiful boy. She plays Michael as free, easy, and sweet, a girl/boy who's kind to her sister, her parents, and her new friend. After she's exposed, she lingers at home, still dressed as the tomboy she's been throughout the film. Her mother doesn't continue to punish her by making her dress as a girl. She's allowed to be who she is – her mother simply objects to her trying to pass as a boy. Laure sees Lisa through the apartment window; her friend stares up at Laure's home, standing under the tree where they've rendezvoused throughout the story. When Laure joins her, Lisa looks at her friend bemused, and says, "So what's your real name?" Michael answers, after a beat of shy hesitation, and the two presumably pick up where they left off.

Thanks to uniformly wonderful performances by its young cast (many of whom are non-actors) and its featured adults, *Tomboy* is a moving, smart film about gender non-conformity and the complications of being a girl who simply sees herself as a boy. Sciamma's script doesn't require psychology or narrative explanations; Michael/Laure's motivation isn't as important as her simple desire to be herself. And herself is a boy named Michael.

JUNE 19, 2012

Part Four: Artistry

The essays gathered here address seven performances, two films, and one television series that exemplify, for me, moments in which their artistry overwhelmed me with feeling. I found each of these representations moving and resonant, presenting as they do a hopeful, renovated vision of human relationships. While each example could easily be slotted into The Feminist Spectator in Action's advocacy, activism, or argument sections, their artistry dominated my thinking and my writing. The Broadway revival of Come Back, Little Sheba, with its color-blind casting, offered reinterpretations of the play's critique of the constraints of gender and race in 1950s America but also utterly moved me with its pathos and insights and the beauty of its stagecraft. Seeing Diane Paulus's revival of the rock musical Hair in Central Park, before the Public Theater moved it to Broadway, was a transporting experience in which the production's location magically aligned with its text.

Anna Deveare Smith's Let Me Down Easy argues about the U.S. health care system as incisively as her earlier work argues about the state of race relations, but the production at New York's Second Stage was beautiful, moving, and hopeful. Peggy Shaw and Lois Weaver's elegiac Lost Lounge argues against the gentrification of the Lower East Side post-9/11, but it also emanates with the melancholy and ironic beauty of the passage of time. Once, Irish playwright Enda Walsh's musical adaptation of the indie Irish film, directed by John Tiffany at New York Theatre Workshop and then on Broadway, demonstrates how a wonderfully intimate production can resist the conventional musical theatre mold. Daniel Alexander Jones's alter-ego, Jomama Jones, in Jomama Jones: Radiate, created some of the most stirring, moving moments in the theatre I've experienced in the last decade, through her huge and open heart and beautiful, magnetic presence. Director John Speciale's interpretation of Shakespeare's A Midsummer Night's Dream reconsidered gender through its vision of the young lovers and especially of Puck, played by the famous drag artist Taylor Mac, all to create an enchanting revisiting of the classic comedy.

The two films discussed here also left me with a hopeful vision of human relationships. *Bridesmaids*, the surprise blockbuster written by Kristen Wiig and Annie Mumolo and produced by Judd Apatow, presents smart, funny women with desires and agency. And Lynn Shelton's much smaller indie, Your Sister's Sister, narrates a simple love story full of new visions of kinship. Friday Night Lights, the network television series that ran for five seasons (2006–2011), remains one of the most beautifully wrought long-form narratives I've ever enjoyed. Its stories about race, gender, and class complications in a fictitious Texas town never failed to move me with their complex humanity, and to persuade me that telling stories is in itself an empathetic act full of utopian potential.

Friday Night Lights

Imagine Television, premiered on NBC Television, 2006

Friday Night Lights debuted to critical acclaim this television season, but didn't pull in the viewers a show ostensibly about football might have predicted. But then again, if it was only a show about football, I wouldn't be watching myself, since I'm the only one in my Steeler-faithful family who wouldn't know a touchdown from a soccer goal if someone showed me captioned pictures of either. The series takes its name and its themes from the feature film *Friday Night Lights*, which was in turn based on the book of the same name, by H.G. Bissinger. The stories concern the lives of families, friends, and colleagues linked by their dedication to the Panther football team at Dillon High School, in a small, fictitious but perhaps typical, Texas town. In the show's central conflict, the new football coach and his family weather the sometimes brutal pressure of the town's expectations for the team, on which Dillon's residents focus all their thwarted wishes and desires.

Shot in and around Austin, Texas, *FNL* never loses sight of its feature film roots. Much of the camera work is handheld and lit without highly theatrical contrasts, which gives it a gritty, authentic look that nicely complements the story's ambiance. The soundtrack, too, evokes dusty rural Texas, but manages to be suggestive without being stereotypical. In fact, the whole show works because of its deep respect for its characters, who are painted with intricacy and depth rarely seen on network television. In situations ripe for caricature, *FNL* manages instead to convey the complexity of relationships, dreams, and desires, and the casual ways in which simple interactions can have lasting, if not cataclysmic, effects.

Although each episode includes at least a scene or two at a football practice or a highly anticipated Friday night game, each week's plot focuses on the characters more than it does the score. Some of the games provide climactic moments, but they rarely end an episode, because the characters' interactions off the field are much more central to the story *FNL* tells. Also unusual for network television, writers provide the actors with plot outlines and key moments, but allow them to improvise their scenes. This gives the actors a great deal of creative freedom and results in dialogue that sounds unfiltered and remarkably fresh.

For example, the banter between recently hired Dillon football coach Eric Taylor (Kyle Chandler) and his wife, Tami (Connie Britton), who now works as the high school's supportive, emotionally and politically intelligent guidance counselor, rings absolutely true to the complications of a heterosexual marriage. Both partners are under public pressure to perform, they both interact with the same people in the same school, they try to parent a teenaged daughter, they're relatively new to Dillon, and the dreams they both harbor for the future sometimes conflict. But we actually see the Taylors work at their marriage while they hang on to their bedrock love and affection for one another.

In the season's finale, the coach contemplates a job offer that would require his family to move to Austin but that would send him higher up his career ladder. Tami and Eric's daughter, Julie (Aimee Teegarden), resist the move, Julie because of her relationship, and Tami because she believes her own work with students at the high school isn't finished and is too important to abandon. Although the coach tries to resort to male privilege and insist his family follow his ambitions, Tami stands her ground and suggests that Eric commute between Dillon and Austin. Even Tami's unexpected pregnancy, which would (in another show) predict that the family should stay together and follow its man, doesn't shake her resolve that somehow, all three of them should get what they want.

Chandler's performance as Eric Taylor is a masterpiece of restraint and barely contained, intelligent energy. Chandler takes his time with Taylor's responses, but he keeps his thinking process close to the surface. I don't think I've ever seen a male actor whose furrowed brow seemed so sincere and so transparent, his confusion and insistence on weighing complicated decisions so true. Chandler chooses unusual vocal rhythms for Taylor; he pauses in unexpected places and speeds through words that other actors would draw out. His quiet intensity makes him fascinating to watch because it's never clear how he'll respond.

Britton, playing Tami Taylor, presents one of the most complex, mature female characters ever played on network television. She's generous with her time and her affections; doesn't mind admitting her mistakes when she makes them; has a useful, ever-present sense of humor; has an open (but not "bleeding") heart; and respects without reservation the students with whom she works. Her relationship with Eric prizes mutual support and respect. She's good at what she does, and while she's impeccably committed to Eric's coaching career, her own work counseling students demands equal time and attention in their marriage. Watching Chandler and Britton create the complexities of this mature relationship offers a real and rare pleasure.

Improvising dialogue is a challenge for actors accustomed to being handed inviolable scripts, but these actors seem to relish the opportunity. The whole cast is peopled with smart artists who can think through their characters' likely responses in a variety of situations within the constraints of a quick moment. They always seem to be truly listening to one another, since they aren't waiting for prearranged cues. Their conversations range from playful to painful, but they're never predictable or pat.

The storylines, too, don't follow conventional television narrative patterns. Multiple plots overlap and develop, and the writers take the characters in unusual directions with rich results. For example, when Dillon's star quarterback Jason Street (Scott Porter) breaks his spine tackling an opponent early in the season, the show spends as much time with his rehabilitation as it does tracking Matt Saracen (Zach Gilford), the soft-spoken, diffident second-string player who tries to fill Jason's shoes.

Jason revitalizes his athletic career despite his paralysis by joining a wheelchair rugby team on its way to the Olympics, giving him a new set of sports aspirations to replace those he lost. When the Olympic team tells him he's too new in his chair to be able to compete this time around, Jason starts hanging around his old football field advising Matt, and eventually gets a spot on the team's coaching staff. The actors play these shifts in fortune with depth and insight, never reverting to predictable responses even to situations that might seem familiar.

The show also confronts the racial politics of small-town Texas without flinching. Running back "Smash" Williams (Gaius Charles) anchors the team's offense. When "Mac," one of the older white coaches, thoughtlessly suggests that the team's African–American players are "like junkyard dogs" who provide its brawn while the white players offer its brains, Smash finds himself forced to address the racism incipient but never before so overt in the team's power structure. He stages a walk-out of all the team's African–American players at a key moment in the season, turning the media spotlight on Mac's unacceptable remarks.

The episode follows Smash as he becomes a reluctant spokesperson for racial oppression and simultaneously wrestles with his own desire to play for a team that desperately needs his talent to win. Everyone has something to lose in this episode; everyone is forced to confront Mac's racism and develop an individual, somehow ethical, response. When Smash decides to end the work stoppage and return to play the crucial away game, he and his colleagues suffer even more racism on the playing field. The white players on the opposing team taunt the Dillon Panthers, the referees make a series of bad calls, and the game devolves into a brawl that stops play. When the refs decide the Panthers get the win, since they were ahead before the fight, the locals throw garbage at Dillon's players as they board their bus for home.

Two local cops follow their vulnerable yellow school bus down a forsaken country road and try to arrest Smash on trumped up charges that he started the melee. Mac winds up confronting the police on Smash's behalf, challenging their intent to arrest him without a warrant. His rather heroic action in very threatening circumstances allows Mac and Smash to come to a wary truce: Mac sees the power of his white privilege, and Smash understands that despite Mac's racism, he means to do the right thing by the team and all its players. The contretemps ends without a moral victory for either Smash or the coach, but rather as a simple moment of understanding that our motivations are never as clear to us as we expect, and that white racism's systemic poison can always seep through, despite people's best intentions.

FNL's open-hearted, even-handed approach to Dillon's identity politics makes it notable television, although strangely, it's white vs. black racial issues that structure the imagined town, rather than Anglo vs. Latino or Mexican–American politics. In the feature film on which this series is based, another of the significant team members was Latino, which helped anchor the story in Texas's demographics. The lack of a Chicano/a lead character seems a peculiar omission for this otherwise perceptive series.

The characters' lives are also crossed by the politics of class, brought home by Tyra Collette (Adrianne Palicki), the high school's "fast" girl, and her mother, who live in a shabby rental while Tyra's sister works as a stripper at a local club. The family bears the burden of "white trash" circumstances: Tyra's father is absent, and her mother beds a series of lowlife men, one of whom Tyra runs out of the house with a kitchen knife after he beats her mother once too often. But when Tyra befriends Coach Taylor's naïve daughter, Julie, it becomes clear that Tyra's shoplifting and other vices are practiced from necessity rather than spite. Tyra, in fact, turns out to be quite smart, her aspirations limited only by the much constrained dreams meted out to people whose class background cruelly stunts their imaginations along with their self-esteem. Watching Tyra come into her own as a capable, strong, bright young woman was one of the many pleasures of this first season.

Likewise, Lyla Garrity, the cheerleader who dates Jason, the disabled star football player, resists stereotypical characterization. Beautiful Lyla (Minka Kelly) comes from a home in which her father – Buddy, the bombastic, glad-handing car dealership owner who heads the Panther's booster club and holds the highest, meanest expectations of Coach Taylor – cheats on her mother. Her painful realization of her father's adultery is handled with careful grace, as Lyla's illusions about her world are dashed one after the other as the season progresses. Even this young character gets fleshed out in complex ways on multiple levels so that, although we see her perhaps a little too often in her figure-flattering cheerleader uniform, she's never dismissed as only a silly, pretty girl.

Lyla stands by her paralyzed boyfriend, even though her life has been turned upside down by his disability, until she catches him kissing a woman he met in Austin at rugby practice. Yet because of her own indiscretion – she slept with Jason Street's best friend, the handsome, rootless, rather dissolute but good-hearted running back Tim Riggins (Taylor Kitsch) after Jason was hurt – she can't take the moral high ground. Instead, she tries hard to make sense of a life completely reconfigured when it was supposed to play out as the typical fairytale high school romance between the quarterback and the prom queen.

Other equally appealing, well-rounded characters flesh out *FNL*'s story, all of whom go about trying to lead their lives the best way they can, given their circumstances. The show's obvious affection for each of them, and its willingness to treat them with both humor and gravity, makes *FNL* one of the most human, humane, radically humanist shows around.

Spectators understand the town through the newly-arrived Taylors' eyes and come to see that people they first thought were forces for evil (like Buddy Garrity, the powerful, garrulous dealership owner) are actually people whose foibles, eccentricities, and weaknesses humanize them and make them compelling and sympathetic. We come to understand, along with the coach and his wife, that these characters truly want to do the right thing, for themselves and for one another, and they're keenly aware of the community in which they live. Their lives intertwine for better or for worse, and they measure themselves against each other's accomplishments with a healthy lack of jealousy or deceit.

FNL is the rare network television drama that treats its diverse characters with respect and empathy, crafting intelligent stories that make us care about their however fictional lives. The filmmakers evoke Texas in all its beautiful natural glory, and contrast its geography with the rough social necessity of Dillon's over-investment in high school football. The series looks straight on at the complexities of gender and race, rethinking conventional masculinity by considering the underside of football's macho glory. And by balancing Tami's goodness and leadership skills with her husband's, the show renders a portrait of heterosexual marriage more thoughtful and equal than any I've seen on television. As Coach Taylor counsels his players, "Clear eyes, full hearts, can't lose." Neither can *Friday Night Lights*.

APRIL 30, 2007

Come Back, Little Sheba

Produced on Broadway, Biltmore Theatre, 2008

William Inge was one of the notables of mid-20th-century American playwriting, often mentioned in the same breath as Tennessee Williams and Arthur Miller, even though his relatively slimmer output garners him fewer words in theatre history surveys (or might that be because he was gay?). After the success of his second play, *Come Back, Little Sheba*, on Broadway in 1950, Inge went on to write *Picnic* (1953), which won that year's Pulitzer Prize, *Bus Stop* (1955), and *Dark at the Top of the Stairs* (1957). He won an Academy Award for his first screenplay, *Splendor in the Grass* (1960), which starred Natalie Wood and Warren Beatty. According to the Inge Center web site, the playwright became depressed after two plays he wrote in the early 1960s were unsuccessful. He left New York for LA, where he committed suicide in 1973.

This Manhattan Theatre Club-produced revival of Inge's 1950s realist drama was first staged in Los Angeles at the Kirk Douglas Theatre. The production opened on Broadway on January 24, 2008, starring S. Epatha Merkerson, affectionately known as Lt. Anita Van Buren on the long-running, original *Law and Order* NBC television series. Merkerson plays Lola, the apparently desperate and deluded housewife whose attempt to keep her marriage intact and "normal" drives the play's plot.

Sheba is a conventional play, to the extent that it's rife with all the tropes of realism: the "secrets" that sour its relationships, the repressed desires that wind up exploding and ruining its characters, the compromises that make the lives it portrays ones of rue and regret. But in this production, rather than providing a recipe for the obvious, director Michael Pressman and his leading woman find distinctions and complexities in these familiar stories that make *Sheba* vital and resonant.

James Noone's soaring set quotes the claustrophobic domestic spaces that Jo Mielziner captured in his original 1949 design for *Death of a Salesman.* The home in which Lola's unhappiness unfolds is a multi-level, multi-room space with doors and stairs and furniture backed up against imaginary walls, a physical embodiment of the porousness between a family's private and public lives. Lola's kitchen is a bright but strangely empty space, with none of the hominess usually ascribed to the home's nerve center of nurture and sustenance. The living room, at the opening curtain, is furnished with mismatched pieces and a threadbare rug, and strewn with the detritus of careless lives: newspapers and magazines, fresh laundry and dirty clothes. The boarder's room off the living room is decorated in detail, as renter Marie's love life is as central to the plot machinations as the room's location suggests. Up the stairs, balanced precariously over the action, is the shared bath and master bedroom, suggested with doors but revealed by the bedroom's lack of walls, where an always disheveled bed figures the entanglements of thwarted desire that thread through the story.

The set changes, which require reorienting props and pieces of the décor in-between scenes, are directed as part of the play's life. As stage-hands come on to attend to various objects, the actors move around the set in character, making transitions in the play's time-scape. The dream-like simultaneity of the play's action and the production's logistical needs let you see the characters in even more of their quotidian reality as they move pensively from one room to the next in the half light. The set suggests both the home's solidity and its precariousness, just as Jennifer von Mayrhauser's costumes lend the characters both dignity and disrepute. Merkerson wears the housedresses that encaged 1950s housewives, all ties and bows and cheap cloth wrapped around the loosening figures of female middle age. Doc (Steppenwolf's Kevin Anderson) wears suspenders to hold up already high-waisted trousers tightly pulled over his expanding waist-line, foiling his attempt at style and leaving him slightly ridiculous looking. This is a couple playing at the conventions of 1950s domesticity and failing, badly.

Shirley Booth originated Lola on Broadway and in the subsequent film version, for which she won an Academy Award. Her simpering, foolish, flighty version of the woman haunts the character, and provides a sharp contrast for Merkerson's reinterpretation. In the play's first act, she puts her own spin on what appear to be Lola's self-delusions about her relationship and her life, playing the woman as more languid and dreamy than Booth's always bustling, high-pitched fussbudget. But as the second act moves through its devastating unraveling, Merkerson reveals Lola as a surprisingly strong but trapped woman trying frantically to hold on to a marriage she knows was a mistake from the start, struggling to be a partner to a husband whose alcoholism destroys them both.

The secrets alluded to at the beginning find the harsh light of day at the end, as Doc's hatred for the woman whose pregnancy trapped him into a loveless marriage explodes in violence. Lola's attempt to maintain the innocence that let her trust her young lover 25 years ago becomes more and more painful, as it's clear their liaison produced only loss. The baby they inadvertently conceived died when they used a substandard doctor to attend to the delivery; their shotgun wedding was obviated by the disappearance of their progeny, its unhappiness exacerbated by the couple's inability to bear another child. Lola calls Doc "Daddy," underlining ironically (although she always says it earnestly) the emptiness of their union.

Marie, their boarder (Zoe Kazan), inflames an already fraught relationship with her flirtatious presence, taunting Doc with casual intimacies that quicken his step. When Marie flaunts 1950s propriety by sleeping with Turk, the young man with whom she cheats on her out-of-town boyfriend, Doc's carefully manufactured moral code falls apart and knocks him off the wagon of sobriety he's maintained for one uneasy year. The language of Alcoholics Anonymous's 12-step program (still relatively new to American culture in 1950, and much more stigmatized than its commonplace presence today) to which Doc and Lola cling barely holds his bitterness and incipient rage in check. Even though he attends meetings and sponsors other alcoholics, helping them through brutal visits to the local hospital's drunk tank, and even though Lola asks him to repeat his daily affirmation, neither Lola nor Doc truly believe his nature has changed.

Director Pressman gradually builds the production's impending doom, letting spectators recognize that what we see as Lola's inanity is really her frantic attempt to shore up the façade of her relationship's normalcy. In 2008, that façade already seems cracked. The production suggests that the conventions of heterosexual marriage were already rotten in the 50s, even as American ideology worked so hard to construct the nuclear family living happily in the suburbs as the sine qua non of such relationships. Both Lola and Doc suffocate in the confines of their home, fabricating intimacy and performing normalcy as they suffer emotional and social isolation. Doc is jealous of Marie and Turk, and funnels his repressed desire into flirting with her under the guise of paternalism. Lola likes to watch the young couple's romantic couplings; she openly admits that she spies on them. While the audience can read her voyeurism as benign longing for her own lost beauty and youth, her watching also reeks of sexual perversion, as though she's doomed to lurk about the corners of other people's passion, feeding her own desire vicariously.

Their neighbor, Mrs. Coffman (Brenda Wehle), who's suspect enough that Lola first wonders if she has poisoned their missing old beloved dog, Sheba, becomes the play's reproving Greek chorus, stepping into and out of their home and the action with her thin lips pinched, tsk-tsk-ing her way through their lives as she first judges Lola's inadequate housekeeping and then pities her victimization. Inge suggests that even those with the most in common – lonely housewives chained to deadening routines – must invest in appearances of decorum instead of reaching out to one another with sympathy and agency. When Mrs. Coffman inadvertently visits after Doc's rampage, she wordlessly helps Lola right the overturned furniture and clean up broken glass, replacing the vestiges of her dignity without suggesting that Lola change anything.

The Marie/Turk subplot offers interesting feminist resonances. Temporarily separated from her socially upstanding boyfriend, Marie embarks on an affair with a man who's all brawn and no brains, whose only option for social intercourse is sexual. Marie clearly feels something for Turk, but she tells Lola that he's "not the marrying kind." Inge neatly reverses the charge usually leveled against "loose" women, painting Marie as the sexual opportunist who knows she'll soon settle down with a more appropriate man. When her boyfriend, Bruce, appears at the house, he's straitlaced, dull, and judgmental, impatient with Lola's fussing and already puffed up by the obligations to which he's carefully calibrated his life. His appearance on the scene underlines Marie's compromises and Inge's intimation that social propriety requires emotional, sexual, and spiritual sacrifice.

Merkerson is a revelation as Lola. Casting an African–American woman in the wife's role without changing a word of the text and casting the rest of the characters as white (with the exception of one of Doc's AA friends, played by African–American actor Keith Randolph Smith) layers the play with racial shadings unavailable when a white woman performs the part. In many ways, Lola's servitude is more readily apparent; in one key scene, when Lola has made a fancy dinner for Marie and her visiting boyfriend to which Doc, out on a bender, fails to show, Lola announces that she won't eat with the couple, but will be their "butler." Her declaration productively underlines Lola's indentured servitude, as Merkerson's race (and her maid-like adornments) suddenly becomes evident in ways it doesn't through the rest of the production. This color-blind casting in fact underlines gender commonality across race. We're no doubt meant to see this choice through a 21st century perspective, since a mixed-marriage in the 1950s would have been scandalous.

Merkerson slows Lola's tempo, reading her lines with a drawling, southern-inflected cadence that points up her race more than trying to obscure it. Her voice is lovely and wistful, rich and warm, while her face seems frozen with her effort to make something nice out of a life wasted in a loveless lie of a relationship. Where Booth seemed convinced of her own revisionist history, Merkerson's performance reveals the labor required to construct such stories, and the psychic and spiritual toll they take. Instead of hiding her sadness behind relentless movement and meaningless domestic busyness, Merkerson's Lola is almost indolent in her melancholy. When we first see her, she's lying in bed in that upper room, wearing a cream-color full slip and staring quietly into space. There's something erotic and charged about Merkerson's lassitude; she could be a heroine from the steamier bloodlines of Williams's oeuvre. In another scene, left alone in the house, Lola turns on *Taboo*, a radio program that promises covert seductions to its lonely-hearted listeners. Lola drapes herself on the couch, preparing to luxuriate in some physical fantasy; her guilt is palpable when she's startled by Doc's unexpected return from work.

Merkerson's performance is fully embodied and sexually charged. Her invitations to the milkman and the mailman and even to Mrs. Coffman to come sit, stay, have a cup of coffee, listen to a story, to just be with her, all have unsettling, slightly unseemly sexual overtones. And yet over the course of the play, the men who first reluctantly enter her home glancing at their watches and rolling their eyes gain affection and respect for Lola. As her domestic strife becomes more obvious, they begin to see her as someone real, rather than a caricature of the happy housewife she once performed for them so aggressively. The mailman writes her a letter just so that she'll get one, and the milkman proudly shows her his picture in a physique magazine (shadings of Inge's homosexuality, as such rags were notorious as the gay porn of their time).

Although Mrs. Coffman would be a highly unlikely sexual liaison for Lola, Lola's situation echoes that of the much more respectable middle-class housewife of the same era Julianne Moore plays in the film version of Michael Cunningham's book *The Hours* (2002). The emptiness and indignities of heterosexual domesticity fan Moore's character's lesbian longing and propel her out of the family nightmare. No such redemption is possible for Lola. Her boredom is stultifying (Doc prevents her from going to work), and she's utterly dependent on others in her version of house arrest. Her estranged family won't take her back, now 25 years after her sexual indiscretion, even though her drunken husband has threatened her life, brandishing a machete in their living room, calling her names, and promising to "cut the fat off" of her with his weapon.

When drink lets Doc drop his mask, the audience sees the horror Lola has put up with for 25 years, and suddenly, her behavior makes a terrible kind of sense. She's terrorized in her own home, with no way to escape. She has no means, no skills, nowhere else to go. Yet as Merkerson plays her, Lola's unflinching resolve to survive outweighs her terror. When Doc returns, chastened, from his short rehabilitative hospital stay, he's pink and pitiful, helpless as a mewling newborn, and begs Lola not to leave him. With one look in response, Merkerson's devastating expression takes in her present and her future, chained to a mercurial alcoholic who will descend into madness and claw his way back to temporary redemption again and again, leaving her to fend off his murderous rage and to soldier through a fake life. She walks Doc to their kitchen table and proceeds to cook for him as they glance at each other warily, pretending, again and always, that their suburban prison houses something real and nourishing.

Pressman's wrenching production makes the realist conventions of Inge's play critical of the very domestic story they structure. This revival is one of the most progressive realist dramas I've ever seen produced, not because the director deconstructed it, but because he and his cast fight their way to the horrible core of the situations it describes. They don't blame their characters, regardless of their ethical or moral failings, but instead indict a culture that insists that heterosexual, coupled, suburban domesticity is the best way to live.

No wonder second-wave American feminism asserted itself a decade after this play was first produced.

JANUARY 24, 2008

Hair

Produced by the Joseph Papp New York Shakespeare Festival, Delacorte Theatre, New York, NY, 2008

Given Ben Brantley's glowing *New York Times* review, *Hair* will no doubt move to Broadway. Although it deserves a wider audience and a much longer run (or re-run, given its original Broadway success), part of what makes the Public's Delacorte Theatre production in Central Park wonderful is that *Hair* finds its natural setting outdoors. Entering the open-air house feels like stumbling on the young, energetic "Tribe" in their natural habitat. It's not that the designers have gone to great lengths to recreate say, Tompkins Square Park, the far East Village Ground Zero for New York's Aquarius generation in the late 1960s. It's that all the designers and the terrific director, Diane Paulus (recently appointed the next Artistic Director of the American Repertory Theatre [ART], in Cambridge), have taken advantage of the freedom and the pleasure and the wonder of being young and alive under the sky, living on the streets as the characters in *Hair* (at least sometimes) do.

The actors enter the small, undecorated stage from the roofless house, roaming the aisles to address the audience. They're not panhandling, but almost; they entreat us not for cash but for our opinions about their hair, their clothes, and their beings. Spectators I noticed at the preview performance I saw August 5th happily went along with their interactions with the cast, turning the whole evening into something of a mutual love fest. And rightly so, since the Public's revival is vivid and fresh, even magical. The designers might maintain a bare bones aesthetic – perhaps inspired by the concert-style version the Public mounted in the park last summer – but the rest of the production is fully embellished with choreography and music. The energetic, geometric, and precise dance moves were devised by Karole Armitage, and Rob Fisher supervised the musical direction by Nadia Digiallonardo of a small band of horns, percussion, and electric guitars (since *Hair* was, as the Feminist Spectator 2 reminds me, the first rock musical) played by musicians decked out in the colorful, eclectic costumes of 1960s' Hippies. The band congregates under a *chuppah*-like cloth canopy perched in the back middle of the intimate playing space. Bare of more elaborate decor, the Delacorte stage is perfectly attuned to the musical's simplicity. The stage floor sports a threadbare layer of Astroturf to evoke the balding grass of the Tribe's arena, and the low fences at the back and sides of the stage become part of the Hippies' hollow, the comfy outdoor encampment in which the characters frolic through a long night or two of the soul.

The night I attended, *Hair* seemed a wonderful nostalgia trip for the audience. As the band played the opening chords of "Aquarius," and Dionne (Patina Renea Miller) wandered up to center stage to herald the approach of the new age, people across the packed audience sang along, grooving in their seats to those old lyrics and a tune that seems embedded in the collective memory of a certain generation of Americans. Even younger spectators rose to the occasion, singing along. Who could fail to be moved by the infectious energy and commitment of the cast; by Paulus's direction, which paces each number and exchange with fail-proof ease and speed; by uniformly excellent singers, who put their own stamp on these classic melodies without offending the audience's recollection of their original delivery; or by dances that manage to seem both authentic to the physical and spiritual freedom of the Hippies' historical moment and sharp and contemporary enough to speak to the movement vocabulary of today's young folks? As "Aquarius" dawned and the song's final chords sounded, I'd hazard to say we were all already hooked.

Hair is really a revue, a string of songs linked along the slight plot. Each number captures a feeling, an attitude that signals the emotions and passions of young people of the anti-Vietnam War, Flower Power, Civil Rights, Psychedelic, Free Love, anti-Establishment era. The characters, such as they are, depict stock figures of the moment: Berger (Will Swenson), the handsome womanizer who can't be bothered to appreciate Sheila (Caren Lyn Manuel), his erstwhile main squeeze; Woof (Bryce Ryness), the about-to-be flamboyant on-his-way-to-being "homosexual" who's in love with Mick Jagger; Hud (Darius Nichols), the Afro-encircled black man bursting with then-new racial pride; and Jeanie (Kacie Sheik), inadvertently pregnant by another man, but thoroughly, unrequitedly in love with Claude (Jonathan Groff of *Spring Awakening* fame), the confused boy torn between fidelity to the Tribe and some misplaced sense of obedience to authority, whether incarnated by his parents or "the law" or "the country." For reasons that haven't been clear in any production I've ever seen of *Hair*, Claude decides not to burn his draft card like his mates, but instead follows through with his Army induction. He cuts his down-to-there hair, goes off to war, and is promptly slaughtered, reduced from an idealistic, attractive young man to just another anonymous body sent home in a box wrapped in just another empty, wasted flag.

The draft-card-burning scene that ends *Hair*'s first act, staged to the reiterative melody of "Hare Krishna," is particularly affecting in the Public's Delacorte production, partly because the outdoor setting lets it viscerally evoke the moment. As smoke pours into the night air from a fire lit in a street-size steel garbage can, each of the cast's men take their turn ritually dancing up to the light. They throw their cards into the flames as drums beat and trumpets blare, and the rest of the cast dances triumphantly, until Claude approaches the can and just ... can't ... do it. As the ritual of refusal comes to an abrupt end, the Tribe backs away from their friend, confused. The spirit of group-think, so pleasurable a force to which to surrender, dissipates, and the Tribe breaks apart, wandering off into the night in pairs or trios.

But as Claude sings the haunting ballad of ambivalence and bewilderment "Where Do I Go?" the Tribe returns for the fleeting, rather sacramental nudity that was part of what made the original *Hair* so radical for its time. Under cover of night and low stage lights, the Tribe gathers back near Claude, casting off their clothes not under the privacy of a large billowing tarp, as they did in the 1960s, but openly, and with a kind of conviction and vulnerability that both underlines and contrasts with Claude's hesitancy. Discarding their outfits to stand naked before the audience gestures to a primal necessity underneath the radical posturing, to the possibility of feelings not sexual, but unmediated and, if you will, pure. Although nudity on stage no longer shocks (at least not in Central Park in New York City), in this production the cast's collective disrobing played as a declaration of authentic present-ness more than it did rebellion or desire.

The moment also works effectively to question the momentum of political feeling in the 60s that sometimes devolved into lifestyle instead of a more considered, analytical program of dissent. In the Public's production, I noticed that the Tribe isn't first and foremost committed to activism, but rather indulges in a way of life that's pleasurable because it's free from the "square" expectations of the moment *and* unfettered by the dogma of its politics. Until it ends with the draft-card burning ritual, the first act establishes the Tribe's preoccupation with personal relationships over the political, in songs like "Donna," "Frank Mills," and "Easy to Be Hard." It both lampoons and celebrates the counter-culture's social practices in "Hashish," "Sodomy," and "Hair," evoking the moment but resolutely embedding it in personal, rather than political, choices. On the other hand, Act One offers its share of social satire, critiquing the sorry state of our skies in "Air," the impenetrability and proliferation of acronyms in "Initials," and the rigidity of the 1950s generation in "My Conviction." Performers Andrew Kober, who plays the drag role of Margaret Meade as well as the uptight, all-purpose "Dad," and Megan Lawrence, who's physically and vocally on target as the stereotypical yet familiar, anxious "Mother," parody the "Establishment" with acerbic physical wit.

Although Claude is a cardboard cut-out of a character, his second act drift away from his community into the maw of the war machine is wrenching, not because the audience has necessarily identified with him or any other character, but perhaps because it's in the last half of the evening when *Hair* becomes most relevant to the present and when analogies with the war in Iraq feel most palpable. This, too, is handled with a light touch consistent with the rest of the production. In the show's finale, the Tribe parts down the middle to reveal Claude, dressed in full military colors, lying still on the stage floor across a large American flag. Their friend's empty sacrifice resonates with those of the many soldiers over the last five years who've lost their lives in Iraq and Afghanistan, for equally suspect political reasons. The second act more specifically echoes the ideological commitments of the moment (then and now). "Let the Sunshine In," as Public Theatre Artistic Director Oscar Eustis notes in the program, was never "a celebratory anthem; it was always a broken-hearted plea by a tribe that has not only failed to stop the war, but failed to keep one of their own from being consumed by it." Taken out of context, the song became a commercialized feel-good hit, but Eustis and this production recalls its origins as a cri de coeur, a heartfelt plea for tolerance and peace.

The Public's production doesn't suffocate *Hair* under overworked contemporary references. Paulus lets the cast's freak flags fly in the exuberance of the lyrics, the costumes, the dancing, and the invigorating night air. *Hair* is by now a "costume piece" – the long-flowing locks on most of the men are obviously wigs, and the fringed vests worn over their bare chests obviously evoke another era's style. In fact, the cast's bodies give away the persistence of the present most emphatically, in the sculpted six-pack abs of the male actors and the svelte physical lines of the women, perceptible even under their long, fluid skirts. The contrast between Hair's premiere 40 years ago and this revival seems embodied in how much tighter, leaner, and, ironically, rather warrior-like the ideal American body has become.

Still, *Hair*'s messages are all here, along with the pleasure of nostalgia, the poignancy of being reminded of how history repeats itself, and the joy of watching young people so physically, musically, and emotionally dedicated to embodying if not fully fleshed out characters, then the simple spirit of a moment now long past, yet close to the present nonetheless. When the cast invited the audience onto the stage to dance as the band played after the curtain call, people of all ages (and colors, although unlike the Public's very diverse staff, working at the Delacorte as security and ushers, the audience for *Hair* was predominantly white the night I attended) bounded down to join them. The dancing was a utopic, performative slice of "now" inspired by an evening's performance that knit audience and cast together in communal fellow-feeling and hope.

I can imagine some readers or spectators disparaging this production as empty nostalgia or easy sentiment, unattached to actions that might actually change or critically note how bereft are the politics of war and imperialism. But I left the theatre buoyed not just by the electricity of memory, or by hearing the enduring if sometimes silly lyrics, but by the production's full-hearted devotion to the present, to making these songs and the representation of an inclusive, open-handed spirit of belonging and rebellion mean something in a time when we don't readily value ideas or movements or even just moments that bring us together so unashamedly.

In their program bios, each cast member ends his or her paragraph with "Love." Just the word, period. Corny, but also sweet, and evidence, perhaps, of how much this cast's generation came to appreciate and even share the sentiments first embodied in *Hair* by the last. Good morning star-shine indeed.

AUGUST 9, 2008

Let Me Down Easy

Produced at Second Stage Theater, New York, NY, 2009

Anna Deavere Smith's *Let Me Down Easy* represents a departure from the typical tone and trajectory of her "On the Road" cycle of monologues. Smith established her talent in the early 90s, after many years working in regional theatres, as an artist/anthropologist who interviews people in community settings and then performs their words verbatim. She argues that people's language and their voices – their syntax, their inflections, the rhythm of their words and their cadence – reveal their character, and that through meticulously recreating their speech acts in the context of often vexed or conflicted community relations, something of the larger character of America is also revealed. Smith's first major success, *Fires in the Mirror* (1992), for instance, addressed the civil strife between the African–American and Chasidic communities of Crown Heights, Brooklyn, after the chief rabbi's motorcade inadvertently hit and killed a young black boy named Gavin Cato. Smith spent time in Crown Heights interviewing people about the incident, all of whom were involved to varying degrees and spoke from opposing points of view. She also interviewed people who simply shared a unique perspective on the tension, including Al Sharpton and Cornel West.

Smith channeled the voices of all the people she interviewed through her own body and vocal impersonations, editing the time she spent with each one into a meaningful bite of sound and then weaving them into a tapestry of character and viewpoints on the central conflict. Smith doesn't presume to "become" any of these (real) characters. Conventional actors typically ask the audience to suspend its disbelief while they make interior emotional connections that allow them to identify psychologically with the fictional character. Smith works from the outside in, mimicking the complexity of individual language and voice as a way to reveal something human, surprising, and true about people we might suspect of being stereotypical and predictable.

In her second large-scale piece, *Twilight, Los Angeles* (1992), Smith brought a similar anthropological outlook to the civil uprising in Los Angeles after local courts returned a "not guilty" verdict to the police officers accused of beating Rodney King for a traffic violation. For

Twilight, Smith's interviews ranged across and among an even larger group of people, as the Los Angeles uprising crossed community lines and included African–Americans, Latinos, Asians and Asian–Americans, and white people as subjects with keen perspectives on the events. In a nuanced reference, "Twilight" refers both to the liminal moment between day and night, the in-between time in which crisis perhaps gives rise to social change, and to the gang member whom Smith interviewed as part of the palette of citizens whose viewpoints enlightened her and her audiences about the LA events.

Let Me Down Easy breaks the mold of Smith's work by foregoing her usual immersion in communities rife with conflict. No "us vs. them" structures the play and no sense of traditional dramatic agon pulls the show from crisis to resolution. Instead, the social crisis of the American medical establishment motivates Smith's examination; as she notes in the program, the play began as a commission for the Yale School of Medicine.[1] But the people she interviews and impersonates demonstrate more subtle and complex standpoints in a social investigation that winds up addressing death, dying, and what we make of our lives before we get there more than it does the failing medical system that purports to give us care. The show, as a result, doesn't ask the audience to take sides or to consider deeply opposing points of view, as did *Fires* and *Twilight*, but lets us muse together for 95 minutes on what defines us as human beings in the face of our inevitable demise.

The people Smith weaves together into this thoughtful human tapestry vary wildly not just by occupation and profession, by geography and locale, or by their relative relationships to social power but also in temperament and character, gender and race, class and accent, which makes each impersonation a pleasant surprise. The play's theme doesn't predict who Smith will consult for opinions, and the juxtapositions of speakers' preoccupations and voices are sometimes funny, sometimes poignant, and always fascinating and compelling. In the first six portraits alone, Smith performs James Cone, a famous African–American theologian who loves to think about language and what it means to his community and provides Smith with her show's title; Elizabeth Streb, a white post-modern dancer who accidentally sets herself on fire while performing for her female partner's birthday party, and finds in her trauma the astonished, boastful pride of a survivor; Lance Armstrong, who sees his body as a nearly mechanical balance of weight and power that demands the most minute calibrations; Sally Jenkins, a sports writer who describes how athletes are driven to burn themselves up in the effort of exertion they make look easy; Eve Ensler, the feminist theatre artist famous for writing the now ubiquitous *Vagina Monologues* and the V-Day activism that supports annual readings of the play, who shares with Smith her suspicion that anorexia is a plot to rob women and girls of their power, since, as she says, it's difficult to get much done when you're only eating a raisin a day; and Brent Williams, an Idaho rodeo rider who wears a cowboy hat and pulls on a beer while he tells Smith about his high threshold for pain.

These characters alone provide a rich collection of stories, insights, accents, and body types. Thinking back, even though Smith is costumed (by Ann Hould-Ward) only with a striped sports jacket for one person, a couple of rings for another, or a hat of some sort for a third, I can see the bull rider's lanky height, Armstrong's arrogant muscular slouch, Ensler's stolid feminist force, Streb's physical euphoria, Cone's expansive girth and gestures, and Jenkins' firecracker countenance and humor as clearly as I remember Smith's white shirt and black trousers, the neutral palette onto which all these people's personalities are painted.

In *Let Me Down Easy*, even more than in her earlier virtuosic performances, Smith seems to have settled into her informants' stories and the possibilities of what they might mean, knit together into an evening. She seems to have less of an ax to grind here, ironically. In an historical moment when health care is debated on the front page of every newspaper, and the fractious debate over public options spouts from so many lips, this show doesn't directly engage the terms of that dispute. As a result, Smith – who vehemently protests her objectivity in productions in which it's impossible not to presume she doesn't take one side or the other – appears even-handed and magnanimous with her characters. She seems to enjoy playing them, speaking as them, sharing their insights. The implicit – and sometimes overt – didacticism of *Fires* and *Twilight* is absent in *Let Me Down Easy*.

Smith's performance seems filled with an outsized joy, which flatters her skillful technique by almost understating her talent. Each character's name and the title of their monologue is projected as a superscript on the frame above the stage. Smith (subtly directed by Leonard Foglia) moves fluidly among them, reaching the final comment of each monologue that usually punctuates and often titles the idea at hand. Then she takes off the character's defining costume piece or prop, lifts the next from the hands of a nondescript female assistant who enters and exits the stage – barefoot, like Smith – delivering each object or bit of apparel, drapes herself in its spell and launches into the spirit she inhabits next. You can see Smith in the interstices between characters. She's a thoughtful, purposeful, precise presence, the guiding spirit of the piece who's moved by her appreciation of the people she embodies and to whom she gives voice.

Let Me Down Easy is as trenchant a political commentary as any of Smith's shows, but because she creates an "us" or a "we" instead of the binary of conflicting "thems," the production feels generous and forgiving, its humor poignant instead of pedantic. Points of view accumulate on stage, rather than replacing one another. The costume pieces and props that index each person literally litter the stage by the play's end, as each character is haunted by those preceding him or her. The collection of things points to a collectivity of people and perspectives that's oddly comforting. The show is about death and dying, loss and grief, but also about how we live in the meantime. As each character Smith performs eats, drinks, smokes, or chats, we see people who are extremely different from one another nonetheless sustaining themselves in simple, basic ways that seem familiar and communal. Smith had a head cold the afternoon I saw one of the last preview week performances (September 30, 2009). Because she removed the same blue hanky from her pocket to blow her nose as she performed several different characters, it seemed as though they all shared the same cold, an inadvertent but moving coincidence. The gesture also made it easy to remember Smith's presence, although in this show, she doesn't seem to want us to forget that she's there, mediating these stories, providing the vehicle that drops each character into our lives and carries them too quickly back out.

The beautifully crafted production offers a lovely backdrop to Smith's impersonations. The spare set (by Riccardo Hernandez) includes a modern white couch and coffee table stage right, offset by a white dinner table and chairs stage left, at which several characters take their meal. The warm, intimate setting is framed by five tall screens/mirrors that tilt from the top over the set, vaguely diffusing what spectators see reflected. Sometimes, Smith is seen live in the mirrors, although her image is swirled by some surface distortion; other times, Smith's character is projected onto the surface as though he or she is looking into a camera. The woody, golden aura is sculpted by subtle, architectural light (by Jules Fisher and Peggy Eisenhauer) and a soft soundscape textures the play's aural mood.

The Wednesday matinee audience with whom I watched the play seemed to appreciate Smith's observations and insights, and she spoke directly to them under the guise of character. Her impersonation of the now late, former governor of Texas, Ann Richards, who nonchalantly describes how she has to preserve her qi for herself is a memorable crowd-pleaser, but spectators also responded enthusiastically to the lesser-known characters. Ruth Katz, a patient at Yale New Haven Hospital whose file is lost through staff ineptitude, garnered particular appreciation, as did the plight of physician Kiersta Kurtz-Burke, describing how she waited to be rescued with her patients at Charity Hospital in New Orleans after Katrina hit, and her dawning realization that no one really did care about the poor, elderly people of color in her charge.

Toward the play's end, a few of the monologues seem superfluous, although thinking back, I can't imagine *Let Me Down Easy* without any one of its stories. But the 95 minutes feel a bit long by the end, the stories a bit repetitive, even in their differences. Or maybe it's that the string of tales makes your heart a bit too tender to bear the narratives for much longer. The penultimate monologue, Trudy Howell's story about a dying young girl in an orphanage in South Africa who packs her suitcase to go off to see her already deceased mother, leaves an indelible image. Likewise, Smith ends the play performing a Buddhist monk, who demonstrates how life finally runs out by overturning a full tea cup into his palm and letting the liquid pool on the stage floor as the lights around Smith turn green and deep blue.

Let Me Down Easy does justice to its title and to its audience, delivering us into the pointed grace of its ending.

OCTOBER 5, 2009

Jomama Jones: Radiate

Produced at Soho Rep, New York, NY, 2011

Jomama Jones: Radiate, an incomparable performance art/concert created by singer-lyricist-performer-playwright Daniel Alexander Jones, is the first downtown theatre must-see experience of 2011. Jones (Jomama and her alter-ego, Daniel Alexander) is a brilliant persona, full of love, light, and beautiful lyrics and stories. The abundance of charisma and good will emanating from the small stage at Soho Rep makes the house feel ten times its size, enlarged by the presence of a personality who could fill a space ten times larger still. Jomama calls herself a "diva" – in fact, one of Soho Rep's supplementary "Feed" events is a panel discussion called "What Makes a Diva?" But while she comports herself theatrically, Jomama declines the imperious narcissism the image implies. Jomama performs with the calculated flair of the constructed personality she is – she's a fiction wholly of Daniel Alexander Jones's creation. But she's got so much heart, and her interactions with her audience, her back-up singers, and her band leader are so genuine and generous, it's easy to forget that she's not, well, real.

Jomama's warmth fuels her delightful singing. She carries her 1980s-brand funk, R&B-, jazz-, and disco-inflected original songs with ease and aplomb, each number revealing a new side of Jomama's soulful performance stylings. Her dancing is casually choreographed, showing off Jomama's great legs and beautiful carriage, which are flattered by costumes (designed by Oana Botez-Ban and Ron Cesario) that shimmer and slink and cut across her shoulders on provocative biases. Jomama boasts three different costume changes (as any diva should – the appearance of each new gown is a small, sweet joke in *Radiate*), each of which heightens her statuesque beauty and her performativity. Her first dress is white, tight, and short, cut straight to hang halfway down her thighs and loosely across her muscular chest. Her next outfit is steel gray, cut on a diagonal, leaving one shoulder bare and her legs freer, which lets her dance with more abandon. Her last costume is a stately gown that extends down to the floor and up to Jomama's neck, bringing her more stature than seems possible, given that she already wears staggering platform shoes that help her tower over her companions on stage. When Jomama appears after the show to greet friends and admirers, she's wearing yet another costume, a feathery, bright red number that seems to make even her huge, round, 1970s Afro glow. To say she cuts a striking figure is a desperate understatement; she's a wonderfully special effect.

But in performance, her theatricality is also effective. Jomama entertains with joyous, infectious abandon that provokes the audience to shout their approval at the end of each song and to join in the clapping and the moving and grooving while she sings. Jomama is also a woman with a mission; her patter delivers hope and social faith that Alexander Jones carries off without sanctimony or excessive sentiment. Thanks to Jomama's ingenuous earnestness, she's entirely winning as she tells the audience how she left the U.S. for Europe in the 1980s because she didn't like where the country was heading politically. She's warily decided to return home to stage her comeback, and to participate in what she wants to believe is Obama's on-going culture of change. Jomama handily creates such an ethos in her performance, making an audience full of strangers into a community of people she encourages to care for one another, however fleeting our moments of connection. Like a lovely, smart, embodied Tinkerbell-cum-drag queen, Jomama invites us to make wishes and to believe along with her, and damn if she doesn't pull it off.

The evening's magical quality begins as soon as spectators enter Soho Rep, where we're met near the box office by the spritely Jing Xu, a slight young performer dressed in a sparkly white costume that seems like a cross between a gymnast's uniform and a riding outfit, a look that seems at once futuristic and fantastical. Clown-white make-up outlines and extends her eyes, which contrasts starkly with her spiky black hair. She encourages us to write a wish on cards she draws from a basket in her arms. Spectators gamely scrawl down their thoughts, leaning up against the theatre's walls or crouching by chairs to write. Later in the evening, toward the show's end, Jomama and her back-up singers, the Sweet Peaches (played deliciously by Sonya Perryman and the dazzling Helga Davis), take turns reading aloud spectators' wishes. These short desires are by turns comic or sincere, but all are announced with the graceful hope that through community, our wishes can in fact come true.

Jing Xu acts as a Puck figure throughout the evening, welcoming the audience and providing the night's benediction much in the spirit of Puck's "If we spirits have offended, think but this and all is mended..." speech at the end of *A Midsummer Night's Dream*. She moves stools on and off the stage for Jomama and the Sweet Peaches, and brings Jomama the occasional glass of water, moving with the fluidity of a dancer and the heightened theatricality of someone who knows she's collaborating in a charmed event. The narrow, deep stage at Soho Rep is set and dressed for a concert. Band-leader Bobby Halvorson (who wrote and composed the music with Alexander Jones with help from Sharon Bridgforth, Grisha Coleman, and Amy Hunt) fronts a five-piece band behind a round platform surrounded by sheer white curtains that Jomama and the Sweet Peaches pull around a track to expose and reveal the band and themselves in different configurations throughout the night. The band and the singers are dressed in neutral shades of white, gray, and khaki which, thanks to lovely lighting designed by Lucrecia Briceno and David Bengali, seem to shimmer and reflect prismatically (occasionally assisted by the disco ball that hangs from the flies like a talisman).

Jomama grounds the heavenly scene, interacting with the musicians, the Sweet Peaches, and what quickly becomes her adoring audience. She's beautiful, her Afro large, her heels high, her long legs striking, her face handsomely made-up, and her body passing convincingly as female. One of the pleasures of Alexander Jones's drag, in fact, is how lightly it's worn. His effortless performance suggests, in fact, that he's not "crossing" gender so much as embracing a femininity that's as much a part of him as masculinity. Neither does he parody women. Alexander Jones's is a lovely, loving, and lived-in performance that lets him revel in his adornments and use them as a vehicle for *affect* more than *effect*. So many drag performances are about surface, about gender as a set of constructed social codes we perform by cultural agreement. But that chestnut of feminist and queer theory isn't Alexander Jones's central point. His achievement with Jomama is how he fills in her outline with affective substance, with emotional care and connection that trumpets his (and by extension our) humanity.

Jomama interacts with the audience like a quick-witted stand-up comic. She asks people their names, playing off their responses with good humor and style. The evening feels improvisational, as good concerts do, persuading us that the performer really is with us in the moment and hasn't told her stories a hundred times before. Kym Moore's, confident direction helps Jomama establish a physical connection with the audience. She comes off the stage into the house halfway through the show to tell part of her story, standing in the aisle for one of her numbers and shaking people's hands. In-between songs, house lights come up on the audience, so that Jomama and the Sweet Peaches can see who they're addressing from the stage. Jomama's patter relates the story of her comeback. Although the character is fabricated, Alexander Jones appeals to the malleable operations of memory to nearly persuade us that we can remember her original performances in the 1980s, and to convince us that we're happy she's back. Jomama's amazing and amusing "realness" brings her fully to life. Alexander Jones believes in his character, and her charisma and caring makes it easy to invest in her presence. He delivers the cabaret-style act with dialogic panache, a Martin Buber-esque enactment of intersubjective attention that ennobles both speaker and listener. Buber, the Jewish philosopher-theologian, also believed in the "wish" as a performative utterance, something transformative for not just the person wishing, but for the world. Jomama and the Sweet Peaches embody just this sort of potential.

I saw *Jomama Jones: Radiate* the day after the *New York Times* ran its favorable review. Many of the wishes Jomama and the Sweet Peaches read out at the show's end were from people on the waiting list hoping to get in to see the performance. But *Times* reviewer David Rooney slightly missed the point of *Radiate*. He compared Jomama to the drag persona created by Justin Bond for the lounge-singing duo Kiki and Herb. The comparison couldn't be less apt. Where Kiki is a liquor-soaked harpy at the piano, mercurial as she swings between contrition and vengeance for her difficult life, Jomama's voice and her presence is all about shining light. Alexander Jones's reference isn't Bond's Kiki, but divas of color like Josephine Baker, Lena Horne, and Teena Marie, who graced the world not just with their strength of their voices, but with the size of their souls. Like each of them, Jomama, too, has struggled; Alexander Jones creates her as a woman for whom being in the world requires persistence, faith, and a spirit of grace.

The on-stage world that he conjures, accompanied so ably by Davis, Perryman, and Halvorson's band, is one of love and hope, embodied in an evening of theatre magic. Alexander Jones's performance is filled with a sharp theatrical and political intelligence that's most obvious when he's improvising with the audience. His eyebrows raise, his voice deepens for a moment with interest, empathy, and a wicked wit, and his foot jumps off up the ground just enough to lift his hip with wry punctuation. But Jomama doesn't invest in irony. Her music and her outfits – and in some ways, her outlook – might hail from the 1980s, but Alexander Jones doesn't parody her anachronisms. On the contrary, she reminds us of something good and right, something we might reach back to and forward toward all at once, to grasp a pre-terror New York when we could with easy confidence be the community Jomama wishes for us throughout the evening.

It's impossible not to be affected by Jomama's example. She radiates the love and hope she wishes for us all.

JANUARY 13, 2011

Lost Lounge

Produced at Dixon Place,
New York, NY, 2011

This elegiac evening with Peggy Shaw, Lois Weaver, and musician Vivian Stoll is a beautiful meditation on change, loss, and aging, delivered as a Sid Caesar/Imogene Coco- or Mike Nichols/Elaine May-style lounge act with post-modern stylings. In Dixon Place's expansive basement black-box theatre – excavated, as Shaw and Weaver imagine, from three stories of layered dirt – the inimitable lesbian pair and their musical partner trade songs and repartee against a visual and sonic backdrop of the city being demolished and (presumably) reconstructed in unrecognizable ways. The images never picture the new; they only show us the wreckage, through an aperture that expands as the evening progresses. *Lost Lounge* testifies to the past, keeping its view of the present and the future only rueful. The show is melancholic, the laughs wistful and poignant. Seeing the performance just a day or two after the death of Ellen Stewart, the doyenne of New York's downtown theatre scene, made the performance even more of a testimony to time's passing, an even more nostalgic, slightly doleful examination of life's fleeting.

Before the show begins, as the audience waits upstairs in Dixon Place's own small lounge, Shaw mingles, asking people what they miss about New York (be it a person or a building) and taking notes on small pieces of square white paper. Dressed formally in a black tux and cumberbund, with a lively black-and-white bow tie topping her on-going illusion of gentlemanliness, Shaw is a woman with a mission – she chats, but she's collecting impressions, ideas, words, and names. When the audience descends to the theatre, Shaw accompanies us. Weaver is pre-set, sitting on a black wooden stool and slumped against the black wire bar that's the evening's only set piece. Weaver wears a wide black-and-white horizontally striped dress adorned with excessive petticoats, a black velvet bodice, and a décolletage deep enough to store some of her (and our) secrets. Stoll, too, is already present, standing sentinel by her electronic keyboard, an unlit cigarette dangling from her lips, white against her purple-black dinner jacket. Throughout the short evening, she plays, sometimes 1950s standards to which Shaw and Weaver sing in off-key, heartfelt renditions, sometimes instrumentals, wistful melodies that set the evening's scene and its tone.

The "lounge" act provides the evening's conceit and its structure, while "lost" provides its theme. Shaw and Weaver play – although *Lost Lounge* is in some ways a "reality" show – an embattled duo who've worked together long enough to be able to predict one another's moves and motives, whose long-term relationship chafes just enough to give their act a testy edge. In fact, when Weaver turns her back, Shaw flicks folded up bits of paper at her, whether to get her attention or to annoy her. Weaver and Shaw have explored these themes before in their duets as Split Britches (they formed the influential, historic feminist performance troupe with Deb Margolin in the early 1980s, and now use the name themselves). Their work together – *It's a Small House and We Live in it Always*, for example – often tracks the emotional complications of a once romantic, life-long working relationship.

But the performance of on-stage intimacy takes on new poignancy in *Lost Lounge*, in part because Shaw and Weaver are now squarely middle-aged, and in part because they perform their own longevity and their relationship's changes against the backdrop of a city transforming in ways they mourn. The video projections of demolition and deconstruction and the clanging, beeping sounds of jackhammers and dump trucks backing up and moving out evoke the work that's been on-going at Ground Zero for the last 10 years. But it also recalls the rest of downtown Manhattan and its many, if less cataclysmic, losses. When, at the show's end, the performers read the slips of paper that describe the losses Shaw collected from us in the lobby, describing what and who we miss, we hear people refer to restaurants and other neighborhood locales that no longer exist, as well as people (more than one referred to Stewart's death). Weaver expresses her own astonishment at how quickly these changes are wrought. One day, she remarks, the Bowery mainstay Marion's is there, flourishing, and the next, the neighborhood restaurant is just…gone. Spectators hiss at the mention of New York University, whose corporate expansion plans have changed much of the West and East Village into a student dorm.

Lost Lounge mourns these changes, but at the same time, it celebrates what endures. Weaver and Shaw (or their "characters") might harp at one another, but they're there, witnessing one another's solo performance turns and helping one another with grace, respect, and love. One of the evening's loveliest numbers is meant to be funny – and generates a few laughs and no doubt a lot of smiles – but it's also deeply moving: Shaw and Weaver dance, partnering one another through iconic ballroom dancing poses and moves. But they need assistance to carry it off. Instead of accomplishing the bends and lifts and twirls with which a younger couple might display their virtuosity, the set's ubiquitous black stool is used as an assistive dancing device for those whose bones and muscles and tendons can't emulate those movements without it.

Weaver lays across the stool as she falls back into Shaw's arms in a conventional swoon, and rather than lifting Weaver when she leaps, Shaw holds up the stool. Weaver reaches up toward it, representing, rather than executing, the balletic moves of a conventional romantic duet. The partners accomplish the scene with the wink and nod that's the signature of *Lost Lounge*, but its melancholic implications are inescapable. These performers are aging women, whose bodies can't quite realize everything for which their imaginations continue to wish. And yet at the same time, they're observant, mordant, and smart, prodding us to see what's lost and what's gained in the inexorable progress of personal and public history.

Shaw and Weaver have always been very physical performers, actors who devise their own choreography (with help from Stormy Brandenberger) and dialogue, fashioning their numbers from a wish-list of images, ideas, and issues to which their desires lead them. *Lost Lounge* lets them mash up the crooning melodies of lounge singers (one of their best duets is "Autumn Leaves") with the direct address of stand-up comics, combined with the feminist insights of the political project that always grounds their work. Their career-long interventions in conventional gender performance and the signs of sexuality continue to flourish here, as Shaw's mercurial gentleman courts and cares for Weaver's femme dynamo. Shaw runs through her quintessential poses, arms up in the air, Richard Nixon-style, pointing and punctuating, fiery and present. Weaver is a solid, dependable presence, hands on her hips around her big hoop skirt, casting her ironic gaze in our direction.

Both performers get down and dirty. Shaw lies on the floor close to the top of the show to listen, she says, to the sounds of the earth, and Weaver falls to the ground later on, her petticoats awry, to deliver a ruminative monologue. They aren't ginger with themselves – Weaver and Shaw's whole-hearted physical investment continues to be risky and delightful, a model for how to dispense with fear of foolishness. These two have always been clowns of a sort, but rather than playing for laughs, they play for insights, creating a community of presumptively like-minded folks. We're something of a coterie crowd, the audience at this performance, an assumption borne out when Shaw, Weaver, and Stoll read what spectators miss about New York, and the performers, invariably, nod in recognition and agreement. Shaw and Weaver see the world through the unique, productive perspective of people who've been around the block and know its history intimately.

A palpable sense of "then and now" infuses *Lost Lounge*. But Shaw and Weaver don't intend to chastise those who know the present better than the past. Rather, they suggest a kind of costs-benefits analysis of what happens when time passes, when neighborhoods change, when the small get devoured by the large. *Lost Lounge* is finally a generous gesture, an opportunity, Weaver tells us, for us to "rest," since we so rarely get the chance. In fact, the show moves more slowly than their other work; several times, a big digital clock is projected on the screen behind the performers, and they stand, silently, while a few minutes tick by in something of a doomsday countdown. Or perhaps it's just a time-out, a real rest, an opportunity to truly lounge, together, inspired and moved by our favorite lesbian feminist downtown performers, who carry our history and help us imagine our collective future.

JANUARY 18, 2011

Bridesmaids

Universal Pictures, premiered 2011

Bridesmaids' release on DVD gave me the pleasure of watching the movie for the third time, after seeing it twice in theatres when it was released last spring. The pure pleasure of a comedy that celebrates, instead of denigrates, women is worth repeated viewings, and the DVD extras, with deleted scenes and spliced-together dialogue that had to be cut from the final version, is well worth watching for the utter hilarity of actors riffing on moments that were necessarily shortened for release. Enjoying the outtakes and extras only underlined what continues to be the movie's importance as a feminist intervention into popular culture.

Written by Annie Mumolo and Kristen Wiig (*Saturday Night Live*) and executive produced by Judd Apatow, *Bridesmaids* lets its women in on the joke instead of using them as its butt. Centered on Annie, Wiig's quirky character, *Bridesmaids* draws a surprisingly complex portrait of a young woman whose life plans have gone at least temporarily awry and now finds herself about to be abandoned by her best friend, who's suddenly engaged to be married. With a mixture of goofy self-deprecation, cutting sarcasm, and sincere sadness and emotional confusion, Wiig creates a character who appears more real, sympathetic, and just plain interesting than many women in recent mainstream films.

In a refreshing twist on the Apatow formula, the jokes in *Bridesmaids* rest mostly on the men. The film opens with a hilarious scene in which Annie has a tryst with her sex-partner, Ted (played by Jon Hamm, nearly unrecognizable in this break from his dour *Mad Men* role). He's a sexual adventurer whose ministrations to Annie are boisterous, wild, and entirely self-serving. After an evening of impossible positions and loud vocalizing, she breaks the rules of their affair and stays the night. In the morning, Ted pretends he regrets asking her to leave, but he's barely able to mask how eager he is for her departure. He even forgets to buzz her out of his driveway gate; Wiig's climb over the fence is one of the film's many moments of physical humor. In Wiig's elegantly embodied and acutely emotional performance, Annie's humiliation motivates a budding self-respect that allows her to move onward and upward in her quest for a life with agency.

Annie and Lillian (the terrific Maya Rudolph), Annie's soon-to-be-married best friend, talk about sex in a coffee shop, where they eat French fries and other fatty foods after trying to crash an outdoor boot-camp-style exercise session in a local park without paying for it. Annie has spent the night with Ted, and Lillian inquires whether he slept in her mouth, asking fairly directly whether she gave him head. The two proceed to act out the weird insistence of a penis approaching a woman's mouth. Wiig closes one eye and tries to be "round," at which she fails, she admits, because her elbows are too angular. But the women's cheerful parody of male anatomy and desire is very funny and quite outré, if only because it's so rarely seen and heard in mainstream film. I'd say this scene competes with the deli scene from *When Harry Met Sally* for the best publicly performed demonstration of sexual ridiculousness.

Although *Bridesmaids* is about a wedding gone way out of control, it isn't about Annie's desire for a husband. It's also not a critique of marriage per se, though most of its married women characters are unhappy. *Bridesmaids* is instead about Annie's grief over losing her very best friend to a wedding that interrupts their intimacy. Wiig and co-writer Mumolo demonstrate how the machinery of conventional weddings pulls brides into its maw and doesn't shake them loose until after the honeymoon. The film takes aim at the excess of the marriage industry, hilariously deflating the pretentions of salespeople who peddle dreams of perfection. It also illustrates that weddings are really about the women anyway. All the preparation and planning, all the celebrating before the big day itself – the shower, the bridal luncheon – is organized and attended only by women, creating a homosocial environment from which to launch them rather unceremoniously into heterosexual marriage which, *Bridesmaids* none too subtly suggests, is no bargain.

On an ill-fated plane ride to a bachelorette party in Las Vegas, for example, we learn that Lillian's friend, Rita (Wendi McLendon-Covey), can't stand having sex with her husband, who hasn't kissed her in five years, and that another friend, Becca (Ellie Kemper), has never been with a man other than her husband, whose OCD is so pronounced that after they clean themselves in preparation for sex, he's too tired to do it. Rita and Becca's confessionals, greased by in-flight cocktails, send them into a make-out session with one another in their first class plane seats. And when Lillian leaves the table for a moment at a luncheon Annie organizes before the women go to select their brides-maids' dresses, Lillian's sister-in-law-to-be, Megan (played to deadpan perfection with stunning physical humor by the wonderful Melissa McCarthy) explains that Lillian is probably crying her eyes out in the bathroom because her brother, Doug, whom Lillian is about to marry, is such an asshole.

Although her off-kilter and off-color comments come from nowhere, the off-handed remark seems to predict the same unhappiness that Lillian's friends suffer in their own marriages. But we have to take Megan's word for it; in the few scenes in which Doug even appears in *Bridesmaids*, he doesn't utter a single line. His silence is a brilliant touch in a very smart film. Wiig and Mumolo slyly suggest that it doesn't matter who plays the groom in this narrative – the girlfriends will be torn asunder regardless, and that's what Annie mourns.

In addition to the pending loss of her best friend, Annie's cake shop has failed and her boyfriend has fled. Because the shop closed, she feels like a failure. And because Lillian's marriage plans leave her lonely and make her feel inept, she can't pull herself together. Annie now works as a salesclerk in a jewelry store where she can't keep herself from puncturing the dreams and romance of its shoppers. An Asian couple who want wedding rings and a teenaged girl eager to buy a necklace for her own BFF all get an earful from the disappointed and dejected Annie until she's finally fired.

Because she doesn't have any money, Annie lives with Gil (Matt Lucas), a bald British man and his slovenly sister, Brynn (the pitch perfect Rebel Wilson), who shows off an absurd tattoo of a Mexican in a sombrero drinking a cocktail that she got from a man working from a van off the curb. When Annie tells her the tattoo is infected and that she should put a bag of frozen peas on her back to subdue the inflammation, Brynn proceeds to bend over and pour the loose peas all over her back and onto the floor. People in *Bridesmaids* do these sorts of things – Brynn isn't even a lead and isn't even in the front of the shot when she enacts this hilarious moment. We get to enjoy Wiig's reaction to her instead; she's masterful at the incredulous but somehow generous eye roll.

All the film's subplots conspire to humiliate Annie and to heighten her sense of entrapped failure. Compounding her depression is that another woman has horned in on her friendship with Lillian. Her fiancé's boss's wife, Helen (Rose Byrne), is wealthy and chic, impossibly thin and over-the-top with her fashion sense, which extends from the gown she wears to Lillian's engagement party to the spectacle of a wedding she throws for her. Helen is tone-deaf when it comes to understanding what Lillian might really want or prefer, even though she means well. Helen isn't a stereotypical alpha female who sails in to destroy everyone in her path. In fact, we eventually find out that she's lonely. Her own husband travels continually – I'm not sure we ever even see him – and she doesn't have other girlfriends. She pulls Lillian away from Annie because she desperately needs female intimacy and is accustomed to simply buying it.

Bridesmaids' scenes of Annie and Helen competing with one another for Lillian's affections are hysterical moments in which the two women try to top one another. At Lillian's engagement party, they battle publicly over who's closer to the bride. Both Helen and Annie keep returning to the dais to add postscripts to their toasts, fighting over the microphone as well as the right to put the period on the evening's remarks. When Lillian urges them to spend time getting to know one another, they wind up on a tennis court, playing doubles in one of the most viciously, hilariously staged matches I've ever seen on film. Annie and Helen are ruthless opponents, sending overheads and forehands into one another's chests and heads, in a montage of a game that's cut frantically from one wounding shot to the next. Yet somehow, director Paul Feig keeps these scenes from being mean-spirited, since it's clear that their friendship with Lillian is somehow at stake. Helen and Annie become her female suitors, one trying harder than the other to keep her affections close.

Since this is an Apatow-produced movie, *Bridesmaids* includes its share of scatological humor. When the women head for the bridal salon to choose their dresses, they've just come from a Brazilian restaurant where Annie hosted their luncheon. As soon as they're zipped into their potential outfits, the friends start to sweat visibly, as food poisoning makes its way through their systems and into their awareness. In the pristine, pretentious white salon, nothing could be more deliciously irreverent than six women in fancy gowns suddenly afflicted with nausea, vomiting, and diarrhea. As the frantic saleswoman shouts that they should use the bathroom across the street, one bridesmaid after another heads for the salon's chic marble facility, where they projectile vomit in the general vicinity of the toilet. When Megan feels her lunch exiting from below instead of above and the toilet is already occupied, she heaves herself onto the sink to relieve herself, implore the others to "Look away! Look away!"

Some critics found the gross-out humor gratuitous. I found it fitting, because it shows women capable of the over-the-top physical comedy that vomit-, shit-, and fart-jokes afford men. And those leaky bodies soiling the bridal salon can't help but comment on the capitalist pretensions of such shops and how they're calculated to make women look as though their bodies are too perfect to be human at all. The wedding does indeed make Annie sick; she's not jealous of it so much as she's suspicious of how little it represents the Lillian she knows and loves. The gross-out scenes, in other words, are nothing compared to the critique of the marriage industry *Bridesmaids* launches. All this lead-up, Wiig and Mumolo suggest, and for what? Rita relates stories about her three boys, how they smell and how they cover everything with their uncontrollable semen. She tells Becca, who's desperate for her own child, that when she's slaving to make dinner and one of her sons is pissed because she won't let him get a pizza instead, he tells Rita to go fuck herself. In reality, the relationships and families that jewelry stores and bridal salons romanticize ground lives in which women service men and slog through the isolated grind of providing a domestic life to ungrateful, selfish families.

But because *Bridesmaids* is, after all, a comedy, its happy ending comes with the appropriate man packaged and delivered. Annie meets an Irish cop named Rhodes (the charming Chris O'Dowd), when he stops her on the street because her car's tail lights are out. He's a gentle and generous man who used to eat in her cake shop and waives her ticket when he realizes who she is and that she's depressed. Improbably but amusingly, their paths cross on the highway more than once, and she impulsively asks him to hang out. That he's "right" for her is obvious when he brings her the ingredients to make a cake the morning after the first night they spend together. But Annie isn't yet ready for a nice guy and sabotages their affair until after Lillian's outrageously spectacular wedding, when she can be free to attach herself elsewhere.

Bridesmaids gets all the details right. The wedding shower's excesses push just over the top the choices that grace many of these events. The chocolate fountain at Lillian's shower is a real, outdoor fountain in which the chocolate flows down three stone tiers; the "best wishes" cookie is so large it sits on an easel; and the party favors for the guests are little yellow Labrador retriever puppies, who wear pink beanies because the theme of the proceedings is French. Wiig and Mumolo tweak the conventions just enough to point out how ridiculous they actually are.

Bridesmaids doesn't really twist the narrative of love and marriage as we know it. Of course Annie and Rhodes will become a couple at the end – part of Annie's trajectory toward really knowing herself is realizing that she deserves him. It's no surprise when he pulls up after Lillian's wedding to take her home, although it's refreshing that they don't reconcile *before* the ceremony. A more conventional film would have had him standing at Annie's side, or would have had her catching the bouquet at the end, excessively signaling that all will be well and that Annie will get the husband she seems to desire. But although the plot outline fills in the dots, the script is sophisticated enough to avoid these obvious clichés. A scene between Helen and Annie at the end also underlines that this is really a story about women. The two former adversaries have nothing to compete over once Lillian's wedding has gone off like a July 4th spectacular, and even the manic Helen (played with wistful comic timing by Rose Bryne) seems rueful as she and Annie say goodbye. Impulsively, they agree to have lunch, which cheers both women more than they expect and implies that a new, real friendship might emerge from all the wedding bother. Their final embrace is a warm, hopeful moment that balances Rhodes' appearance with his cop car. In this case, the girl might get the guy, but she's going to hang on to her girlfriends, too.

JUNE 23, 2011

Once, The Musical

Produced at New York Theatre Workshop, 2011

When you enter New York Theatre Workshop's space on E. 4th Street to see *Once,* the musical adaptation of the 2007 Irish indie film, the well-worn theatre suddenly feels like a party hall. The stage has been transformed into a bar, replete with distressed old mirrors and sconce lights, and a low counter that serves double-duty as a place for spectators to get a pint before the play proper starts and as a secondary acting platform for the considerable talents of this musically distinguished and emotionally empathetic cast. In Irish playwright Enda Walsh's faithful adaptation of the film, the Dublin community on which the story focuses is bound by its music-making. The cast is small by musical theatre standards, since the community here, usually represented by dozens of supernumeraries, is the close-knit one of Dublin street buskers and musicians soulfully devoted to music as an expression of their pining spirits.

Steve Kazee plays "the guy," a recently jilted, emotionally and artistically ambivalent singer/songwriter who, at the show's beginning, after a wrenching solo, has decided to abandon his battered guitar on the street as a kind of remnant of his own lost soul. But "the girl" (like "the guy," also nameless, an odd conceit borrowed from the film) overhears his ballad and brings him emphatically back to his music and to his life. Played by the lovely, energetic Cristin Milioti (last seen at NYTW in Ivo Van Hove's *Little Foxes*), she drags him to a music store where she borrows a piano on which to accompany him in her resonant, equally soulful style. Through sheer will and a bit of artfully withheld romance, she encourages him to resume his music-making in America, where he can reconnect with his departed girlfriend and have a wonderful life.

As in the film, music expresses the duo's personalities and their yearnings. The musical's loveliest and most haunting number remains the Academy Award-winning "Falling Slowly," written and performed in the film by Glen Hansard and Markéta Irglová, the original guy and girl who remain credited for the music and lyrics of this adaptation. The ballad grows as a duet between the couple, whose voices blend perfectly as their separate instruments play a kind of syncopated, already sad flirtation. Although the pair fall in love as soon as they begin harmonizing together, the musical keeps them apart rather than uniting this typically central heterosexual couple as more conventional musical narratives are wont to do. One of the pleasures of *Once* is watching it resist this stereotypical formula. The community that typically mirrors the central couple's initial opposition – like the cowboys and the farmers who should be friends in *Oklahoma* – here are already united.

Walsh manufactures some humorous initial conflict between Billy (Paul Whitty), the music store owner, and the bank manager (Andy Taylor) to whom the girl and guy turn for a loan to make their album. When the banker turns out to be a closeted musician (and a not-so-closeted gay man), he gives the couple the money and joins the band, overcoming Billy's suspicion of capitalists to become part of the singing and playing ensemble. That band of sympathetic brothers and sisters is one of the sweetest things about this very sweet show. Director John Tiffany (*Black Watch*, The National Theatre of Scotland) keeps his instrument-playing and singing cast on stage throughout *Once*, John Doyle-style. He guides them toward saloon-style chairs that line the wide proscenium stage in-between numbers. From there, they watch the action intently and provide the occasional musical punctuation or undertone. The several acoustic guitars, an electric bass, a banjo, an accordion, a ukulele, a bass, and two violins, as well as a drum set employed in the climactic studio-recording scene, compose the orchestra, all played by members of the cast. The mournful ballads underscore the fated love story and the musicians provide pre-show and intermission Irish pub music to persuade the audience into the Dublin world of *Once*.

And the audience loves it. They approach the bar on stage willingly before the show and during the intermission, where cast and crew pull pints of Guinness and other beers. Several spectators the night I attended danced with the musicians who sang together center stage, stomping their feet Riverdance-style and making that particularly Irish sort of merry before the central story got underway. The pre-show party is a fun theatrical choice, shaking up, as it does, the conventional separation between performer and spectator. Creating a pub environment that lets the show be small and intimate signals from the start that *Once* is not aspiring to be a standard musical spectacle that would mock the more personal commitments at the film's heart.

The guy lives with his father (David Patrick Kelly), a crusty old Dubliner called "Da," above the vacuum repair shop they run together. When the girl finds the guy losing heart on the street, she asks him to fix her Hoover, insisting that he make the machine "suck." Because she's Czech – and Walsh gets a fair amount of mileage from her Eastern European seriousness – she soberly sets about the task of re-inspiring the guy toward his own talents. He's grudging at first, floundering on the shoals of lost love and confusion about his own ambitions. But she's insistent. In the first act, in fact, she's a bit too single-minded in her intention to repair his heart and appears to be the stereotypical girl in the service of a guy's future rather than her own. But Walsh gives the character more nuances in the second act. She has a child and a husband who's on his way back to Dublin from a trial separation. And although she's drawn to the guy, she has a stalwart morality that requires her to try to make her marriage work. That the guy and the girl clearly love one another but don't become lovers is a refreshing tactic for a musical. Their attraction shimmers around the show, and their sad but appropriate failure to consummate their love makes *Once* wistful and somehow true about those complicated affairs of the heart.

Bob Crowley's evocative set and costumes are lit beautifully by Natasha Katz, who graces the actors with romantic, introspective warmth that seems to deepen their emotional complexity. Many of the show's scenes take place in squares of light that mark off the space, carving it into private encounters between pairs of characters: the guy and his father; the guy and the girl; Billy and his date. *Once*, as a result, is an intimate, surprisingly quiet affair, in which between the numbers the characters spend time simply talking to one another about their desires, hopes, and dreams.

The show's choreography is light and unobtrusive, but occasionally inspired, as when the girl and the guy, in separate images, seem to sculpt the air with their arms, providing circles of warmth and closeness into which one of the other performers walks. For instance, the girl, downstage center, curves her arm out in front of her, and one of the other women moves into her embrace, leaning her back into the girl's chest and circling her arm around her waist so that the girl can lay her chin on the other woman's shoulder. In another light but poignant dance moment, when the girl listens to the guy's music on a pair of large headphones, the two other young women in the cast (both of whom play the violin) mirror her as she moves about the stage, their hands outstretched into the air with the exhilaration of listening to sounds you love.

Once is a charming production, currently selling out at NYTW and poised to move to Broadway in February. The show premiered at Diane Paulus's American Repertory Theatre in Cambridge before the move to

NYTW; its investors have apparently always planned on a Broadway run. When the show moves to the Bernard Jacobs Theatre, I only hope it finds a way to retain its appealing intimacy for a larger audience. It would be a shame to sacrifice the pub-like atmosphere of the theatre and the quiet simplicity of the acting and the singing, or to make the show wholly bigger for a Broadway crowd. The charm of *Once* comes from the appropriate scale of its ambitions – to tell a story through lovely ballads, sung from broken, yearning young hearts.

DECEMBER 19, 2011

A Midsummer Night's Dream

Produced at Classic Stage Company, New York, NY, 2012

The Classic Stage Company in New York invariably uses their odd, three-quarter semi-thrust stage with imagination and innovation, but director John Speciale's glorious production of Shakespeare's classic comedy pushes the potential of the space even further. Speciale and set designer Mark Wendland render the play's court and forest settings with great visual and physical wit. A mirrored back wall that extends from the floor to the flies slants over the stage, carved with rectangular squares that open unexpectedly to reveal characters and to allow unseen stagehands to pass props into the playing space. The stage floor is covered with rough black rubber mulch, which gives the actors bounce and verve and creates an evocative base from which the production's design and performance colors pop.

Against the dark mulched landscape and that glittering, beautifully lit mirror, Speciale and costume designer Andrea Lauer dress the cast in contemporary (if vaguely Edwardian) clothes in muted colors of beige and grey for the men and white for the women, except for the formidable Hippolyta (Bebe Neuwirth). She sports a skin-tight, black riding outfit complete with a fearsome crop for her opening scene, in which she mourns for her stolen Indian boy and scowls with derision at Theseus's (Anthony Heald) affectionate protestations. Theseus's white suit and black tie fit the barrel-chested Heald tightly. He looks like a square box of a man, his courtly power emanating from his trunk and his voice, which resonates through that impressive chest as he articulates Shakespeare's chewy words with kingly clarity. Hippolyta, by comparison, has to use her costume to derive her power, because Neuwirth is as thin as a piece of paper.

Midsummer's well-known comedy is most often played for laughs at the expense of Hermia and Helena, whose squabble over their men drives the romantic love plot. Hermia is betrothed to Demetrius but loves Lysander; Helena pines for Demetrius even though he scorns her. Helena offers to be his "spaniel," so that Demetrius can beat her and otherwise mistreat her but still enjoy her devotion. Demetrius and Lysander are typically interchangeable, and in conventional productions can seem handsome but listless, since directors assign much of the comic business to the women. Speciale plays the men's bland sameness to comic effect, giving them nearly twin-like appearances and mirrored Adonis-like physiques.

The women are slightly more distinct. As Hermia, Christina Ricci sports the raven-colored hair that's mocked when Lysander, cruelly enchanted by Puck's potion, falls out of love with her during their night in the forest. As Helena, Halley Wegryn Gross is Hermia's blond counterpart, wearing her long hair in a swathe across her forehead that she brushes aside as self-consciously as a Valley girl. In her first entrance, Helena seems startling fragile, her tooth-pick-sized arms poking from a short white shift that barely covers her torso. Both women are stunningly thin. But Speciale plays off the slight stature of Hippolyta, Helena, and Hermia to make mockery of the men. Though Demetrius (Nick Gehlfuss) is slightly taller, as the night of amorous confusions proceeds and all the lovers are stripped of their pretensions (and their clothing, until finally, all four cavort madly in their underwear), he and Lysander (Jordan Dean) become visually interchangeable, their carrot-colored hair, white skin, six-pack abs, and bulging biceps mirroring one another in joyously homoerotic and physically flamboyant performances.

The night's madness, fueled by Puck's potions, moves Lysander and Demetrius to heights of emotion, where they express their love for Hermia and their antipathy for Helena in tornadoes of self-flagellation and exertion that leave their impressive bodies shimmering with sweat. The physical investment of all four lead performers contributes to the production's great fun. The very strong men wrestle and the very small women use their would-be mates to box with one another. Seeing Ricci and Gross perched on Gehlfuss's and Dean's shoulders for the catfight is hilarious but also gives the women their own purchase on tall power. When Theseus finds the lovers at dawn the next morning, pulling back a stage-sized silk covering to reveal them, the four remain in their underwear, piled together with limbs intertwined like puppies. Hippolyta, too, has been transformed, appearing for the morning in a less severe riding outfit, persuaded to love Theseus despite his machinations with the Indian boy.

Part of *Midsummer*'s fun is its meta-theatricality, funneled through the rude mechanicals and their rehearsals in the forest for the duke's nuptials. The five joiners and tinkers and workers double here as Titania's fairies in the forest, and then serve triple duty as waiters in the court scenes, where they're dressed in white shirts and dark pants and aprons, and move around the wire and wood chairs used to represent Theseus's court. The chairs look exactly like those scattered about Bryant Park and the Times Square mall in mid-town Manhattan, which brings the production a nice contemporary, intertextual reference to large urban settings. The simple light chairs also let Speciale move his actors around and then into the forest with a minimum of scenic fuss.

As for the rude mechanicals, Steven Skybell is terrific as the scenery-chewing Bottom, bringing all the appropriate effusive histrionics to his demonstrations of thespian prowess, but also finding a welcomed pathos at the end of his strange and wondrous evening as an ass romancing Titania in the forest. Skybell makes Bottom adorable and in his own right talented. He puts his own stamp on Bottom's signature death throes in the Pyramus and Thisbee scene, using sounds and gyrations to demonstrate Bottom's inability to exit the stage. David Greenspan plays Francis Flute/Cobweb/Thisbee, in one of Speciale's two campy queer casting choices. Greenspan does his renowned swanning about, playing Francis Flute as a forgetful but ruminative mechanical, and an appropriately wistful and quiet Thisbee to Bottom's blustery Pyramus.

In another coup of queer casting, Taylor Mac plays Egeus/Puck. Practically unrecognizable as the angered, bearded father in the opening court scene, Mac transforms into Puck with outrageous performative mugging. Ordered about the forest by the imperious Oberon (Heald transformed into a more macho king of the fairies, with knee pads and layers of silky dark clothing), Puck enters every scene with a new outfit and persona that have nothing directly to do with the proceedings at hand. In one, he's dressed as something of a milkmaid; in another, he's a clown with a large golden Afro and a bodysuit of bold red and white stripes (which most resembles Mac's typical drag-freak style). He enters to correct the lovers' star-crossed liaisons in a strange stuffed animal-like outfit, with big elephant ears sticking off the side of his head and then forming the dress of his outfit, while his chest is bare but for a pair of suspenders. In another, he appears naked except for a pair of tight striped briefs. In each of his appearances, Mac plays the drag queen, speaking Puck's lines and performing his actions but also improvising with the audience, tossing off extemporaneous asides, and playing the ukulele, which he asks a spectator to bring him from the case that's hidden under her seat.

Puck-as-drag-queen works beautifully to highlight the sexual transformations the night brings to the forest, in which Titania loves an ass, the lovers' stars temporarily cross, and Puck and Oberon become the puppet masters who put the evening's shenanigans in motion then sit back to watch them unfold. As they watch the lovers quarrel through the night, Oberon and Puck arrange themselves on beach chairs under the mirrored stage wall, in which a square opens and disembodied hands pass through popcorn and sodas which the fairy king and his henchman enjoy as they observe the passing show of the couples' conflagrations. It's a smoothly executed moment, another meta-theatrical witticism that reminds spectators that we, too, are enthralled by the evening's adventures. And enthralled we are. The audience was reduced to fits of laughter throughout and thanks to Mac's willful and frequent breaking of the fourth wall – throwing clothing and other props at first-row spectators in CSC's intimate space – often implicated in the madness.

The production's original music – by Christian Frederickson and Ryan Rumery – also added nice undertones. Erin Hill, as both Robin Starveling and "First Fairy," and as the only female mechanical and fairy, wearing a gossamer, fanciful dress and sporting a ginger beard, played a harp and sang to accompany some of the music. Rob Yang, as Peter Quince, played a guitar melody underneath his recitation of the story of Pyramus and Thisbee and accompanied Bottom and Flute as they performed their scenes. Incidental music throughout helped modulate the production's mood.

With a game cast and a coherent comic vision, this *Midsummer* proved a wonderful evening of gender performance and play, an earnest, energetic engagement with revelries of sexual confusion and reassessment. Even if by the morning all the relationships are set aright and heterosexuality and marriage reasserted, the glorious theatrical freedom to evoke a queer night lingers over the scene and reminds us that all is never necessarily as it seems.

APRIL 23, 2012

Your Sister's Sister

Ada Films, premiered 2012

Lynn Shelton's lovely, intimate film was written in collaboration with her actors, who are credited as "creative consultants," mostly because Shelton gives them a rough outline of a scene and then lets them fill it with dialogue, personality, and character. Mark Duplass, Emily Blunt, and Rosemarie DeWitt are terrific as three people whose lives are knit together in surprising and complicated ways. The film feels like a short story; it's compact but rich, full of detail and the authenticity of lives lived in a raw present moment. Hannah (DeWitt), Iris (Blunt), and Jack (Duplass) form points on a triangle that becomes a circle by the film's end. Iris once dated Jack's brother, Tom, whose memorial service, marking a year after his death, begins the film. Jack's emotions about his brother's loss are still raw; he behaves badly enough among his friends that Iris suggests he retreat up to her father's cabin on an island near Seattle (where the film is set) to get his head together.

When Jack arrives at the cabin – by bicycle, as Iris insists, knowing better than he does what he needs – he finds it already occupied by Hannah, Iris's half-sister, who's come to escape her own emotional woes. She's left a seven-year relationship with a woman named Pam after realizing that whatever had held them together was long gone. Although Hannah and Jack have never met, they've heard about one another from Iris, who adores them both. The two rather lost souls spend an evening getting drunk, hit it off, and on a whim, find themselves in bed together. Iris arrives at the house unexpectedly the next morning and Jack insists that he and Hannah keep their dalliance secret. Hannah doesn't understand the need for subterfuge, until she and her half-sister go for a walk on which Iris confesses that she's in love with Jack. Pained by her inadvertent betrayal, Hannah realizes she has to come clean about their evening together. But it turns out Hannah had ulterior motives – she's decided she wants to have a baby and used sex with Jack as an insemination strategy. Although it might not have meant anything at first, as the trio's emotional complications heighten, the one-night stand looms much larger in all three character's lives.

Narrated schematically, the film could sound melodramatic and glib, but it's performed with such grace and generosity that *Your Sister's*

Sister stays winning and true. All three actors have wonderful chemistry. Watching Blunt and DeWitt perform as half-sisters made me realize how rarely we get to see intimacy between women – as friends or family – on screen. How nice to see Blunt and DeWitt play scenes in which their familiarity is physical as well as emotional; Iris and Hannah unselfconsciously curl around one another in bed and hook arms together as they walk.

Hannah and Jack's inadvertent betrayal of Iris prompts the film's crisis, but director Shelton's camera simply watches as the anger and tension between the women morphs back into love and trust. They're related; they adore one another. Even about something that feels so monumental, they can't stay mad. Blunt and DeWitt are wonderful in nearly silent scenes in which their glances dart toward and away from one another, until finally they're secure enough to rest in each other's gazes again. When Iris crawls into Hannah's bed to offer to raise the baby with her, if Hannah is indeed pregnant, the moment is moving and hopeful, performed simply and intelligently but with great heart by Blunt and DeWitt, and filmed from above, with a camera that simply watches the exchange.

Fearful of family conflagration, Jack leaves the house after Iris learns he's slept with Hannah, his own feelings confused and inexplicable. He camps out around the island, haplessly riding his bike and putting up a make-shift tent and sleeping in coffee shops. But when he returns to the cabin, he's found enough emotional resources to admit his love for Iris, and to offer to somehow be in the baby's life if Hannah is pregnant. Jack is unemployed, and he's still something of a mess over his brother's death, but something in the triangle appeals to his bedrock sense of possibility and potential. His willingness to be part of Iris's and Hannah's lives is adult and hopeful; the three of them hug one another when he returns, and the film ends with the trio crammed into a small bathroom, waiting for Hannah's pregnancy test to turn color.

Your Sister's Sister could be a play, since it's really a well-observed character study built on the small but key gestures of relationship made by people who know one another very well. But the peaceful remoteness of the island setting provides the isolation of a place where Hannah, Iris, and Jack can forge something new on their own. In Seattle, surrounded by friends, committing to one another and a reinterpretation of family might have been more difficult. And then there's the location – the beautiful cabin on a lake in the woods, where spirits can be restored and psyches reordered.

As I watched the film, I found myself wondering why we care so much who people have sex with. That is, in this story, Jack and Hannah fall into bed hugely drunk, he comes very quickly, she's left unsatisfied and, the next morning, mortified that they had sex at all (except, of course, that she's poked holes in the condom hoping she can use Jack's sperm to make her baby). But their brief moment together changes everything, at first for the worst and then for the best. That's what's hopeful and rather brilliant about Shelton's small, affecting movie – that she turns a cliché into a possibility for reinventing how families are made. It's not revolutionary, but it's something.

JUNE 30, 2012

"How-To" Guide

How to Practice Feminist Criticism and Spectatorship

My own career as an arts writer began through feminism. When as a sophomore in college I regretfully gave up acting because of how it constrained my own gender expression and because of what I intuitively felt as its gender-enforcing strategies and norms, I turned to criticism. Feminism was just seeping into the cultural arena in the mid- to late-1970s in the U.S., but the whiff I caught of the zeitgeist was enough to persuade me that being a feminist critic would become my replacement calling. I've practiced feminist criticism and spectatorship now for 35 years, which has naturalized it a bit in my own viewing and reception practices.

The following prompts are meant to parse my own strategies for seeing through a feminist lens and as a "how-to" guide for writing feminist criticism – or for seeing theatre, film, performance, or television from a feminist perspective, whether or not you write about it – that I hope will be helpful for teachers, students, and aficionados alike. Writing, of course, is a way to hone and clarify thinking, and the availability of instant web-based publishing makes the kind of citizen criticism I discuss in the introduction an appealing outlet. But any thoughtful spectator might use these prompts to enhance his or her viewing experience, and to clarify, in discussion, what she or he thought and felt about a play or a film or a television episode. In fact, I hope these prompts inspire discussion of all sorts. Learning how to talk to one another about what we see – one-on-one as well as in classes or informal groups or over meals – is as important to the health of the arts as good critical writing. I've addressed these prompts to a general "you," hoping that any reader might find them provocative and generative, and applicable across multiple situations. I've also used "we" here to conjure a community of feminist spectators and critics, readers and writers, who I hope will include people of all genders, races, ethnicities, classes, and ages.

Looking at gender and race

In some ways, feminist criticism simply requires a keen awareness of how gender, race, and other identities frame relationships in a film, theatre production, or television episode. While many reviewers and critics write about story or narrative structure, and sometimes direct our attention to design choices, camera angles, shot composition, and editing, a feminist critic also looks at the frame for what it tells us about gender and race. Start with who the story is about: Is the play or film about a woman? A white woman? A man? A person of color? An LGBT person? A differently abled person? Although focusing on who a story is "about" might seem narrowly specific, the best stories tell us something about our lives. The best help us imagine different ways to live in relationship to one another; the worst, from a feminist perspective, reinforce old pieties about gender and race. In the most conservative representations, women are mothers, virgins, or whores, the unholy triumvirate that feminist film and theatre critics described and deconstructed beginning in the 1970s. And in some of those same representations, people of color are either nowhere to be seen, or serve the white people's story (typically the white heterosexual man's story) without having power, agency, or desires of their own. When you shift your critical perspective to consider gender and race, and when you see maleness as also gendered and whiteness as also a race, it's remarkable how many representations continue to fit these conservative examples.

Part of a feminist critic/spectator's responsibility is to broaden his or her own frame of reference for what to see, for which cultural products to seek out and consume, to think or write about. Some of the most mainstream products now offer hope for more progressive representations of gender (see *Bridesmaids* and to a certain extent *Brave*, which I discuss in earlier chapters) and sometimes race (see the television series *Scandal*, also discussed above). More and more independent films and off Broadway plays and performances feature women, LGBT people, and people of color in central roles that move the narrative. A feminist critic/spectator's work begins with what we decide to see and consume; our dollars directly influence the future of theatre and film production. And because more and more producers follow blogs and audience responses, the citizen criticism or more formal writing we produce and circulate has a direct effect.

Feminist spectators and critics should consider our spectating choices from a range of perspectives, all of which have real consequences. In summer 2012, for example, a feminist spectator could make a number of decisions about what to see and why, selecting from films alone. She or he might see *Magic Mike*, a Hollywood release about male strippers, but write or talk about it from a feminist perspective. He or she could see *Your Sister's Sister*, an indie film in which the two women characters drive the narrative, and whose relationship to one another and the male friend they both love is nuanced and intimate. Feminist spectators could see *The Amazing Spiderman*, the latest installment in the on-going blockbuster series, or *Ted*, starring Mark Wahlberg as a man with a trash-talking teddy bear as his best friend. We could see Charlize Theron and Kristen Stewart in *Snow White and the Huntsman*, a mainstream film that stars two talented female performers, or *The Dark Knight Rises*, the latest Batman film, which stars only one (but she's the terrific Anne Hathaway). As a feminist spectator, vary your consumption and reception practices. Enjoy what you see – in fact, make enjoyment the central plank of your viewing platform. But discuss and write about what you see from a keen, incisive feminist perspective. Your input and insights will help drive up the level of discourse about the arts. Your response matters.

These questions might help you develop a feminist critical spectating practice of your own:

◆ How does the production frame or the camera organize how we view the narrative that unfolds in front of us? Feminist critics have long identified the "male gaze" in both fields – where do we look to see its operations? In film, camera angles and frame compositions are sometimes easier to see, as they focus our gaze more specifically. Are women in the frame represented as whole bodies or are their parts isolated? How does the camera detach which parts of women's bodies? Are the women characters sexualized? Are they backdrops against which the action of the male characters unfolds? As Alison Bechdel would ask, Do the women in the frame speak? To one another? About anything other than a man?

◆ Likewise, where is race represented in the production or film frame? Are all the bodies on view white? How can you tell, and what does this mean to how we see the relationships unfolding? Are people of color full characters or tokens who simply serve to vary the environment of a scene? Do they speak? About their own desires and agency, or to provide a background for the action of white characters?

♦ Direction in theatre productions and performance is less hegemonic than film cinematography and editing because a spectator is free to look anywhere at all within the frame of a live performance. But a director nonetheless attempts to corral our attention through how a scene is paced; through blocking, in which actors move through the stage space in ways that illustrate their objectives and their relationships to one another; and through the placement of actors' bodies on stage, in which the downstage and center positions are considered more visually and emotionally powerful. How is a production directed to feature a character's gender and race? Are white male characters always the ones standing in the powerful downstage center position? Are women and people of color central to the production's visual field as well as to the narrative's unfolding?

Reviewing the reviews

Too often, we read reviews uncritically, giving over the power of determining where we spend our dollars or how we think about cultural production to those who've been anointed by mainstream, dominant outlets. *The New York Times* for theatre and the arts, the *Los Angeles Times* for film, and a host of other mainstream newspapers and websites best serve this purpose nationally, but regional newspapers also remain trusted sources of information about what to see and why. A feminist critic/spectator contributes to arts discourse by reading reviews critically, to consider what they don't see and what they often explicitly refuse to address, and by noticing what they leave out of their discussions. Do the critics you read address gender and race? When and why and how? Sharpen your awareness of the critical discourse in which you engage and write back to the reviewers you read. I've heard many critics complain that they never hear from readers. Write to them to tell them when you agree or disagree with their assessments and why.

♦ Which critics do you read? Why? In which public venues do they write (or speak, if they're broadcast/podcast critics)? What do you like about their style? Do they engage with the cultural and social meanings of the things they discuss? How might you improve what they do? How might you emulate them as a critic or viewer?

◆ What purpose do you think criticism serves in the world? Are the reviewers you read "political," whether or not they identify themselves as such? Which ideological line does the reviewer seem to toe? What do their reviews accomplish in the world, as well as for the arts in general and for your personal spectating habits in particular?

◆ What do you think should be feminist criticism's specific contribution to arts discourse? Is it corrective? Is it an amplification of critical discourse? What does it add to the world? Is it always critical of what's not there in the frame, or does it also point out what is or might be there in the stories we regularly see, hear, and consume? Feminist criticism has a reputation for negative critique, but I believe this is a stereotype that's been constructed to neutralize its power. How can feminist critics/spectators launch positive critical engagements with culture?

◆ Focus on one or two reviews written by a critic you like, detest, or read frequently. What captured you about the review? Why did you keep reading it? Because you care about the artists who created the work? The subject matter? A performer or designer who worked on it? What makes you gravitate to a review and read it all the way through? What's missing?

◆ Describe the reviewer's strategies. What does he or she think is important? Why? On which aspect of the production does she/he focus? Is the writing "consumer reporting"? Why or why not? What is it meant to make the reader do?

◆ Who is the presumptive audience for the review? Any publication has a specified readership. *The New Yorker* presumes a different readership than *People Magazine* (though some people might read both – I do). But individual writers for each publication often assume their own sense of their readers. Is the reviewer addressing you? How can you tell? If you feel consistently ignored by the critics you read, what might you do about it? If you don't see your own or other people's perspectives represented in criticism, how might you respond?

Description without judgment

When I was in graduate school in performance studies at New York University in the early 1980s, one of my professors, the late Michael Kirby, taught what he called "structuralist" criticism, which required simply describing what you saw in a production and suspending any and all judgment. Working with him in those years (1981–1985) as the managing editor of *The Drama Review*, I practiced the objective description Kirby required, even as these practices chafed against my own feminist predilections. Thinking back, however, I learned a lot from trying to merely describe what I saw. Reviews or criticism can easily get bogged down in plot summary; learning how to combine a discussion of *what* happened with a description of *how* it happened in a play or film is a skill worth practicing. Serving what you've seen by describing it clearly and well is also a crucial part of responsible feminist criticism. I challenge myself to evoke what I saw, especially for people who might not get to see the theatre production I experienced or even for those who might see it but not feel it as I did. I want my words to call up very specifically the aesthetic, political, and emotional quality of what I experienced at the movies or at the theatre. Doing so is more difficult than it sounds.

Since feminist critics/spectators are still too often accused of being partial or (worse) strident, evoking and describing without judgment is an important rhetorical strategy. I encourage emotionally acute responses to art and would never suggest a critic or a spectator hide their anger or enthusiasm for what they see. I hope it's clear that I don't believe in objectivity. But I do think that learning to evoke and describe is a political tactic that will convince people to listen to feminist responses to theatre and film.

◆ Think of a play or production or film or television episode or series that galvanizes you for some reason, about which you'd like to write, speak, muse, or discuss with others. Set some parameters, as an exercise: Who will be your audience? Friends? Of what penchants or tastes? Readers? For what publication? What will or won't they "get" about what you've seen? Is it a blockbuster? Or an avant-garde performance presented in someone's apartment in Williamsburg? Are your interlocutors feminists? Do their identity coordinates – race, class, sexuality – matter?

◆ For how long will you be able to speak to them? That is, will you monopolize the evening's conversation to make your point or do you only have 10 minutes before dinner is served? If you're writing, how many words do you get? Or are you blogging and self-imposing your word count? Do you typically take up space or air time this way? What's the occasion of this writing or speaking and why is it important?

◆ Although these questions are important for any piece of writing or commentary, use them here to set the circumstances for your thoughts. Then assign yourself to simply describe what you saw. Reserve value judgments, although it's fine to be enthusiastic (or not). But do whatever you can to evoke the play/production/film/television show to your readers/listeners without editorializing.

◆ What will you cover? The plot? Genre? Character interactions or details? How the story moves through time and/or space? Will you describe where you saw this or with whom? When? Why? Are these details important? Journalists typically address five issues: who, what, where, when, and how. Critics and spectators might do well to keep these basics in mind.

◆ How can you evoke what you saw and how it made you feel, using only the words you speak or write? How difficult is it to describe something without judging it? What does this prohibition force you to do?

Thinking in context

Conventional reviewing and criticism often looks at a production or a film strangely out of context. That is, a reviewer of a Broadway production usually doesn't describe the audience or the theatre (even though all Broadway theatres aren't the same). The same reviewers rarely point out the differences among production contexts. As I noted in the introduction, seeing a play at Playwrights Horizons on 42nd Street between 9th and 10th Avenues in Manhattan is a different experience than seeing a performance at New York Theatre Workshop, a comparable off Broadway theatre on E. 4th St. between the Bowery and Second Avenue downtown, partially because the geography of the neighborhoods in which these theatres reside is so different. Likewise, seeing a movie in IMAX at a multiplex is different than seeing a film at an art house that doesn't have stadium seating, or than watching a film on DVD or video-on-demand in your living room (or on an iPod, iPad, or laptop). How, where, and with whom we watch a play, performance, television show, or film influences our reception experience and is worth detailing when we write about or discuss what we think about what we saw.

For example, I saw Ethan Lipton's multi-genre cabaret *No Place to Go* at Two River Theater Company in Red Bank, New Jersey, in fall

2012, after its successful run six months earlier at Joe's Pub, part of the Public Theatre complex in the East Village of Manhattan. In the performance, Lipton speaks and sings original songs about his current state of unemployment, describing how adrift he feels as a citizen without the anchoring labor (and paycheck) of a job. Backed by three additional musicians, who join him on sax, guitar, and bass, Lipton wears a suit and speaks directly to the audience, relating mournful stories of being laid off from a mid-level, white-collar position by a firm that decided to move to, well, Mars.

The black box space at Two River Theater had been transformed into a cabaret for the performance. The theatre notified the audience in advance that food would be available for purchase before and even during the performance. But because of New Jersey's liquor licensing laws, no alcohol was served in the theatre. At Joe's Pub, by contrast, a full bar (and a two-drink minimum in addition to the ticket price) means that spectators who imbibe are probably loosened up and open to hearing Lipton's poignant but sometimes non-linear musings. At the Two River Theater, the audience the night I attended looked mostly above 55-years-old and predominantly white. They did take advantage of the food. But without the extra warmth and camaraderie wine, beer, or alcohol might provide, Lipton worked noticeably hard to cajole spectators to follow his flights of employment fantasy. How was *No Place to Go* different at Joe's Pub, a performance space whose name announces that it's a bar, and whose audiences are frequently young, hip, and, given the programming, notoriously open to artistic mélange and experimentation? Space and place are political; they signal power and position, taste and cultural influence. Sociologist Pierre Bourdieu would suggest that they provide the "habitus" – a set of taste practices – for what we choose to consume. For a feminist critic/spectator, widening the discussion beyond the stage and screen to the place and space of viewing opens up the context in all its sociological and cultural complexity.

◆ How does the film's or production's context and venue influence what it means and how you and other spectators react?
◆ What's the history of this production? Did it begin at this theatre? Will it tour? What does this indicate about its presumed audiences? Might this performance mean something different in another location?
◆ Can you judge the audience composition at the performance you attended? How might that matter to the performance's reception? Likewise, films draw different audiences, sometimes at different

showings in different venues. Watching a film with a few people at a matinee might be different than going on a Saturday night at 7:30 or 10:00. Does that change your reception of the movie?
◆ Where is the theatre located? Which activities available before and after the performance might influence how it's received by the audience? How do spectators arrive? Subway? Taxi? Car? Train? Walking? Do they have to park? Where do they appear to go afterwards? Are they "natives" to the theatre's neighborhood or do they travel in and then depart for other neighborhoods after?

Isolating production choices

Every element of what we see on stage or screen has been considered and carefully constructed to tell a story or to promote a certain kind of experience. Describing the narrative or summarizing the plot are the bare essentials of how a feminist critic/spectator might begin to parse out the elements of a film, television show, or theatre production to derive what it meant at this particular historical moment. Narrowing the lens from the whole production context to the choices made on stage (or behind) or on screen lets us consider their implications at a micro-level.

This micro-level provides a fruitful interstice at which to think about gender, race, and class. In how small a gesture, for example, can we see gender produced? If an actor moves his or her wrist this way, do you see him or her as more feminine than if he or she moves it that way? If an actor arranges him or herself on a chair in a particular way, how is she or he performing gender? If an actor speaks with a certain inflection, how is he or she performing race or ethnicity? How can we tell? These questions demonstrate that each choice – from the largest to the smallest – has implications for how spectators read a performance, whether or not they're consciously looking from a feminist perspective.

Any representation, whether its artists intend it to or not, tells a story about gender and race. Sifting through production choices can let the feminist critic/spectator determine which actions created what kind of meanings. The critical questions posed to live performance or film and television are infinite, but here are several with which to begin:

◆ In what style was the production, film, or television episode performed? Realism, naturalism, broad comedy, affect-free post-modernism, physical theatre, dance-movement-based style?

◆ Was the "fourth wall" observed? If it was broken, by whom and why? How were spectators addressed by the performers?
◆ What pace did the direction establish? How did the director work to hold spectators' focus and on which characters or issues? How did gender or race figure into how they created compelling or unusual stage pictures? Did the performers seem like an ensemble? How did gender and race contribute to the on-stage collaboration and collectivity?
◆ How did the set, lighting, and costume design create an environment for the performance of gender and race the production advances? Which visual aspects – period, color, mood, atmosphere, and the movement of light and fabric, furniture and walls – were most salient to your reading?

Writing about artists

The women behind the activist project "History Matters: Back to the Future" argue that because we've forgotten our female forebearers, we're continually reinventing the wheel of gender equity in theatre. As relatively more women become known as theatre and film artists, the new canon of work to address increases exponentially. But it remains important to publicize work by women artists, as the preponderance of reviews, media profiles, and interviews are written about or conducted with artists who are white, heterosexual men. Likewise, we need more biographies of accomplished women artists and more compilations of their work. If you've followed closely a mid-career woman artist, test the waters for writing a biography or a critical edition of her work. The University of Michigan Press publishes a series called Michigan Modern Dramatists, conceived as companion editions for theatre-goers interested in reading about a playwright and her key texts. Smith and Kraus, Methuen, and Palgrave MacMillan publish similar series. If you're looking for a substantive writing project (or need a topic for a dissertation or an MA or honors thesis), consider researching a woman (of color, queer, or any combination of identities) theatre or film artist.

Interview and write about the artists you admire. Artists love to be contacted about their work; don't be star-struck or shy about reaching out online to those you respect and whose work you think should be broadly known. Ask for 20 minutes of their time on the phone or Skype, or if you plan a more extensive essay or profile, or a longer interview, ask if they'll spare an hour over a meal. Approach your work with an angle: What's unique and interesting about this artist? Not just that she's a woman (white or of color), but what is it about her vision of the world and how she creates her art that you think should be publicized? Why should people be introduced to her? What's your argument? Specifics to consider:

◆ Who tends to be interviewed in the mainstream press? Who "trends" in any given day or week? How can you interrupt these tendencies by focusing on someone who's not in the public eye?

◆ Who will you interview? Why? What interests you about her work? What's your slant?

◆ Who is your audience? For which publication?

◆ What format will your writing take: Question and answer (Q&A)? Profile? Feature story?

◆ How many words will you be assigned or propose? Or will you post on a blog or do a podcast for a particular readership or listeners?

Talking about performance and film

Just as mainstream critics and reviewers are never urged to unmask their own critical presumptions, feminist critics/spectators for different reasons often hesitate to name their perspectives. To popularize our viewpoints and to persuade others that seeing as a feminist is both viable and pleasurable, we need to hone our conversational skills as carefully as our written critical ones. Be self-conscious about yourself as an interlocutor. How do you present your ideas in discussion? How can the most casual conversation afford an opportunity to name and advance a feminist perspective on a film, play, or television show? Feminist criticism doesn't have to be a conservational burden. Instead, it can be a pleasurable act of engagement that demonstrates your own agency and models for others how to consume and receive culture from an active, incisive, productive critical perspective. Here are some proven tips for thoughtful, sensitive feminist discussion strategies:

◆ Speaking publicly is an important part of the public discourse on the arts. Be mindful of your ability to succinctly, carefully, and clearly articulate your thoughts, passions, and ideas. Consider this an aspect of your own performance of yourself as a feminist critic. Think about how you would like to sound as a radio or television commentator, or if you developed your own feminist arts criticism podcast. What, literally, should your voice sound like? How will you project your critical persona?

◆ Bring your perspicacious observations to informal conversations and discussions with friends and colleagues. Project enthusiasm and confidence. Criticism demands opinions and perspectives; don't feel obliged to hide or soft-pedal your own. At the same time, a discussion or conversation might encourage you to change your perspective. Listen to others carefully, allowing room for constructive disagreement and debate. Be aware of "air time" – that is, how much time have you taken relative to others? Has everyone spoken once before you speak for the second or third time? How might you encourage others to speak if they seem less willing (or able) than you? How can you encourage the feminist principles of respectful speaking and listening among your peers? Feminist coalition building demands sharing the floor and making room for multiple, even conflicting, perspectives.

A portfolio of critical production: things you can do

The world needs more feminist reviews, whether you pitch them to an editor at a newspaper or web site or you decide to blog on your own or write for a school newspaper. We also need to hear more about women and LGBT artists and artists of color. Learning to interview people and write Q&A-style pieces or profiles based on these conversations is an important contribution to arts discourse. When people say there aren't any good women playwrights, you should have a list of names and titles that you can write or reel off in conversation, putting to shame those who suggest otherwise.

Editorials or "op-eds" (columns by contributing writers that run opposite the editorial page in newspapers) are also important venues for critical cultural writing. The Op Ed Project, a non-profit organization determined to increase the number of women and people of color represented in what they call U.S. "thought leadership," regularly observes whose voices are heard in the largest, most influential public platforms (see their website address in the list of further reading). They suggest that media outlets are hungry for more work by women and people of color, who don't submit their writing in the same numbers as white men. Visit the Op Ed Project web site; take one of their hands-on workshops; practice inhabiting your own authority as a person with something to say. Write opinion pieces that argue for or against artistic trends; weigh in on *Bridesmaids* or *Magic Mike* or *Brave* and what they mean for women, people of color, and queer people. Use your expertise and your unique perspective to influence others.

Write a manifesto about artistic, critical, or reception practices and publish it on the growing number of web sites now devoted to theatre and film production. Manifestos are statements of belief and possibility that can inspire readers to think differently about creative and critical practice. They're utopian interventions in what *is* that outline what *could* be, and represent important imaginative exercises in thinking beyond current constraints. Read other manifestos not just for writing models but for working models, of how to be an artist, critic, or spectator.

Write a grant or create an advocacy project to address the issues about which you care the most. Look at non-profit organizations or foundations like Animating Democracy, the American Alliance for the Arts, Creative Capital, and the Soros Foundation to investigate the kinds of projects they fund. Though the economy is weak and the federal government is always eager to reduce arts and humanities funding, private foundations and non-profits continue to support innovative projects and ideas. Be creative and entrepreneurial. And think about critical writing as persuasive rhetoric easily adapted to grant proposals or project descriptions for potential funders.

Write a speech that you can peddle to community and school groups. Make contacts with your alma mater, synagogue, or church and offer to speak about feminist critical and art practices. Develop your own lecture show and take it on the road. People love hearing others speak about their passions and love being challenged to see differently. Offer to speak at your public library or community center, and tailor your ideas to groups across gender, race, class, and age. Always be aware of your audience; speak directly to what you think might be their interests while you also challenge them to expand their critical and reception horizons. Practice the art of happy argument, so that you can engage politely and enthusiastically with the inevitable naysayers while still scoring your feminist points. Rehearse defending your ideas without sounding (or being) defensive. Enjoy the intellectual and political exercise of a good argument, which lets you marshal your examples and your evidence to persuade people. Be specific, clear, and anecdotal so that people will remember your ideas and adopt them for their own viewing practices.

The feminist critic's journal

Many writers suggest using a notebook in which to keep track of your thoughts and potential writing projects. Collect your ideas in whatever format you'd like. You could set aside a notebook, three-ring binder, folder, document holder, or anything that works for you, in which to record your thoughts and accumulate bits of writing that inspire or enrage you. The journal might include:

◆ Writing that intrigues you or that you'd like to emulate, with notes that suggest why
◆ Rough drafts of articles/reviews/news pieces on which you're working
◆ Scattered thoughts about projects you'd like to start and notes on ideas that compel you
◆ A running commentary on your pleasures in and frustrations with your own work, charting your progress through projects and ideas
◆ Cultural issues about which you'd like to comment, about which you've formed arguments, or debates you'd like to join

A few final pragmatics

Writing and spectating as a feminist resembles any kind of writing or seeing. The same basic practices typically structure this experience, with perhaps a few key differences. Feminists are often more willing to collaborate with other artists, thinkers, and writers, though this, too, is a generalization. Second wave U.S. feminism prized collaboration, collectivity, and coalition. Feminist writing groups can be as valuable for critics as they are for scholars and creative writers. Sharing your ideas and your writing drafts with people who see culture in similar ways can enhance your style and your sense of yourself as someone with a clear, persuasive point of view.

For those of you who will write about what you see, it's worth being self-conscious about your process. Anticipating your habits abates anxiety about deadlines and lets you better predict the time, space, and circumstances you need in which to do your best work. Think about how you write – literally. Do you write with pen and paper? Do you draft on screen? Do you move back and forth between formats? Where do you like to write? Do you write in private or in public? At what time of day? Are you driven by deadlines? How do you remember things? Do you have to write them down? When? When you see a play or a film, will you have to take notes as you watch? Will you have to see something twice? Do you remember by talking through things or by seeing things? How do you collect ideas? When and where? How do you keep track of what you think?

Practice short writing preliminary to drafts of longer pieces. Automatic writing is an excellent way to generate ideas, as it allows you to connect with your writing process without editing your thoughts. My friends in the Rude Mechs theatre collective encourage what they call "brain dumps," in which they ask people, often in preparation for grant writing, to just send them all their thoughts around a particular topic without necessarily being coherent or structured. Brain dumps and automatic writing represent rough thinking on paper and can be very useful to break through writer's block or to begin a piece that at first seems inchoate or intimidating.

Consider writing as revising. Pay close attention to the shape and evolution of your drafts to be self-conscious about your process and your style. Keep careful track of each draft, numbering and dating them in a header or footer. If you chart your thinking, especially as you begin fashioning yourself as a feminist critic, you will be able to perceive your on-going development as a writer. When you look back over early drafts, you'll begin to gather a sense of when your voice emerges; when you're ready to embellish your style; and when you tend to land on your strongest arguments. Understanding your own idiosyncratic writing process lets you manage the stress inherent in the work.

Any beginning writer worries about when they're expert enough to speak into a larger public forum. With the proliferation of venues for writing, launching yourself might seem either easier or even more intimidating. But you have your own unique perspective to add to the public discourse. What particular new angle can you offer through which to look at performance or film from a feminist perspective? What background do you bring to your viewing that will make your insights different from, for instance, mine? I'm a middle-aged, Jewish, white, lesbian, woman professor who lives in the northeast (among other identities I might list). My background, tastes, and expertise form my perspective. Your identity and experience will give you a different outlook. Yours is as useful to public debate as mine.

Every feminist critic has different tastes. What theatre, performance, film, and television do you like to see? How might you expand your critical horizons as a cultural consumer? How do you hear about things about which you might write? To which web sites or RSS feeds do you subscribe? To which others might you add your address? How do you track internet sites? I collect information and ideas using Evernote, an application that I can access through my several desk- and laptop computers as well as on my phone and iPad, as it syncs across platforms. I can create folders for project or essay ideas and clip web sites, emails, and any other information I want to track. I also use Instapaper, another cross-platform, synced application that lets me save articles and web pages that I'd like to read later, creating an archive I can consult whenever I log on. Numerous apps are available that serve similar purposes. Be aware of what works best for you.

Just to be old-fashioned, I'll end with a shout-out to books about writing that I've used in classes and for my own work. An introductory journalism class I took in the mid-70s as an undergraduate at Boston University first introduced me to the wry exhortations of Strunk and White's *The Elements of Style*. Although I don't think many of my students have ever found it as clever and relevant as I have, I continue to find their list of rules for good grammar and especially their injunctions on style useful and inspirational. Strunk and White taught me to omit needless words, which those of us writing to word limits must learn how to do. They also remind me that clear writing doesn't have to sacrifice complexity, but that simple word choices and sentence structures are often the most direct route to a strong, multi-leveled argument.

William Zinsser's book *On Writing Well* has also been a useful source over the years, especially when I taught research methods for graduate students. The rules for academic writing should be no different than those for good "popular" critical writing. We can't reach people with new ideas if they can't follow our thoughts. Stephen King's instructions for would-be writers in *On Writing: A Memoir of the Craft* have also been useful, despite his often misogynist tendencies (a feminist critic/reader will quickly find them in his prose). But because I believe in "poaching" – lifting good ideas or strategies from anywhere at all to use for feminist ends – I ignore the sexist medium and use the message, which is often, like Zinsser and Strunk and White, to write clearly, succinctly, and evocatively. I can't think of a more feminist practice than that.

Finally, as any writer would suggest, the way to write better feminist criticism is to write more. And the way to hone your feminist spectating skill is to see as much as you can. Write about it, even if you never share your words publicly. Catalogue what you see; track genres you like or don't, directors whose work you admire and want to champion, writers who you think don't get enough attention, performers whose work is overlooked. Keep writing and keep refining your expertise. And keep proclaiming your idiosyncratic feminist perspective as a vital, instructive, important, and fun framework for engaging with culture.

Appendix

The 34 essays in The Feminist Spectator in Action *are organized according to four categories that might distinguish the critical work they attempt. But they could also be gathered in other ways, according to – for only several examples – theme, genre, and authorship. I've listed below various strands under which the essays might find alternative placements as another way to guide the reader through this collection.*

Themes

Adaptations
◆ *Mamma Mia!*
◆ *For Colored Girls*
◆ *The Hunger Games*
◆ *Once*
Fathers and Sons
◆ *Death of a Salesman*
◆ *Clybourne Park*
Guilty Pleasures
◆ *Mamma Mia!*
◆ *Black Swan*
◆ *The Hunger Games*
◆ *Brave*
Mothers and Daughters
◆ *The Kids Are All Right*
◆ *Circumstance*
◆ *Tiny Furniture*
◆ *Mamma Mia!*
◆ *For Colored Girls*
◆ *Black Swan*
◆ *Brave*

- *Tomboy*
- *Nurse Jackie*

Queer Desire

- *Dynasty Handbag*
- *The Kids Are All Right*
- *Circumstance*
- *Black Swan*
- *The Normal Heart*
- *The Children's Hour*
- *Tomboy*
- *Hair*
- *Bridesmaids*
- *Lost Lounge*
- *Jomama Jones: Radiate*
- *A Midsummer Night's Dream*
- *Your Sister's Sister*
- *Nurse Jackie*

Revivals

- *The Merchant of Venice*
- *The Normal Heart*
- *The Children's Hour*
- *Porgy and Bess*
- *Wit*
- *Death of a Salesman*
- *Come Back, Little Sheba*
- *Hair*
- *A Midsummer Night's Dream*

Shakespeare

- *The Merchant of Venice*
- *A Midsummer Night's Dream*

The Male Gaze

- *Black Swan*
- *The Social Network*
- *Wit*

Genres

Broadway or West End Theatre

- *The Merchant of Venice*
- *The Normal Heart*
- *The Children's Hour*

- *Porgy and Bess*
- *Wit*
- *Death of a Salesman*
- *Clybourne Park*
- *Come Back, Little Sheba*
- *Once*

Hollywood Film

- *The Kids Are All Right*
- *The Hurt Locker*
- *Mamma Mia!*
- *For Colored Girls*
- *Black Swan*
- *The Social Network*
- *The Hunger Games*
- *Brave*
- *Bridesmaids*

Indie Film

- *Circumstance*
- *Young Adult*
- *Tiny Furniture*
- *Tomboy*
- *Your Sister's Sister*

Off- or Off-Off Broadway Theatre

- *Dynasty Handbag*
- *The Dog and Pony Show*
- *Jomama Jones: Radiate*
- *Hair*
- *Let Me Down Easy*
- *Lost Lounge*
- *A Midsummer Night's Dream*

Solo Performance

- *Dynasty Handbag*
- *The Dog and Pony Show*
- *Jomama Jones: Radiate*

Television Series

- *Friday Night Lights*
- *Nurse Jackie*
- *Homeland and Girls*
- *Scandal*

Authorship

By People of Color (as writers or directors)
- *Circumstance*
- *For Colored Girls*
- *Porgy and Bess*
- *Let Me Down Easy*
- *Jomama Jones: Radiate*
- *Scandal*

By Queer People (as writers or directors)
- *Dynasty Handbag*
- *The Kids Are All Right*
- *The Dog and Pony Show*
- *Mamma Mia!*
- *The Normal Heart*
- *Wit*
- *Lost Lounge*
- *Jomama Jones: Radiate*
- *Nurse Jackie*

By Women (as writers or directors)
- *Dynasty Handbag*
- *The Kids Are All Right*
- *The Dog and Pony Show*
- *The Hurt Locker*
- *Circumstance*
- *Young Adult*
- *Tiny Furniture*
- *Girls*
- *Mamma Mia!*
- *For Colored Girls*
- *The Hunger Games*
- *Brave*
- *The Children's Hour*
- *Porgy and Bess*
- *Wit*
- *Tomboy*
- *Let Me Down Easy*
- *Bridesmaids*
- *Lost Lounge*
- *Your Sister's Sister*
- *Nurse Jackie*
- *Scandal*

Notes

Introduction

1. Rebecca West, "Mr. Chesterton in Hysterics: A Study in Prejudice," *The Clarion*, November 14, 1913, reprinted in *The Young Rebecca: The Writings of Rebecca West, 1911–1917,* Jane Marcus, ed. (Bloomington: Indiana University Press, 1989).
2. Polly Carl, "A Boy in a Man's Theatre," *HowlRound*, April 23, 2012, http://www.howlround.com/a-boy-in-a-mans-theater-by-polly-carl/, accessed July 12, 2012.
3. Ryan Gosling, despite this performance in a pretty sexist film, is a complicated example here, partly because he's made his career playing a conflicted version of white, straight male masculinity. See this discussion of the popular meme in which images of Gosling are overlaid with references to feminist theorist Judith Butler on the *Huffington Post* at http://www.huffington-post.com/2011/10/10/feminist-ryan-gosling-blog_n_1004158.html and the Tumblr images themselves at http://feministryangosling.tumblr.com/post/11171240616, both accessed October 14, 2012.
4. See "The Bechdel Test Movie List," www.Bechdeltest.com, accessed July 12, 2012.
5. See, for example, discussion about the Guthrie Theatre's announcement of a season comprised only of white male playwrights in "Diversity Drama in the 2012–2013 Season," The Feminist Spectator, http://www.thefeministspecta-tor.com/2012/05/22/diversity-drama-in-the-2012–2013-season/, accessed July 12, 2012.
6. See David Cote, "Critical Junction," *American Theatre Magazine* (November 2011), http://www.tcg.org/publications/at/nov11/critical_juncture.cfm, accessed October 14, 2012.
7. See information about the Nathan Award and a list of winners through 2012 at http://www.arts.cornell.edu/english/awards/nathan/, accessed October 14, 2012.
8. Theresa Rebeck, ART/NY Laura Pels keynote, March 2010; see http://womenandhollywood.com/2010/03/16/text-of-theresa-rebeck-laura-pels-keynote-address/, accessed July 12, 2012.

9. Bruce Weber, "Like Father (a Writer), Like Son (an Actor), and Neither is Likable," *New York Times*, October 4, 2000, http://theater.nytimes.com/mem/theater/treview.html?html_title=&tols_title=BUTTERFLY%20COLLECTION,%20THE%20(PLAY)&pdate=20001004&byline=By%20BRUCE%20WEBER&id=1077011432318, accessed July 12, 2012.

10. See Charles Isherwood's review, "Student Meets a Mentor She has Met Before," *New York Times*, January 18, 2011, http://theater.nytimes.com/2011/01/19/theater/reviews/19how.html, accessed July 12, 2012.

11. Sarah Schulman, "Supremacy Ideology Masquerading as Reality: The Obstacle Facing Women Playwrights in America," *Theatre Journal*, 62 (4) (December 2010): 567–570.

12. The present generation of feminists has gravitated to the internet to launch its own trenchant cultural critique on sites that address politics and culture in concert, refusing the distinction between them that often hobbled my generation's arguments about culture's centrality to feminism. Blogs like *Feministing* (www.feministing.com), for example, address pop culture in all its manifestations. Melissa Silverstein's *Women and Hollywood* blog (http://blogs.indiewire.com/womenandhollywood/) combines film reviews with interviews and informational and feature essays on women filmmakers. Third-wave feminist magazines like *Bitch* and *Bust* collect feminist writing on popular culture, but neither regularly covers theatre or performance. Television is sometimes discussed in online forums such as www.afterellen.com, a lesbian-oriented web site launched after Ellen DeGeneres' public coming-out, but often from a more colloquial, fan-friendly point of view. Other reviews are accessible on sites like www.rottentomatoes.com, but only one of the 165 critics it aggregates self-identifies as feminist.

13. See Laura Mulvey, "Visual Pleasure and Narrative Cinema," *Screen*, 16 (3) (Autumn 1975): 6–18, for her discussion of the psychoanalytic mechanisms, including "scopophilia" (pleasure in looking), that she suggests organizes the gendered differences of spectatorship.

14. See Katie Roiphe, "Why Criticism Matters: With Clarity and Beauty, the Weight of Authority," *New York Times Book Review*, December 31, 2010, http://www.nytimes.com/2011/01/02/books/review/Roiphe-t-web.html?pagewanted=all, accessed July 12, 2012.

15. See Abraham Joshua Heschel, *Man Is Not Alone* (New York: Farrar, Straus, and Giroux, 1976).

16. Michael Kaiser, "The Death of Criticism or Everyone Is a Critic," *The Huffington Post,* November 14, 2011, http://www.huffingtonpost.com/michael-kaiser/the-death-of-criticism-or_b_1092125.html, accessed July 12, 2012.

17. Andrew Horwitz, "Why Aren't Audiences Stupid," *Culturebot*, November 16, 2011, http://culturebot.org/2011/11/11716/why-arent-audiences-stupid-andy-version/, accessed July 12, 2012.

18. Chloe Veltman, "Chloe Veltman on Arts Criticism," *HowlRound,* March 27, 2012, http://www.howlround.com/chloe-veltman-on-arts-criticism/, accessed July 12, 2012.

19. Karen Fricker, "First Past the Blogpost: Why Jill Dolan's Theatre Criticism Award Matters," January 9, 2012, http://www.guardian.co.uk/stage/theatreblog/2012/jan/09/jill-dolan-theatre-critic-award, accessed July 12, 2012.

20. Michael Feingold, "3C: Bad Company," *The Village Voice*, June 27, 2012, http://www.villagevoice.com/2012–06–20/theater/3c-bad-company/, accessed July 12, 2012.
21. See "Wisconsin News Anchor Talks About Critical Weight Email on CBS This Morning," at http://newyork.cbslocal.com/2012/10/03/wisconsin-news-anchor-talks-about-weight-bully-on-cbs-this-morning/, accessed October 14, 2012. The site includes a clip of Livingston's on-air response to the email.
22. See my *Utopia in Performance: Finding Hope at the Theater* (Ann Arbor: University of Michigan Press, 2005).

2 Activism

1. See, for example, http://www.newyorker.com/online/blogs/books/2012/03/hunger-games-and-trayvon-martin.html. *Jezebel* has several excellent articles about *The Hunger Games* tweets controversy, in which dozens of fans expressed appallingly racist concerns about the casting of Rue and Cinna: http://jezebel.com/5896408/racist-hunger-games-fans-dont-care-how-much-money-the-movie-made and http://jezebel.com/5896688/i-see-white-people-hunger-games-and-a-brief-history-of-cultural-whitewashing. See also "Race and Fandom: When Defaulting to White Isn't an Option," *Racialicious*, June 7, 2012, http://www.racialicious.com/2012/06/07/race-fandom-when-defaulting-to-white-isnt-an-option/ and other useful posts on the web site at http://www.racialicious.com/tag/the-hunger-games/.
2. See, for example, Caroline Kitchener's editorial, "Casanova on the Street," *Daily Princetonian*, October 6, 2010, http://www.dailyprincetonian.com/2010/10/06/26460/, accessed March 18, 2013..

3 Argument

1. Frank Rich, "Post-Racial Farce *New York Magazine*," May 20, 2012, http://nymag.com/news/frank-rich/racism-2012-5/
2. See Norris quote in Ann M. Shanahan's review, *Theatre Journal* 64 (2) (May 2012): 284.

4 Artistry

1. See Susan Dominus, "The Health Care Monologues," *The New York Times Magazine*, September 30, 2009, http://www.nytimes.com/2009/10/04/magazine/04smith-t.html?pagewanted=all&_r=0, accessed March 18, 2013..

Suggestions for Further Reading

Note: This is a short list of further reading. These materials have all been inspiring, foundational, or thought-provoking to me over the course of my own career as a critic. Some taught me feminist theory in the 1980s; others model critical collections of writing that set a high standard for my own.

I've divided the material into five categories. The first, "On Arts Writing and Interviews," includes books and a few articles that either discuss or exemplify good writing about the arts or gather interviews between the author and an artist. Collections of interviews seem to be rare these days; the ones I cite are quite good and demonstrate the fine art of the one-on-one interview published in a question-and-answer format.

The category "Feminist Theory" offers a smattering of foundational material in theatre, film, and television. I've tried to cite the scholars who really helped begin the trend of research and writing in these three categories; many, many more people would be on this list if space permitted. With the "Criticism" category, I've included several collections of writing I find significant, mostly in theatre and film. I don't necessary agree with these critics' style or their values, but I read them and find that their writing one way or another helps me shape my own.

The few volumes listed under "On Writing" have been quite useful to me over the years. Cameron's sounds New Age-y but actually includes very practical exercises for facing the blank page or screen; Lamott's is a beautiful exegesis of what it means to write; Strunk and White is mandatory for any serious writer, and the illustrated version is funny and fun; and *Eats, Shoots, Leaves* is a book of humor with a serious point about the power of language.

The few web sites that end these recommendations direct you to organizations, bloggers, or journals that I find relevant to the project of feminist criticism.

I hope these suggestions prove the beginnings of your own list of sources you consult regularly to ease your way through your own feminist critical practice.

On Arts Writing and Interviews

Bogart, Anne. *Conversations with Anne: Twenty-Four Interviews*. New York: Theatre Communications Group, 2012.

Cohen-Cruz, Jan. *Engaging Performance: Theatre as Call and Response*. New York: Routledge, 2010.

Eichenbaum, Rose. *The Dancer Within: Intimate Conversations with Great Dancers*. Middleton, CT: Wesleyan University Press, 2008.

Ferguson, Marcia L. *A Short Guide to Writing about Theatre*. New York: Pearson/ Longman, 2008.

Greene, Alexis. (ed.) *Women Who Write Plays: Interviews with American Dramatists*. New York: Smith and Kraus, 2001.

Ivey, Bill. *Arts, Inc.: How Greed and Neglect Have Destroyed Our Cultural Rights*. Berkeley, CA: University of California Press, 2008.

Margolin, Deb. "Count the I's, or, the Autobiographical Nature of Everything," *Women & Performance Journal* 10:1–2, #19–20 (1999): 24–32.

Miller, Tim, and David Román. "Preaching to the Converted." *Theatre Journal* 47 (2) (May 1995): 169–188.

Savran, David. *In Their Own Words: Contemporary American Playwrights*. New York: Theatre Communications Group, 1988; rev. ed. 1998.

Feminist Theory

Banes, Sally. *Dancing Women: Female Bodies on Stage*. New York: Routledge, 1998.

Case, Sue-Ellen. *Feminism and Theatre*. Houndmills, UK: Macmillan, 1988; rev. ed., Palgrave Macmillan, 2008.

———. *Feminist and Queer Performance: Critical Strategies*. New York: Palgrave Macmillan, 2009.

———. (ed.) *Performing Feminisms: Feminist Critical Theory and Theatre*. Baltimore: Johns Hopkins University Press, 1990.

Diamond, Elin. *Unmaking Mimesis: Essays on Feminism and Theater*. New York: Routledge, 1997.

Doane, Mary Ann, Patricia Mellencamp, and Linda Williams. (eds) *Re-vision: Essays in Feminist Film Criticism*. Frederick, MD: University Publications of America, 1984.

Dolan, Jill. *Presence and Desire: Essays on Gender, Theatre, Performance*. Ann Arbor: University of Michigan Press, 1993.

———. *The Feminist Spectator as Critic*. Ann Arbor: University of Michigan Press, 1991; rev. ed. 2012.

———. *Theatre & Sexuality*. New York: Palgrave Macmillan, 2010.

———. *Utopia in Performance: Finding Hope at the Theatre*. Ann Arbor: University of Michigan Press, 2005.

hooks, bell [sic]. *Black Looks: Race and Representation*. Boston, MA: South End Press, 1992.

———. *Homegrown: Engaged Cultural Criticism*. Cambridge, MA: South End Press, 2006.

———. *Outlaw Culture: Resisting Representation*. New York: Routledge, 1994.

———. *Reel to Real: Race, Sex, and Class at the Movies*. New York: Routledge, 1996.

Kaplan, E. Ann. (ed.) *Feminism and Film*. New York: Oxford University Press, 2000.

———. (ed.) *Regarding Television: Critical Approaches—An Anthology*. Frederick, MD: University Publications of America, 1983.

———. *Women and Film: Both Sides of the Camera*. New York: Methuen, 1983.

Modleski, Tania. *Loving with a Vengeance: Mass-Produced Fantasies for Women*. Hamden, CT: Archon Books, 1982; rev. ed. New York: Routledge, 2008.

Phelan, Peggy. *Unmarked: The Politics of Performance*. New York: Routledge, 1993.

Rich, B. Ruby. *Chick Flicks: Theories and Memories of the Feminist Film Movement*. Durham, NC: Duke University Press, 1998.

Rivera-Servera, Ramón. *Performing Queer Latinidad: Dance, Sexuality, Politics*. Ann Arbor: University of Michigan Press, 2012.

Solomon, Alisa. *Re-Dressing the Canon: Essays on Theater and Gender*. New York: Routledge, 1997.

Warner, Sara. *Acts of Gaiety: LGBT Performance and the Politics of Pleasure*. Ann Arbor: University of Michigan Press, 2012.

Williams, Linda. *Screening Sex*. Durham, NC: Duke University Press, 2008.

Wolf, Stacy. *A Problem Like Maria: Gender and Sexuality in the American Musical*. Ann Arbor: University of Michigan Press, 2002.

———. *Changed for Good: A Feminist History of the Broadway Musical*. New York: Oxford University Press, 2011.

Criticism

Banes, Sally. *Writing Dance in the Age of Postmodernism*. Hanover, NH: University Press of New England, 1994.

Bentley, Eric. *What Is Theatre: 1944–1967*. New York: Hill and Wang, 2000; Antheneum, 1968.

Brantley, Ben. (ed.) *The New York Times Book of Broadway: On the Aisle for the Unforgettable Plays of the Last Century*. New York: New York Times, 2001.

Carr, C. *On Edge: Performance at the End of the Twentieth Century*. Hanover, NH: Wesleyan University Press, 1993; rev. ed. 2008.

Daly, Ann. *Critical Gestures: Writings on Dance and Culture*. Middleton, CT: Wesleyan University Press, 2002.

Dolan, Jill. *The Feminist Spectator*. www.TheFeministSpectator.com.

Jenkins, Jeffrey Eric. *Under the Copper Beech: Conversations with American Theatre Critics*. New York: Foundation of the American Theatre Critics Association, 2004.

Kael, Pauline. *I Lost It at the Movies*. Boston: Little, Brown, 1965.

Kalb, Jonathan. *Free Admissions: Collected Theatre Writings*. New York: Limelight, 1993.

Kellow, Brian. *Pauline Kael: A Life in the Dark*. New York: Viking, 2011.

Kuftinec, Sonja, Tim Miller, Bill Rauch, and David Román. "Critical Relations: The Artist and Scholar in Conversation." *Theater,* 33 (3): 119–131.

Lerman, Liz. "Toward a Process for Critical Response." *Community Arts Network*. www.communityartsnet/readingroom/archivefiles/2003/10/toward_a_process.php.

Rich, Frank. *Hot Seat: Theatre Criticism for the New York Times, 1980–1993*. New York: Random House, 1998.

Schwartz, Sanford. (ed.) *The Age of Movies: Selected Writings of Pauline Kael*. New York: Library of America, 2011.

Shellard, Dominic. (ed.) *Kenneth Tynan: Theatre Writings*. New York: Drama Publishers, 2007.

Williams, Jeffrey J. *Critics at Work: Interviews 1993–2003*. New York: New York University Press, 2004.

On Writing

Cameron, Julia. *The Artist's Way: A Spiritual Path to Higher Creativity*. New York: J.P. Tarcher/Putnam, 2002.

Lamott, Anne. *Bird by Bird: Some Instructions on Writing and Life*. New York: Anchor Books, 2005.

Strunk, William, Jr. *The Elements of Style*. Fourth Edition. Boston: Allyn and Bacon, 2000.

———. *The Elements of Style*. Illustrated by Maira Kalman. New York: The Penguin Press, 2005.

Truss, Lynne. *Eats, Shoots & Leaves*. New York: Gotham Books, 2003.

Helpful Web Sites

Artivate: A Journal of Entrepreneurship in the Arts, www.artivate.org. Disseminates new thinking and perspectives on arts entrepreneurship theory, practice, and pedagogy.

Culturebot, www.culturebot.org. A web site devoted to arts, culture, and ideas that aggregates and authors interviews, reviews, and essays.

GLAAD, the Gay & Lesbian Alliance Against Defamation, www.glaad.org. Amplifies the voice of the LGBT community by empowering real people to share their stories, holding the media accountable for the words and images they present, and helping grassroots organizations communicate effectively. GLAAD promotes understanding, increases acceptance, and advances equality for LGBT people worldwide.

HowlRound: A Journal of the Theatre Commons, www.howlround.com. Builds open platforms for knowledge sharing and aligning resources for theatre artists and organizations.

Jumper, www.artsjournal.com/jumper. A blog by Diane Ragsdale on what the arts do and why, and the relationship between economic strategy and mission in the arts.

League of Professional Theatre Women, www.theatrewomen.org. A not-for-profit organization that seeks to promote visibility and increase opportunities for women in the professional theatre.

The OpEd Project, www.theopedproject.org. The project's mission is to increase the range of voices and the quality of ideas we hear in the world. A starting goal is to increase the number of women thought leaders in key commentary forums to a tipping point.

VIDA, Women in Literary Arts, www.vidaweb.org. VIDA seeks to explore critical and cultural perceptions of writing by women through meaningful conversation and the exchange of ideas among existing and emerging literary communities.

Women and Hollywood, www.blogs.indiewire.com/womenandhollywood. Blogger Melissa Silverstein writes about films by and about women, collecting facts, resources, and aggregating relevant features, interviews, and reviews.

Women's Media Center, www.womensmediacenter.com. Amplifying women's voices and changing the conversation. Determined to make women visible and powerful in the media by training women and girls to be media ready and media savvy. The center curates original content from women writers; monitors and calls out media sexism; and holds the media accountable for an equal voice and equal participation.

Index

Printed in China